P9-DNQ-845

Taxpayers' Hayride

Taxpayers' Hayride

THE FARM PROBLEM FROM THE NEW DEAL
TO THE BILLIE SOL ESTES CASE

BY

JULIUS DUSCHA

LITTLE, BROWN AND COMPANY · BOSTON · TORONTO

*Published simultaneously in Canada
by Little, Brown & Company (Canada) Limited*

PRINTED IN THE UNITED STATES OF AMERICA

FOR

My Mother

Author's Note

THIS BOOK is about a clever, uncomplicated Texan and an unbelievably complex Government program. The man is Billie Sol Estes, whose gargantuan financial exploits turned him into a world-famous figure and led to fines and jail sentences. The program is the system under which American farmers are guaranteed high prices through Government subsidies. It is a program which few Americans understand, even though more Federal funds are spent on it than on any other domestic, nondefense Government program. Billie Sol Estes understood it, however.

The book grew out of my coverage of the Billie Sol Estes case and of the Government's agriculture programs in the course of my work as a reporter for the Washington *Post*. Most of the material on the Estes case itself is based on my own firsthand reporting in Texas and Washington. The statistics on farm subsidies, income, production and population are from official United States Department of Agriculture, Budget Bureau and Census Bureau publications. The conclusions drawn from official sources are of course my own.

The book was written for laymen. The jargon of the Agriculture Department and of economists has been dropped in favor of simple language. It is my hope that if more Americans understand the farm program, it can be made to work in the interests of the nation rather than in the interests of a few big farmers or of a man like Billie Sol Estes.

J. D.

Contents

Taxpayers' Hayride

1

"Just a Farm Boy"

IT WAS quiet in the palatial Estes home on the outskirts of Pecos. Outside, the cool evening breeze rustled the tops of the three royal palms standing like sentinels in the carefully tended front yard. It was going to be a nice desert night. Billie Sol was not home yet, but his wife Patsy and their five children expected Daddy any minute now. After putting up the girls' hair for the night, Mrs. Estes relaxed with them before the television set. They were a good-looking family, the four girls and little Billie Sol, Jr. For them the modern American dream had come true. They had a comfortable house, a Cadillac and two airplanes, and their father was one of the best-known businessmen and farmers in Texas. He was a Christian gentleman, admired for the exemplary life he led.

The television program they were watching was interrupted for a news bulletin. Their father, the television announcer breathlessly reported, had just been arrested by the FBI.

Patsy could not believe it. The children could not understand it. The news was as shocking to the rest of the people of Pecos as it was to Mrs. Estes. Her husband was the most important man in this little West Texas town of twelve thousand. He was the very embodiment of the American success story — a millionaire fifty times over; a poor farm boy who had reached the heights of business success at the age of thirty-seven. He paid the best wages in town and was a friend of rich and poor alike. Everyone in town knew of someone Billie Sol had helped in time of need. He was a faithful family man, an elder and a lay preacher in his church. He knew much of the Bible by heart and laced even his business conversations with apt Biblical quotations. He neither drank nor smoked — he did not even curse. He frowned on dancing and would not allow boys and girls to swim together in his spacious backyard pool.

The people of Pecos did not know it on the night of March 29, 1962, when two FBI agents picked up Billie Sol, but he was indeed an unusual man who would not soon be forgotten. He was the first man to realize the full potentials of the multibillion-dollar farm subsidy programs. His vast business empire had been carefully built on ever-expanding Government subsidies to farmers and to businessmen who handled farm commodities. He had turned the farm subsidies born of the desperate days of the depression thirty years earlier into an unbelievable bonanza. His meteoric business career demonstrated that programs designed to help all farmers keep up with the rest of the economy can also be used, both legally and illegally, to make a few men very wealthy indeed.

In a dramatic, personal, easy-to-understand way, the Billie Sol Estes case raises basic questions about the thirty-year-old farm programs: What have the programs accomplished? What have they done to the nation's farm economy? Who really benefits from the astonishing array of farm subsidies? And what is to be done about the costly, often mismanaged farm programs?

The second of six children, Billie Sol Estes was born in 1925 on an isolated West Texas farm three miles northwest of the little town of Clyde. His parents were sturdy people, poor but hard-working and self-reliant. He was named for an uncle — in the Southwest, Spanish names such as Sol (sun) are common. To help meet the payments on their farm his mother churned butter and sold it from door to door in Clyde. His father was a lay preacher in the fundamentalist Church of Christ. By planting cotton and wheat and raising sheep, hogs and cows on his arid land, he managed to make just enough money to feed and clothe his family and to pay off a substantial mortgage.

Billie Sol helped his father with the farm chores and attended a one-room schoolhouse where he got a rudimentary education. At the Estes home the atmosphere was spartan and religious. Living in rural isolation in the mid-twenties, the Estes family relied on the Bible for guidance and spiritual sustenance and on the hard work traditionally associated with farm life for economic well-being.

It was the kind of puritanical life that was supposed to bring out the best in people and to mold men and women of strength, courage and unchallengeable honesty. For generations Americans had viewed the bucolic existence on farms like the one where Billie Sol was raised as one of the basic underpinnings of the American way — and dream. America was great because the people in its cities and industries had sprung from strong, uncorruptible rural roots.

The year around the farmer battled the weather. It always seemed to be either too dry or too wet. If the rains did come, they were too early or too late. Hail, windstorms and drought were particular problems in West Texas.

The vagaries of the marketplace were even worse than

those of the weather. By 1920, less than two years after the end of World War I, the farm economy was plunged into the midst of yet another rural depression. Since the end of the Civil War these depressions had periodically swept across the countryside. No one knew how to prevent them. There was no way for the millions upon millions of farmers producing crops and growing livestock to control the market. Their only response to low prices was to produce more, but such expansion in production led only to additional surpluses that further depressed market prices.

By the time in the early 1930's when Billie Sol Estes became conscious of the world around him, businessmen and workers as well as farmers were mired in the slough of the worst depression the nation had ever known. Out of this depression would come a new life for farmers and for the rest of the nation, but it would be a life far different from that which Billie Sol had known in his boyhood days. Billie Sol was not only a child of the depression; he was born and raised in a fading rural atmosphere that has all but disappeared from the United States during the last thirty years.

On his thirteenth birthday in 1938 Billie Sol got his start in farming and business. His folks gave him a lamb. When the lamb grew up Billie Sol sheared her, sold the wool, and bought more lambs. With his profits from sheep he started raising hogs and finally got into the cattle business in a small way. By the time he was eighteen, Billie Sol has boasted, he had $38,000 in the bank. Over the years Billie Sol carefully nurtured and embellished the story of his business precocity. His account of his teen-age success has been hotly disputed by people in Clyde and Baird, Texas, the nearby county seat of Callahan County, who knew Billie Sol as a boy.

"He was just a farm boy like the rest of us," Dan South,

the Clyde postmaster who went to school with Billie Sol, has said. "We were all poor boys trying to get along."

Bob Norrell, a banker in Baird who also knew Billie Sol as a boy, has described him as a "very energetic youngster," who, however, showed no "great distinction in a financial way."

Billie Sol is still remembered at the Clyde High School as the fellow who demonstrated his energy and budding business acumen one summer by organizing youths to clear prickly-pear cactus from ranches and by contracting during another summer to supply some hands, including himself, for the wheat harvest in Kansas. In his junior year Billie Sol's schoolmates selected him as the "King" of their class. Patsy Howe, the girl he would later marry, was named "Queen" of the same class. Billie Sol graduated from high school in 1943 in the midst of World War II, and that year won a national 4-H Club achievement award for his extensive and highly productive victory gardens.

Estes was unable to get into the armed services during World War II because of bad eyesight and also because one of his legs is a bit shorter than the other. When the war was won in 1945 he did join the Merchant Marine and for two years served in the Atlantic as a mess attendant and wiper on merchant ships. His sternly religious upbringing did not prevent him from engaging in — and winning — many shipboard poker games.

Estes did not go on to college. He did not have time for higher education. Instead, he turned his talents to the buying and selling of surplus housing from military bases. He needed little money to purchase the old wooden barracks and was generally able to sell them at a good profit. He bought and sold the buildings, which usually had to be moved from the bases, in Arkansas, New Mexico, California and the State of Washington as well as in his own West Texas. The barracks were converted into apartments that were then rented to war veterans or were cut apart to be rebuilt as individual homes.

It was after his fling in surplus housing that Estes, a pudgy, near-sighted young man of twenty-six, moved to Pecos in 1951 to seek his fortune. He said that he hoped to become as rich as the Murchisons. The Murchison family is one of the wealthiest in Texas, where it has large land and oil holdings. When Billie Sol arrived in Pecos he had accumulated $28,000 from his surplus housing deals. W. M. Holcombe, a portly Pecos banker who befriended Estes and loaned him money when he was struggling to get started as a cotton farmer, has said that a year after Billie Sol arrived in town his own financial statement showed he had assets of $185,000 and debts of $68,000, leaving a net worth of $117,000. The statement was not a certified audit of Estes' finances, but Holcombe, an astute banker, verified the statement to his own satisfaction.

"There are two things Billie Sol can do real fast," a Pecos businessman once said. "He can quote the Bible and he can whip a financial statement out of his pocket with the speed of lightning. Several months ago he took a piece of paper out of his pocket and asked me: 'Would you like to know how much money I made last month?' "

To the cross-country travelers who quickly pass through Pecos on U.S. Highway 80, the flat, sun-baked town hardly looks like the place to make a fortune. Two hundred miles to the west and south lies cosmopolitan El Paso, while eighty miles to the north and east are the booming oil cities of Odessa and Midland. The cluster of concrete and wooden buildings that make up most of Pecos offers little to the traveler except a quick break in the flat, monotonous desert country of West Texas. The streets are wide, clean and never crowded. They seem to run off into the countryside for endless miles until they meet the hazy horizon.

From early in the spring until late in the fall the desert sun beats down mercilessly on the town, sending temperatures above 100 degrees day after day. It is the dry heat of the desert that produces little perspiration and tricks the unwary visitor into thinking that he can easily withstand the midday sun. It takes only one or two days for the visitor to understand why most of the people of Pecos spend the sunlit hours in air-conditioned houses, air-conditioned automobiles and air-conditioned offices. Even the meanest and grubbiest houses bulge at their sides with air-conditioning units.

Not all of Pecos has the flat, adobe look of the downtown business district. There are new residential blocks that are as pretty as a picture-book suburbia. There is even a sprinkling of trees on these streets, where successful farmers as well as prosperous businessmen live.

Everywhere in Pecos, however, the wind begins to blow during the latter part of most afternoons. From the west the winds often bring gritty dust and biting sand, but seldom rain.

The town boasts that it is the birthplace of the rodeo. Pecos also proudly displays a replica of the saloon from which Judge Roy Bean, one of the Old West's notorious hanging judges, is supposed to have dispensed justice as the only law west of the Pecos River. Judge Bean held court some miles south of the present town of Pecos.

Billie Sol Estes and the other men who crowded into Pecos in the late 1940's and the early 1950's were interested in neither the lore nor the law west of the Pecos. A new West

Texas crop, cotton, brought them to town. From the time Pecos was settled in the late nineteenth century until the end of World War II, the little farming that was done in the area centered around cattle and fruits and vegetables. It did not take many head of cattle to turn the patches of grassland found by the early settlers into clumps of sagebrush. Juicy melons still come out of the Pecos Valley, but few other fruits and vegetables thrive on the sand and the wind.

Shortly after the end of World War II water was discovered in Reeves County, of which Pecos is the county seat. In the arid regions of West Texas water is welcomed almost as if it were oil. In Reeves County an underground river of clear, sparkling water was brought to the surface, to turn the dry desert into soil as rich as the cotton land of the Mississippi Delta or the cornfields of Iowa. But the water was expensive. The desert entrepreneurs needed to take great care in choosing a crop for the irrigated acres that would not only quickly repay the high cost of drilling a well twenty to thirty thousand feet deep but would also yield a substantial profit. Long-staple cotton, which brought a premium price because it could be woven into the best and the strongest cloth, seemed to grow extremely well on the newly irrigated fields. Generous amounts of fertilizer had to be added to the land along with the water, but cotton prices were good. What is more, the Federal Government in far-off Washington, that Government which spent so much money to the public distress of so many Texans and other Americans, guaranteed the twentieth-century Pecos prospectors a handsome price for their cotton.

When Estes came to town he had a battered and bulging briefcase filled with ideas and plans. The briefcase was a rather unusual status symbol in a rough-and-ready cowtown like Pecos. A high-crowned hat that Estes neglected to crease easily identified the stranger in town as he trudged the streets seeking advice and credit. Both were plentiful in the Pecos of the early 1950's. First of all, Billie Sol let it be known, he wanted an honest real estate man. He found one who not only was highly recommended but belonged to the Church of Christ, the faith in which Estes was raised by his God-fearing mother and father. Cotton was the crop, Estes learned, and it did not take him long to borrow enough money to buy a section of desert land (a section is 640 acres — a square mile). His credentials as a farmer were good enough. His father had been a farmer; he had grown up on his father's farm and he had lived in West Texas all of his life.

With the help of two of his brothers, Word and Bobby Frank, and the cheap labor of Mexican field hands, Billie Sol soon cleared the tangle of mesquite and sagebrush from the land. Then a well had to be drilled, an automatic pump installed, and a concrete irrigation ditch built to channel the valuable water to the fields. Meanwhile, the fields were plowed and carefully prepared for the tiny cotton seeds that would be planted in neat rows and then flooded with life-giving water. Finally came the chemical fertilizer which, when correctly and judiciously applied, would make the desert bloom with cotton. The miracle fertilizer was called anhydrous ammonia, a form of nitrogen. It makes plants, whether cotton, wheat or grain sorghums, grow bigger, better and faster. Into the soil go the seeds, water and fertilizer and out come the beautiful white bolls of cotton.

This was farming quite different from the kind that Billie Sol had done as a boy. For his success as a cotton planter

Estes depended heavily on technology as well as on the Government. He also needed large amounts of capital. Merely to drill a well deep enough into the desert cost twenty to thirty thousand dollars. Tanks were needed to haul the new miracle fertilizer to the fields so that it could be mixed with the water or injected directly into the land at the exact moment when the cotton plants had to draw additional nourishment from the soil. Through its price guarantees on cotton as well as on other crops, the Government gave Estes and other farmers a much-welcomed reassurance that their labor would not be in vain.

Billie Sol's father depended largely on his own labor for his success as a farmer. Billie Sol seldom did any physical labor in his fields once they had been cleared. The work was done by Mexicans who came across the border each year to work in the cotton, fruit and vegetable fields and the orchards of the Southwest. The Mexicans plowed the fields, planted and weeded the cotton, and finally picked it for those farmers who felt that they could not yet afford a mechanical cotton-picker mounted on a tractor.

The farmers who flocked to Pecos from as far away as Alabama and Mississippi to get in on the postwar cotton boom did not love the dreary West Texas landscape. Few of them lived on the land. They preferred the air-conditioned comfort of modern ranch-style homes in Pecos. Trusted Mexicans lived in ramshackle houses in the fields, where they watched over the valuable wells, pumps, irrigation ditches and cotton. For the men who owned the farms, life was infinitely better in Pecos than it could ever be on the windswept plains. These modern farmers were quite willing to pass up whatever virtues there still might be in the good rural life in favor of a more comfortable in-town life.

Within two years Billie Sol Estes became the talk of Pecos. His farming operations prospered and he began to branch out into such business ventures as a general store in a nearby town, a well-digging company and a ditch-lining service. He was a man who talked big, but he seemed to back with action his natural Texas affinity for bragging. He had bought a nice enough house on the edge of town and he had proved to be a religious man who never missed a service at the Church of Christ.

So it was not surprising that in 1953 some of his friends suggested to the Pecos Junior Chamber of Commerce that Estes be honored by being nominated as one of the five outstanding young Texans of the year. The suggestion was turned down, but his friends nominated him without the official sanction of the Pecos Junior Chamber of Commerce. Billie Sol was named one of the five young men of the year in Texas and then was chosen as one of the ten outstanding young men in the nation.

"Through his tireless energy and brilliant insight," the National Junior Chamber of Commerce selection committee said, "Billie Sol Estes has done much to revolutionize the production, the conservation and expansion of agriculture in the Pecos Valley. He is well known in Texas for his outstanding contribution and leadership in church work and the betterment of conditions of Negroes and Mexicans in Southwest Texas."

Estes was just twenty-nine years old when he was honored at a lavish banquet in Seattle in January 1954 as one of the ten outstanding young men of the year. Two other members of the group were Governor Frank Clement of Tennessee, who became a close friend of Billie Sol's, and Douglas Stringfellow, a Utah Congressman who was being cited partly for his outstanding war record. Later it was discovered that Stringfellow's war exploits had never occurred and his short-lived career in public life came to an abrupt end.

Estes was not an imposing-looking man. He was five feet, eight inches tall and beginning to put on weight. He wore glasses to correct his near-sightedness but had not yet adopted the thick black rims that were later to become so well known to the nation. His face was too fleshy for him to be handsome. He walked a bit awkwardly and with ever so slight a limp. He spoke with a thick Texas accent. His bad grammar and occasional misuse of words betrayed his scanty education in the one-room schoolhouse and small-town high school. He was a modest and at times almost retiring man, but he was fond of quoting his own homely bits of philosophy drawn from the Bible — "The only book," a friend of his once remarked, "that Billie Sol knows anything about."

"When people comment on something they think I have done," Estes told an interviewer at that time, "I want to tell them that by himself a man can accomplish nothing. A man can never do more than he can visualize," he went on. "Some of my ideas have been crazy, but you have to have vision and imagination and believe in both of them. There are more opportunities in every field today than ever before. You have to walk out on a limb to the far end — for that's where the fruit is. If it breaks, you learn how far to go next time."

Estes did not even seem to be particularly disturbed about the new Government cotton allotment program, which in 1954 forced him to cut back his cotton plantings from 1,440 acres to 400 acres. "We will diversify and will experiment with other crops this year," he said. "The surface has hardly been scratched on the agricultural possibilities of the Pecos

Basin. Actually, we are limited only by our own imagination and our own courage."

Government restrictions on wheat as well as on cotton production forced the farmers of West Texas to diversify their crops. Many of them planted their idle acres to grain sorghums, a crop that was almost as good a cattle feed as corn. There were no Government controls on sorghums, and new hybrid varieties had been developed to withstand the harsh, dry climate of West Texas. Like cotton, however, the sorghums did need plenty of anhydrous ammonia fertilizer.

So Estes went into the fertilizer business. At the beginning his operations were little different from those of scores of other fertilizer dealers in the small towns scattered across West Texas. Early each year the dealers signed agreements with farmers in their areas to supply fertilizer throughout the growing season. The anhydrous ammonia fertilizer was stored in large tanks, and taken directly into the fields in smaller, portable tanks about the size of an automobile. Each dealer had a few of these portable tanks.

By the end of 1958 the Estes fertilizer operations began to spread throughout West Texas. Billie Sol and his associates always seemed to be able to sell fertilizer cheaper than their competitors. Also, Estes was a convincing salesman who could easily persuade farmers to do business with him. Billie Sol talked a language the farmers understood.

Government farm subsidies were encouraging surplus production of the new hybrid sorghums in West Texas. To get their Government guarantees under the complicated subsidy program, farmers had to store their crops in grain elevators and warehouses meeting Government specifications, and they were producing surpluses at such a high rate that more and more storage facilities were continually in demand. With his fertilizer sales booming, Estes now moved into the grain storage business.

The entire West Texas farm economy was booming, but Billie Sol seemed to be expanding at a considerably faster rate than his competitors. His extraordinary success was looked upon with envy by rival farmers and businessmen. By 1961, when he was only thirty-six years old, Estes owned or had an interest in forty-one business enterprises: Agricultural, Inc., Agriculture, Inc., Allied Elevators, Billie Sol Estes Enterprises, Colonial Chapel, Del Norte Courts, Delta Homes Investment, Equipment Service, Estes Brothers, Estes Building, Farmers Butane, Farmers Company, Farmers Ditch Liner Service, Farmers Grain and Warehouse, Farmers Storage, Farmers Water Well Drilling, Farmers Water Well Service and Supply, Fort Stockton Implement, Gillette Pipe and Supply, Hale County Grain, Lester-Stone, Midland Concrete, Palo-Duro Grain, Pecos Growers Gas, Pecos Printing, Pecos River Land and Gravel, Pecos Tire Service, Pecos Transit Mix, Roy Lindsay Construction, Sabine Surplus, South Plains Grain, Sudan Storage, United Elevators, United Fertilizer and Chemical, United Grain, United Salvage, Verhalen Credit, Verhalen Mercantile, Western Flying Service, Wheeler Fertilizer, and Woodcrest Apartments.

He also maintained forty-six bank accounts, thirty-seven of them at the First National Bank of Pecos, seven at the Security State Bank in Pecos, one in San Benito, Texas, and another at Fort Stockton, Texas.

Like most other men who become successful, Estes made enemies along the way. He was a man of paradoxes. As a businessman he seemed to take pride in a reputation for ruthlessness. He openly boasted that he was trying to drive rival fertilizer dealers out of business so that he could control the chemical fertilizer market in West Texas. He also had plans for expanding his grain storage business so that he would have a receiving station for grain at almost every crossroads in West Texas. His hard-driving business methods were resented by many of his rivals, but most of the farmers with whom he dealt liked him because he seemed to be a man who tried to do a large volume of business at the smallest possible profit per unit.

Billie Sol had something of both the high-powered evangelist and the successful salesman in him. With his expensive dark-blue suits, his dark ties, his white shirts and a monogramed handkerchief protruding from his breast pocket, he reminded some people of an earnest and successful Bible Belt preacher. The alligator shoes he favored were not what an elder of the church would expect his preacher to be wearing, but the expensive and ostentatious footwear would not have shocked the elder either.

Some of the divided church opinion of Estes was revealed in the fall of 1960 when he was elected an elder of the Church of Christ only after a bitter controversy among the congregation. "We just opposed him because he was not qualified to be an elder," one of the members of the church said. "He was trying to run people out of business and was undercutting them."

One of his opponents quoted I Timothy 3:7 on the qualifications of the leader of a church: "Moreover he must be well thought of by outsiders, or he may fall into reproach and the snare of the devil."

Despite the opposition, Billie Sol was elected an elder, as was his father before him. From all outward appearances

Estes was a God-fearing man. Often he would hurry through important business conferences in a nearby town or even in Dallas or Washington so that he could fly back to Pecos to be at church that night or the next morning.

When W. S. Boyett came to Pecos in September 1960 to become minister of the town's Church of Christ, Estes gave him a white Cadillac. Estes was known to be a big contributor to the church and was said to be the largest contributor to the Pecos Community Chest. He also gave a building to the Negro branch of the Church of Christ in Pecos and helped Mexicans in the town build a chapel.

"I don't think Billie Sol has any deep-seated ill-will in his heart toward anyone," Boyett has said. The minister also said that he had heard Estes pray "for some of the most bitter enemies he's had." "Last year," Boyett added in a conversation with a reporter in 1962, "there was a Mexican family here in dire circumstances. Billie Sol didn't even know the people, but when he found out about it, he sent one of his employees over there who could speak Spanish. It was during the winter and it was cold but the family's lights and gas had been cut off and they hadn't had anything to eat in several days. There were five children in the family. Sol sent his employee to pay all the utility bills and get the lights and gas turned back on, then brought them over thirty dollars' worth of groceries and gave them money for medicine. And he told the man to come to his office the next morning and he gave him a job. There are dozens of cases like that."

Estes not only liked to do good works; he also wanted the world to know that he had a generous Christian spirit. He collected newspaper articles about himself in a pamphlet which he entitled *Success*. Included in it was a flattering picture of Estes looking thoughtfully at a globe — presumably to see what other worlds there were for him to conquer.

The caption was from the Book of Proverbs: *Where there is no vision, the people perish.*

The interviews reprinted in the pamphlet were studded with such Estes aphorisms as:

"If a sparrow cannot fall without His notice, it is impossible for an empire to rise without His aid."

"You win by losing, hold on by letting go, increase by diminishing and multiply by dividing. These are the principles which have brought me success.

"Just keep God's commandments and fear no man."

"You can shear a sheep every year; you can't skin him but once."

He also liked to quote the golden rule: "As ye would that men do unto you, do you likewise unto them."

As the Estes farming, fertilizer and grain storage operations prospered, Billie Sol channeled some of his restless energy into politics. For several years he had contributed to the campaign funds of Democratic Senator Ralph A. Yarborough of Texas and Democratic Congressman J. T. (Slick) Rutherford, who represented the West Texas district that included Pecos. In 1956 Estes was an ardent supporter of Adlai Stevenson in his second campaign for President. Estes seriously suggested to a Pecos banker that he help finance a plan to train parakeets to fly over the United States squawking, "I like Adlai!" (a plan which never got off the ground). In 1960 Estes widened his political interests by also giving money to the national Democratic Party in Washington.

Yarborough was the honored guest at a huge barbecue Estes gave on the two tennis courts in the backyard of his home on the Sunday afternoon before Election Day in November 1960. Estes bragged about his barbecue pit, large even by Texas standards, which he said could easily accommodate three steers. At the November political party were two thousand guests, including many Mexicans and Negroes — unusual in race-conscious Texas.

By then the Estes house had twice been enlarged and had become the showplace of Pecos. It was said to be worth $200,000. The original square, two-story stucco house, which was built over an old swimming pool on an abandoned wartime army base, had sprouted two luxurious stone wings. Old wooden ammunition boxes were used for the walls of the original structure.

In one of the new wings was an ornate, fifty-two-foot palm-bedecked living room that even included a small artificial waterfall. A visitor said that the room looked like a dance hall. The other addition to the house was known as "the Truman wing." It was said that Estes rushed the wing, which is a self-contained guesthouse, to completion in 1960 in anticipation of a visit to Pecos by former President Harry S. Truman. The visit was canceled, and Truman never slept there.

After John F. Kennedy was elected President there were rumors in Pecos that Estes might be appointed Secretary of Agriculture. The rumors proved to be false, and he had to settle for a position on the Agriculture Department's National Cotton Advisory Committee. After the Kennedy Administration took office, Estes was a frequent visitor to Washington. He attended $100-a-plate Democratic fundraising dinners on three occasions and became acquainted with some of the top officials in the Administration. From December 1960 to January 1962, a period of only thirteen months, Estes contributed a total of $12,300 to the national Democratic Party alone. In January 1962 he wrote out a check for $5,000 for fifty tickets at $100 each for the Kennedy Inaugural anniversary dinner in Washington's National Guard Armory. Among his guests at the dinner were Yarborough, members of the Senator's staff, and employees in the office of Vice President Lyndon B. Johnson.

Estes sat at one of the best tables at the dinner, in front of one of the two head tables. Alex Dickie, Jr., Yarborough's administrative assistant, was at the same table. Dickie recalled that Estes "didn't smoke or drink, and I never heard him say a cussword. He was soft-spoken and polite to everyone, and he was very religious."

Another Texan who saw Estes at the dinner remembered that he "was table-hopping all over the place" and was "very attractive to everybody."

Estes began accumulating impressive pictures on the wall of his office in his new one-story headquarters building a few blocks from his home. There they were looking down on Billie Sol — autographed photographs of President Kennedy, former President Truman, Vice President Johnson, Stevenson, and even Democratic Senator John L. McClellan of Arkansas, the Senate's No. 1 investigator, who later would turn his full attention to Estes.

It was about this time, Yarborough later recalled, that dozens of Texans urged him to get behind a movement to help draft Billie Sol as a candidate for the Democratic nomination for governor of Texas. Yarborough described those Texans pushing Estes for the nomination as substantial people in the state, but the Senator said that he turned down the suggestion because he did not think Estes would be a politically feasible candidate, even though he was assured by Estes' supporters that Billie Sol could spellbind his way into the statehouse.

In his only try for public office Estes suffered defeat. This was in 1961, when he ran for the Pecos school board. Estes was beaten by a write-in candidate. Many voters apparently felt that Estes would work to prohibit high school dances and other social events because of his puritanical beliefs. When there had been school parties that included dancing, Estes would throw a big party of his own at his home to try to keep boys and girls from going to the school social event.

Billie Sol's forays into the political world did not distract him from his business operations. His fertilizer operations were expanding so fast, he told other farmers and business-men, that he had exhausted his own credit and would like to borrow their credit to finance the purchase of additional fertilizer tanks to keep up with the demands of his custom-ers for service. Most of the farmers and businessmen he ap-proached were happy to oblige, because Estes was good enough to cut them in for 10 per cent of the money he was borrowing from them. In less than three years his fertilizer tank borrowing skyrocketed to $34 million.

It was late in 1960 when Estes began a rapid expansion of his cotton acreage by using a sale and lease-back arrange-ment to obtain cotton allotments not being used by other farmers. Like the fertilizer tank deals, the cotton allotment plan was advantageous to both Billie Sol and the farmers with whom he was doing business. Through these compli-cated allotment arrangements Estes was able to plant more cotton, and the farmers whose allotments he was leasing were paid for the use of planting permits for which they had no available land.

In the summer of 1961 Estes branched out into two other businesses. First he bought a printing company and started his own newspaper, the Pecos *Daily News*. He did this largely because of the increasing opposition to him and to his business activities from the long-established Pecos *Inde-pendent and Enterprise*, which was published twice a week.

For one thing, the *Independent* had opposed his election to the school board. Estes did not know it at the time, but the *Independent* also was about to embark upon an extensive investigation of his fertilizer tank deals. His other new enterprise was a funeral home, thus fulfilling a forecast of his high school yearbook, whose editors predicted he would become a funeral director.

The Pecos boom that Billie Sol was riding reflected a curious mixture of the frontier spirit of West Texas and the eagerness with which the people of this part of the country have been able to extract every available bit of Government assistance.

Ever since the land was settled late in the nineteenth century it had yielded little to man without a fierce struggle on his part. When a man obtained something from it, he did so only at great cost and effort, and what he got was his and his alone. The settlers changed the land and, as so often happens, the land also affected the men and women who chose to live on it. Sharp business practices remained a part of the every-man-for-himself atmosphere of West Texas. Men went to church every Sunday, but they were all business the other six days of the week.

Although the ever-expanding spending programs of the Federal Government were regularly and religiously denounced in West Texas, they were not ignored if money could be made from them. However much the Federal Government in the abstract may have appeared to be a bad man to the hard-bitten businessmen and farmers, they seldom overlooked any advantages that might accrue to them from the programs.

It was in this intensely independent and fiercely competitive yet solemn churchgoing atmosphere that Estes operated his business enterprises and manipulated the multibillion-dollar farm programs to his personal advantage. In its intensity it was an atmosphere perhaps peculiar to Texas, particularly to still isolated West Texas. Yet to a considerable degree this same attitude, which winks at sharp and often highly questionable business practices and views Government programs as an evil to be taken full advantage of, has permeated much of the modern American business and farming community.

Billie Sol Estes was arrested, indicted and later found guilty by a Texas court because he had defrauded his friends as well as some of America's largest companies. He was also fined because he had violated Agriculture Department regulations. In many respects the Estes operations were in the classic tradition of American swindling. Here was yet another shrewd but highly respected man who had proved himself both as a businessman and as a farmer before embarking on illegal schemes. Like so many swindlers before him, he had an impeccable reputation. He was a churchgoing family man who suddenly seemed to go wrong. His friends agreed that he was smart and lucky enough to have been an honest millionaire, but Estes overstepped the bounds of legality and propriety in his rush to be richer than the Murchisons.

Estes would now be forgotten, however, if he had been just another swindler. He has not been forgotten because his case turned the complex farm subsidies that cost taxpayers more than $5 billion a year into flesh-and-blood problems that suddenly were much easier to understand. The Estes case threw a penetrating spotlight on the vast 100,000-man Agriculture Department bureaucracy, on the Senators and Representatives who write farm legislation, on the farmers who take advantage of every loophole in the loosely drawn laws, and on the businessmen who have a vested interest in farm surpluses.

For thirty years the Federal Government has subsidized the farm economy through costly programs that have undergone few basic changes over the decades. During these years, however, the farm economy has been drastically altered. Despite an unprecedented migration from farm to city since the early 1930's, agricultural production has continued to exceed the nation's needs. New machinery, better seeds, improved planting, cultivation and harvesting methods, and new fertilizers and pesticides have resulted in record production year after year on an ever-declining number of acres.

The nation's antiquated farm legislation was written for an agricultural economy that is as out of date as the Model T Ford. As a result, farm subsidies have encouraged unwanted production at a cost of billions of dollars to taxpayers. In fact, Americans are hit twice in their pocketbooks by the farm programs. They pay for them first in taxes and again when they buy food at the supermarket.

The magnitude of farm subsidies can best be understood when it is remembered that the $5-billion-a-year cost of the subsidies amounts to nearly 40 per cent of the net income of farmers, which came to $12.6 billion in 1962. Not all of the $5 billion in subsidy money goes to farmers; at least $1 billion has been needed each year to finance the cost of storing surplus commodities.

Today's farm programs were developed in the 1920's and put into operation in the 1930's. They grew out of the farm protest movements that took on national political and economic significance beginning in the 1870's. The subsidy programs were drawn up to solve the farm depression problems that plagued the nation throughout the 1920's and most of the 1930's. These were problems quite different from those of the 1960's; yet the farm subsidy tools are essentially the same today as they were thirty years ago.

To understand what has happened to the farm program it is necessary to go back far beyond even the rural depression of the 1920's — to recall the struggle of the Grangers and the other farm protest movements of the late nineteenth century. In those movements were the seeds of the farm program that brought riches and then disaster to Billie Sol Estes.

2

More Hell—and Corn

"WHAT YOU farmers need to do," Mary Elizabeth Lease told Kansas audiences during the 1880's, "is to raise less corn and more hell."

Mrs. Lease was the wife of a farmer who had gone West to Kansas and found life on the frontier hard and unrewarding. She and her husband were among the hundreds of thousands of Americans who took advantage of the Civil War homestead laws to stake out a farming claim on the extensive Government lands of the West. Under the law, land was given to settlers who agreed to farm it. Other Americans had gone West in response to the enticing advertisements and bids of the new Western railroads being built largely with Federal land subsidies.

During the bitter winter months the farmers of Kansas and the other Great Plains states lived in drab isolation. Snow and cold virtually cut them off from the rest of the world. Roads became impassable and travel was all but impossible.

Since the beginnings of the Republic the sturdy, honest, happy, hard-working and resolutely independent yeoman had been one of the most indestructible pillars of the American myth. By the middle of the nineteenth century agriculture, like much of the rest of the American economy, was changing. New machinery, beginning with the McCormick reaper and including the thresher, mower and iron plow, was starting to transform the farm from a self-sufficient, self-contained economic unit into a specialized business. The farmer found himself selling much of his crop for cash and gradually depending on stores in town for many of his needs. The farmer was not, however, sharing in the fruits of the new industrialized society that emerged in the years after the Civil War.

The failure of the agricultural economy to keep pace with the rest of the nation led to a series of farm protest movements, beginning in the 1870's and culminating in the 1890's with the formation of the Populist Party. Mrs. Lease was a Populist who became a well-known prairie orator during the 1880's and 1890's, exhorting farmers to action.

Billie Sol Estes was as different from Mary Elizabeth Lease as the Texas of today is from the Kansas of the 1880's. Yet the roots of the New Deal farm programs that are still the basis for today's extensive network of agricultural subsidies can be traced to the rising rural discontent following the post-Civil War Reconstruction days. In those far-off and simpler times came the first suggestions that the Government should step directly into the farm economy and guarantee agricultural prices through the purchase of commodities. Nearly all of the nineteenth-century proposals for assistance to farmers were for indirect measures designed to cut down the many real and fancied enemies farmers believed were seeking to destroy American agriculture.

For most of the last ninety years American farmers have been raising a lot of hell — but they have not been raising less corn. They have been planting and harvesting more corn, wheat, cotton and other commodities than could be absorbed at profitable prices in domestic and foreign markets. The one constant in the history of American agriculture since the end of the Civil War has been overproduction. Both the farmers and the Government have frequently failed to recognize surpluses as the farm problem. As domestic and international demand fell off, farmers seldom reduced production. Furthermore, production per acre has increased, except in times of particularly bad drought conditions. For almost a century now the only exceptions to this persistent surplus production trend have come during periods of war. There have been other periods of farm prosperity, but they have seldom increased agricultural prices as much as war has raised them.

The unprecedented international demand for wheat after the start of World War I in 1914 led to a vast expansion of wheat production throughout the American West. The plows that broke forty million new acres on the plains in the arid regions of the West not only turned thin soil best suited for grass into wheatfields; they also turned precarious agricultural ventures into profitable farming operations. The farmers later paid their own price when agricultural prices fell disastrously in the 1920's. The rest of the nation paid its price during the 1930's when the Western soils blew across the country in terrible dust storms.

The beginning of World War II in 1939 and the American entrance into the war two years later pushed farm prices upward once again after the lean and hungry decades of the 1920's and the 1930's. Under the pressure of war the surplus stocks of Henry A. Wallace's "ever-normal granary" of the late 1930's were quickly and, as Americans later were to discover, fortuitously drained away. The surpluses started to stack up again when World War II ended in 1945 and Europe was on its way to recovery by 1948. When in 1950 the

United States suddenly found itself fighting a war in far-away Korea, surplus stocks once more disappeared as farm prices increased.

Despite the folklore of husbandry and the supposedly innate and superior intelligence of the yeoman, one generation of farmers never seemed to learn from its fathers or grandfathers. When agricultural prices were considered by farmers to be too low — and they never thought that prices were high enough — they always increased production as the only way to higher income. The farmer traditionally thought that the more he grew the more he would get when it came time to market his crop.

Still another factor working against the farmer is the relatively inelastic demand for food in the United States. As the nation has become more industrialized and as incomes of working people have increased, better-quality food has been consumed by more Americans than ever before. Even with the increase in population in the United States, total food consumption has not kept pace with the ability of farmers to produce ever-increasing quantities of commodities on each acre. If it were possible to end poverty in the United States and to provide an adequate standard of living for all Americans, the consumption of food could not be increased enough to eat up the surpluses.

Although the basic farm problem through the years has been surplus production, with its depressing effect on prices, the efforts of farmers and of their organizations to stabilize production and to get more money for their commodities have followed many political paths and economic byways. Railroads were the earliest targets of farm protest movements because farmers were dependent on them to move their crops to market.

Many railroads also controlled warehouses where farm commodities were stored before being shipped East for processing or for further shipment across the Atlantic to Europe. So warehouse regulations as well as Government restrictions over railroad rates were among the early goals of farm organizations.

The middleman, whether he was president of a giant, impersonal railroad, owner of a warehouse or processor of a commodity, has generally been the object of farmers' discontent. If farmers were not seeking to regulate the man who moved their commodities from the countryside to the wicked cities where the middlemen lived, they were trying to dislodge the alien middleman with enterprises of their own. In the 1870's during the early days of farm protest movements as well as fifty years later in the 1920's, farmer-owned and farmer-operated cooperatives, organized to market agricultural commodities, were looked upon by many farmers as the answer to their problems. In some areas of the farm economy, particularly wheat and dairying, farm cooperatives became strong enough to give their members a greater return on their labors; but for the most part cooperatives were no more effective in solving the problems of overproduction and low prices than were efforts to regulate railroads and warehouses.

Throughout the history of the farm protest movements sporadic attempts were made to solve the farmers' problems through direct Government intervention in the agricultural economy. Such a drastic step was first suggested in the 1880's, but it was not until the depths of the great depression in the early 1930's that the Federal Government became deeply involved in the agricultural economy by placing floors under farm prices.

The first of many national farm protest and reform organizations that sought to channel rural discontent in the United States into meaningful action was the National Grange of the Patrons of Husbandry. The Grange was founded in 1867 by an Agriculture Department clerk named Oliver Hudson Kelley. During a trip through the South he became deeply concerned over the isolated and drab life led by most farmers. Kelley resolved to do all he could to help the farmers to a better life. Through the ritual of a lodge he hoped to bring both farmers and their wives to community meetings for social, cultural and educational activities as well as for discussions of the new machines, methods and marketing techniques of the scientific agriculture of those days. He was trying to develop rural communities and to bring some form and substance to them.

The Granger movement did not become a force in American agriculture until after the depression of 1873. As times got tougher farmers flocked to Grange meetings. By 1875 the movement claimed a membership of more than eight hundred thousand in twenty thousand lodges scattered over practically every state. The greatest Granger strength was in the South and Midwest, and it was in the Midwestern states that the movement was turned from a cultural and educational effort into a militant political organization. In the summer of 1873 farmers throughout the Midwest heard the "Farmers' Declaration of Independence" read at Granger meetings on the "Farmers' Fourth of July."

With far more enthusiasm than good business sense, Grangers organized cooperatives to market milk and cream, to store grain and other commodities, to insure farmers, to sell them supplies and even to manufacture stoves and machinery. The farmers who ran the cooperatives turned out to be better philosophers than businessmen. The cooperatives were badly managed and were faced with great hostility from the middlemen with whom they were competing. Few of the cooperatives prospered and most of them disappeared about as quickly as they had sprung up. The most successful enterprise to come out of the Granger movement was the very sort of big business the farmers were trying to attack. In 1872 Montgomery Ward and Company was founded to help bring to farmers through a mail-order merchandising system the goods they needed and wanted.

The Granger attack on railroads and warehouses quickly resulted in what seemed to be considerable success. Senators and Representatives sympathetic to the Granger program were in the majority in many legislatures in the Midwest in the early 1870's. Beginning in 1871, first in Illinois and then in Minnesota, Iowa and Wisconsin, Granger-dominated legislatures passed laws regulating railroads and warehouses. These railroad and warehouse commissions, which survive today in many states, led to the establishment by Congress in 1887 of the Interstate Commerce Commission to regulate railroads on a national basis.

Through attacks in the courts, administrative restraints on the commissions and restrictive legislation, the railroads succeeded in blunting the effectiveness of the Granger-inspired regulations and reforms. The Granger movement itself went into eclipse, not so much because of the failure of its ambitious reform program but rather because of the return to the countryside of relative prosperity.

The Granger movement exists today, largely in New England and New York State, but it never again attained the influence it had in the 1870's.

By the 1880's, when farm prices next declined, two new organizations became the focus of the farm protest movement. A farm organization in the North and West was founded in 1880 by Milton George, editor of *Western Rural*, a farm paper published in Chicago. He called his organization the National Farmers' Alliance, but it was better known as the Northern or Northwestern Alliance. In the South the Farmers' Alliance and Industrial Union grew out of an organization founded by Dr. C. W. Macune. It had its beginnings in a group of Lampasas County, Texas, farmers who banded together to catch horse thieves as well as to buy supplies on a cooperative basis.

At first the Alliance movement, like the Grangers before it, emphasized cooperatives and social and educational activities. The Alliances quickly shifted their sights to politics, first in the North and then in the South. They tried to get state legislatures in the Midwest to approve measures to grade grain, to prevent foreclosure of mortgages on farms, and to regulate railroads.

As a third party movement in the North and West, and as an insurgent group in the South challenging the Bourbon control there over the Democratic Party, the Alliance forces swept into control of a dozen state legislatures in 1890 — four in the Midwest and eight in the South. The Alliances also elected six governors — among them "Pitchfork Ben" Tillman of South Carolina — four Senators and fifty Congressmen, including the colorful Tom Watson of Georgia. The magnitude of the victories by the radical Alliance forces surprised the farmers themselves and shocked the dominant conservative forces in American politics.

The time had come for the formation of a third party representing the interests of the people and opposed to the forces of monopoly. In July 1892 more than thirteen hundred jubilant reformers met in Omaha to form the People's —or Populist—Party. Alarmed conservatives saw the Populists as the most serious threat to the American political status quo since the Civil War. Not since the days of Andrew Jackson had the people created such a political stir.

Seventy years later the Populist program hardly seems radical; most of its proposals have long since been enacted into law. For the 1890's the program was radical, even though it was made up of proposals that had long been part of the plans of urban as well as rural reformers. To the Populists the principal solution to their problems was reform of the monetary system. Most farmers were debtors and were not frightened by inflation. The Populists wanted more paper money, to be issued by the Government and not the banks. They also wanted unlimited coinage of silver. The silver question was later to dominate the programs of the earnest but practical rural reformers, many of whom realized that the silver-mining interests of the West represented a practically inexhaustible reservoir of campaign funds.

The Populists also wanted the Government to take over the railroads and the telephone and telegraph systems. If the Populists had their way, the railroads would also be forced to return to the people most of the public lands generously granted to them by Congress to encourage the westward expansion of the country. Other reforms backed by the Populists included the secret ballot, direct election of

Senators, the initiative and referendum, an income tax, a shorter work week and the establishment of postal savings banks.

In addition, the Populists had a farm program — the forerunner of the present-day farm price support system. The Populists proposed that the Federal Government operate a network of national warehouses where farmers could store grain, cotton and other nonperishable commodities. The farmers who owned the commodities would be allowed, under the Populist sub-Treasury plan, to borrow from the Government up to 80 per cent of the value of the stored commodities. The money would be given to the farmers in special Treasury notes. This was part of the flexible Populist monetary program, which immediately raised fears of uncontrollable inflation. What was significant about the Populist farm program was the effort being made through it to give farmers some control over their prices by allowing them to store commodities until the market price was right. The New Deal price support and loan programs of the 1930's were not very different from the Populist proposals of forty years before.

The Populists looked at the world and saw in it a conspiracy against the farmer. His enemies were the bankers of New York and London who kept interest rates high and money dear. Aligned with the bankers were the businessmen who ran the railroads and profiteered with their warehouses.

If the nation were indeed run by a gang of conspirators, as the Populists charged, the leaders of the new party were unable to convince the people that their rulers should be overthrown in favor of the radicals from the South and West. In the presidential elections of 1892 the Populists nominated James B. Weaver of Iowa. The Republican candidate was William McKinley of Ohio, and Grover Cleveland of New York was running on the Democratic ticket. Cleveland was seeking a second term; he had been President from 1885 to 1889. Cleveland was elected and Populist Weaver showed little strength, carrying just four states — Kansas, Colorado, Nevada and Idaho. The poor showing made by the Populists in the Midwest and the failure of the party to carry a single Southern state were bitter disappointments to the leaders of the movement.

Populism was at its high tide in 1892. Four years later, when the Democrats ran William Jennings Bryan against McKinley, the Populists supported Bryan rather than nominate a presidential candidate of their own. The Populist silver issue was Bryan's rallying cry, and the Democratic platform of 1896 advocated much of the Populist program of four years before. McKinley defeated Bryan, but in Bryan the agrarian reformers had found the leader that they had been searching for during the previous two decades. Bryan was to run two more times for the presidency, but he was destined never to be elected.

The agrarian reformers themselves never tasted the sweetness of a national electoral victory, but those who lived on into the twentieth century had the satisfaction of seeing their proposals accepted as law. The railroads have never been nationalized, and it took forty years for a farm program to be implemented along the lines of the original Populist proposals. Except for these notable omissions, most of the rest of the agrarian reform proposals that the Populists first turned into national issues in 1892 were enacted into law by the time World War I broke out in 1914.

From the first Bryan campaign in 1896 to the beginning of World War I eighteen years later, American farmers were never completely out of trouble. Yet later generations were to look back upon those two decades as a golden age. The New Deal farm program took the years 1910-1914 as the base period to be used in determining when farm income and the prices of goods bought by farmers were in a proper relationship.

The two decades from the mid-1890's to the start of World War I marked the beginning of the migration from the countryside to the city that continues today. During this period millions of Europeans were also pouring into America's cities, creating expanding markets for the remaining farmers.

During World War I the demand in Europe and other parts of the world for food, particularly wheat, became so great that for a time men were rushing back to the land rather than away from farms to the cities. "Suitcase farmers" went West from Chicago and other Midwestern cities and even some Eastern cities to plant the Great Plains to wheat. For a few years they reaped a bountiful harvest that could easily be sold for good prices in a world torn by war.

By 1920 the short-lived boom was over. Europe once again could feed itself without depending upon the large American imports the war had made necessary. Then the worst and longest agricultural depression in the history of the country began settling over a shocked, hurt, bewildered and embittered rural America.

Not only did farm production increase in Europe, thus sharply diminishing what had become a lucrative market for American farmers; also the European countries began purchasing commodities from exporters other than the United States. India and Egypt took much of the European cotton market away from the farmers of the American South.

Within a year, from 1919 to 1920, the price of cotton in the
United States declined by more than one half, from 38 to
18 cents a pound. The loss of European wheat markets to
Argentina, Australia and Canada as well as to the European
farmers themselves forced American wheat prices down
50 per cent to one dollar a bushel. Corn prices also sharply
declined, reaching their lowest point since the middle of
the 1890's.

The first legislative efforts to solve the depression that
choked rural America in the early 1920's followed traditional agricultural reform lines. At the request of farm
groups, now led by the American Farm Bureau Federation,
Congress passed legislation exempting farmer cooperatives
from the antitrust laws and granting them tax advantages.
It was believed that strengthened cooperatives would help
farmers get prices for their commodities which would assure
them an adequate return on the capital and labor they had
invested in their farms. Farmers also clamored for high
tariffs to keep foreign commodities from competing with
American crops.

In addition, Congress allowed the Federal land banks to
lend more money on farm mortgages, permitted Federal
loans to farmers on livestock and on crops about to be
marketed, and passed legislation providing for Federal regulation of packing houses, stockyards and commission merchants to try to prevent price manipulations and other practices judged to be unfair to farmers. The middleman
continued to be the farmers' villain.

While the nation's industrial economy first boomed and
then roared during the 1920's, farmers continued to struggle
to earn an adequate income. Prices farmers got for their
products declined throughout the decade while prices they
had to pay for tractors and other equipment essential to

efficient operations increased. Efforts during the 1920's to expand production succeeded only in further depressing farm income. So farmers turned from cooperatives and other indirect attempts to raise their income to seek direct Government intervention for the agricultural economy.

Through the efforts of Senator Arthur Capper, a Republican farm paper publisher from Kansas, and other members of Congress from Midwestern and Southern agricultural states, a loosely organized farm bloc that was to endure through the early 1950's was formed on Capitol Hill. For the first time Senators and Representatives from the cotton, peanut and tobacco states of the Old South formed a working legislative partnership with their colleagues from the corn, cattle, hog and wheat states of the Midwest and the West.

The farm bloc concentrated its efforts on the McNary-Haugen bill, based on a program developed by George N. Peek, a Moline, Illinois, plow manufacturer. Charles L. McNary was a Republican Senator from Oregon and Gilbert Haugen a Republican Representative from Iowa. From 1924 to 1928 they sponsored a plan that at first covered only corn, wheat and other grains but later, to gain Southern support, was expanded to include cotton, tobacco and rice.

The McNary-Haugen bill proposed that a Government corporation or farm board buy surplus American production at domestic prices, which were generally higher than the world prices for the same commodities. The Government would sell — or "dump" — the surpluses at the lower world prices. Thus there would be no dangerous, price-depressing surpluses hanging over the United States market and driving down farm incomes. The program would be financed through an "equalization fee" collected by the Government from farmers.

The plan sought to apply to agriculture many of the same principles that had long been used to protect American industry from disastrous foreign competition. The Republican Administrations of the 1920's had supported a high protectionist tariff. Nevertheless, in 1927 and again in 1928, President Calvin Coolidge vetoed the McNary-Haugen bill. On the day in 1927 when Coolidge rejected the farm legislation because he said it constituted interference with laissez-faire economic principles, he signed a bill increasing by 50 per cent the tariff on pig iron.

Farmers had raised hell, Congress had passed legislation, but Coolidge had vetoed it. So farmers continued to raise more corn and other crops in a vain effort to increase their incomes. For farmers this was still the age of laissez-faire.

Under the McNary-Haugen plan the Government's role in underwriting the farm economy would have been as great as any dreamed of by the early Grangers or by the more radical Populists. Many conservative men throughout the farming areas of the South and the Midwest supported the McNary-Haugen plan of the 1920's because the nation's agricultural economy so badly needed help.

During the Hoover Administration, which began in 1928 only eighteen months before the nation plunged into the great depression, a Federal Farm Board was finally established. The Farm Board was too little and too late.

A congressional act of June 1929, passed little more than four months before the depression began, set up the Farm Board to encourage the formation of cooperatives, to seek voluntary limitations on the production of crops, and to spend up to $500 million to stabilize farm prices by purchasing commodities in surplus. The Farm Board did buy up large quantities of wheat and cotton, but these purchases failed to stop the decade-long decline in farm prices.

From 1920 to 1932 net farm income dropped from $9 billion to $2.5 billion, a decrease of more than two thirds. A bushel of wheat sold for $1.82 in 1920 and 38 cents in 1932. During the same period corn prices dropped from 61 to 32 cents a bushel. Cotton, which had brought 16 cents a pound in 1920, sold for 6 cents in 1932.

When Franklin D. Roosevelt took the oath of office as President in March 1933, no one was worse off than the farmers. They had endured not three years of depression, as had the rest of the country; they had suffered for more than a decade. It was not surprising that the first piece of legislation President Roosevelt sent to Congress during the first hundred days of his Administration was an agricultural recovery program.

The legislation put the Government squarely into the farm economy, and the Government has remained there ever since. The ideas planted by the Grangers, the Alliance movement, the Populists and the McNary-Haugen forces were now bearing fruit in the New Deal farm program.

3

Millions of Pigs, Billions of Dollars

THE NEW DEAL farm program began in 1933 with the plowing up of ten million acres of cotton and the slaughter of more than six million pigs. No one objected to the destruction of the cotton, even though millions of unemployed Americans were without proper clothing. It was the killing of the pigs that outraged the nation. The remarks of a Midwestern minister were typical of the outcry heard across the country. He told a church conference that "the destruction of foodstuffs in the present want" was "downright sinful."

"It just makes me sick all over," a woman wrote Secretary of Agriculture Henry A. Wallace, "when I think how the Government has killed millions and millions of little pigs, and how that has raised pork prices until today we poor people cannot even look at a piece of bacon."

During a *National Farm and Home Hour* radio address in November 1935, more than two years after the pigs were slaughtered, Wallace noted: "People are still interested in the six million pigs that were killed in September of 1933. In letters I have received following these radio talks, the pigs are mentioned more often than any one thing except potatoes."

The decision to kill the pigs was made in August 1933.

The slaughter was suggested by corn and hog producers at a meeting in Chicago because there was such a surplus of hogs that they had been selling for less than three cents a pound. The supply of pigs was so large that both farmers and Agriculture Department economists could foresee only a further depressing of hog prices when the pigs were ready for market in the fall or the next spring.

So the Emergency Hog-Marketing Program was put into effect. The Government's new Agricultural Adjustment Administration agreed to buy pigs and sows at prices designed to withdraw enough pigs from the market to prevent a further decline in hog prices. A total of 5.1 million small pigs, 1.1 million heavier pigs and 222,000 sows were sold to the Government by farmers in forty-one states. The farmers received $30.6 million for the pigs and sows, an average of nearly $4.80 per animal.

This does not seem like much money, but in the previous winter many farmers kept their homes warm by burning corn instead of coal. Coal cost money, which the farmers did not have. Corn was available in large quantities. It could be fed to hogs and cattle, but seldom at a profit. So why not at least use it to keep warm?

Farmers turned over their pigs to Agriculture Department representatives at eighty processing and meat packing plants throughout the country. The farmers were paid and the pigs were killed. They were turned into more than ninety-seven million pounds of dry salt pork, twenty-one million pounds of inedible grease, and five hundred tons of fertilizer. The pork was distributed to families on relief. The grease and fertilizer were sold to commercial dealers for $604,000.

"I suppose," Wallace said two years later in commenting on the hostile public reaction to the slaughter of the six million pigs, "it is a marvelous tribute to the humanitarian instincts of the American people that they sympathize more with little pigs being killed than with full-grown hogs. Some people may object to killing pigs at any age. Perhaps they think that farmers should run a sort of old folks' home for hogs and keep them around indefinitely as barnyard pets. This is a splendid attitude, but it happens that we have to think about farmers as well as hogs. And above all, we must think about consumers and try to get a uniform supply of pork from year to year at a price which is fair to farmer and consumer alike."

No matter how often Wallace tried to explain the slaughter of the pigs, Americans still found it difficult to understand why part of a hungry nation's potential food supply should be destroyed. By 1935 it was even more difficult to convince Americans that the 1933 decision had been the right one. In 1934 a severe drought cut the corn crop in half. Farmers quickly reduced their hog production because of the shortage of feed. As fewer hogs were marketed, pork prices increased and consumers complained.

Wallace explained again and again that the pigs which were killed in 1933 would have been marketed in 1934 and not in 1935, when the drought-induced pork shortage developed. He also noted that if the pigs had not been killed they would have eaten sixty million bushels of corn. Instead, he added, the corn was available to help ease hog-feeding problems during the 1934 drought and into 1935. Millions of Americans remained unconvinced.

Henry Agard Wallace was raised in a rich Iowa agricultural tradition. His father and his grandfather before him had edited the respected farm paper *Wallace's Farmer*, in Des Moines. A graduate of the Iowa State Agricultural College, Wallace was not only a writer and editor; he was also a plant geneticist and an agricultural statistician. He understood both the science and economics of agriculture. He helped develop hybrid corn, which made possible the high corn yields of the 1950's.

When in 1921 his father, Henry C. Wallace, became Secretary of Agriculture in President Warren G. Harding's Cabinet, young Henry took over the editorship of the family paper, although he was still only in his early thirties. As the editor of one of the best-known farm publications in the country, Wallace was an active figure in the agricultural reform efforts of the 1920's.

Born and raised a Republican, he became increasingly disenchanted with his party after seeing his father's attempts to help farmers frustrated by other members of the businessman's Republican Cabinet of the early 1920's. In 1928 Wallace formally broke with the Republicans and supported Democrat Alfred E. Smith for the presidency against Herbert Hoover.

President Roosevelt was attracted to Wallace because of his intense idealism. When Wallace entered the Cabinet at the age of forty-five he was a shy, rumpled-looking man with an unruly shock of hair. He was neither a smoker nor a drinker and sometimes even abstained from meat. He exercised regularly and sometimes violently, favoring hikes at dawn in Washington's Rock Creek Park.

There was nothing polished about Wallace. His conversation was devoid of small talk, his clothes never seemed to fit, and he was never comfortable at the numerous cocktail parties and official dinners he had to attend as a Cabinet member. He was at home, though, with the problems of agriculture: here he knew what the farm problem was and what he wanted to do about it.

The slaughter of the little pigs would haunt Wallace and the Roosevelt Administration throughout the 1930's. Nevertheless, if farm income was to be increased, the production of hogs as well as corn, wheat, cotton and other commodities had to be reduced and brought into line with national and world needs.

The lessons of sixty years of intermittent farm distress were clear. Surplus production was the primary cause of the nation's lingering farm problem. The surpluses could be reduced either by greatly increasing the already substantial migration from farm to city or by forcing all farmers to cut back their production. In the midst of the nation's worst depression farmers could not be moved off the land to the cities, where they would only increase the already large relief rolls. So the only answer in 1933 seemed to be Government programs to reduce farm production.

To farmers, the establishment of the Agricultural Adjustment Administration in the spring of 1933 was a great victory. A Congress and a New Deal Administration sympathetic to almost any legislation that held out the promise of relief and recovery for a stricken nation had sought to answer at last the cries from farmers for direct Government help.

Some Americans thought the New Deal farm legislation, passed by Congress in May 1933, had come none too soon. In the Midwest, particularly in Iowa, leaders of the Farmers' Holiday movement were urging farmers to go on strike. Under the direction of an energetic farm leader named Milo Reno, members of the movement tried to get farmers to withhold their commodities from market. They overturned trucks and dumped milk onto highways.

The lives of judges who ordered the foreclosure of mortgages on farms were threatened. When farms or the possessions of farmers were sold at auctions, the Farmers' Holiday leaders made certain that the auctions were flooded with farmers pledged to bid no more than a penny or two for any item. When the auction had ended the successful bidders handed the farm and its furnishings and equipment back to their grateful owner.

The possibility of a rural revolt probably was greatly exaggerated, but the Farmers' Holiday movement and its sympathizers unquestionably spurred on both Wallace and Congress to take action quickly.

The original New Deal farm legislation was written largely by the leaders of the farm organizations themselves. The American Farm Bureau Federation, which had three hundred thousand members even in the midst of the depression, had become the dominant farm organization. Founded in 1920, it had developed from the Agricultural Department extension program set up in 1914, in which Government agents were sent into every rural county to show farmers how to be more scientific and efficient. During the 1930's the president of the Farm Bureau, which had and still has its greatest strength in the Midwest and the South, was Edward A. O'Neal of Alabama. The Populist movement had left its mark on O'Neal, but he was neither an economist nor a philosopher. All he wanted was higher prices for farm commodities. He was willing to accept production controls in exchange for price guarantees.

Although the new farm program was looked upon by many Americans as a radical development in agricultural policy, it was for the most part an adaptation of the McNary-

Haugen domestic allotment plan that had been before Congress for almost ten years. Under the New Deal farm program, producers of cotton, wheat, corn, hogs, tobacco, rice and milk were to be guaranteed minimum prices if they agreed to reduce production. The Government would lend money on the crops at the minimum price guarantees and take over the commodities if farmers did not choose to pay off the loans. The program was financed through a processing tax levied on these seven so-called basic commodities. The levy on processors was passed on by them to consumers, who were thus paying for a subsidy program that would increase farm prices and would also raise food prices.

The initial New Deal legislation worked moderately well during its three-year history. Cash incomes of farmers rose as more than $1.8 billion was poured into the agricultural economy. Partly as a result of drought in the West and Midwest from 1934 to 1936 and partly because of the utilization of acreage controls in the South, production was cut back. Cotton production, for example, was reduced from 13 million bales in 1933 to 9.6 million the next year, but by 1935 it was back up to 10.6 million bales. Farmers were taking their worst land out of production and then intensifying the cultivation of their remaining acres, a practice that would continue to plague farm control programs.

As farmers, economists and politicians argued over the results of the New Deal agricultural relief measures, the program was challenged before the United States Supreme Court in a case involving the Hoosac cotton mill of Massachusetts. It refused to pay processing taxes that the Government declared were due on cotton the mill had turned into cloth. In a decision that swept aside the New Deal farm program the Supreme Court held in 1936 that the processing tax was an integral part of an unconstitutional plan to regulate agricultural production. Such power, said the Court, was not granted to Congress by the Constitution.

Without the funds raised by the tax the farm program could not continue. The program had been enough of a success, however, for no one to talk seriously of again abandoning agriculture to the highly uncertain forces of the marketplace. Instead, the farm bloc in Congress, the farm organizations outside Congress, and leaders in the Roosevelt Administration quickly sought a workable substitute for their now unconstitutional program.

A new program would have to be financed with direct appropriations rather than through a special levy such as the processing tax. The 1936 agricultural legislation provided for Federal payments to farmers who agreed to carry out good soil conservation practices. The payments were set up to encourage farmers to reduce production of commodities judged to be soil-depleting crops and to increase their acreages of soil-conserving crops. Thus the emphasis was still on the reduction of surplus production. Whatever progress had been made in this direction during the previous three years, it was already becoming clear that surplus production was a problem that would confront farmers again if constant efforts were not made to hold down acreage.

The 1936 legislation was a not too successful stopgap effort, and by 1938 Congress was ready to approve a farm program that remains today the basis for the costly agricultural subsidies. The 1938 act combined what were thought to be the best features of the previous two New Deal efforts to increase farm income through price guarantees given to farmers who agreed to reduce production when it outran the needs of the nation.

The principal instrument of American farm policy became the price support system. Using the 1910-1914 "golden" period of American agriculture as a base and a goal, the program established within limits set by law what were considered to be fair prices for commodities — prices farmers should receive for crops which would not only cover production costs and assure a profit but would also provide incomes on a "parity" with business and industrial workers' incomes.

To accomplish this delicate and at times difficult balance the Government stood ready to lend money to farmers on their commodities at from 52 to 75 per cent of the parity price. The farmers could redeem their loans within a specified period of time, but if the farmers did not do so the Government had no recourse except to take title to the commodities through its Commodity Credit Corporation. Here was the ever-normal granary concept long advocated by Wallace and many other farm leaders. The commodities taken over by the Government under the price support and storage program would be valuable insurance for the lean years that the Old Testament had warned against and that the United States itself had become concerned with during the drought of the early 1930's.

Another key part of the 1938 legislation gave the Secretary of Agriculture authority to impose restrictions on the production or marketing of a surplus commodity. These provisions would presumably prevent the agricultural program from becoming an open-end subsidy for farmers. The price guarantees constituted the carrot on the end of the control stick.

The loan and purchase programs were confined to crops that could be stored for many years, such as wheat, corn, cotton, tobacco and rice. For such perishable commodities as milk and fruits and vegetables the Government was authorized to establish direct purchase programs. The results were the same, whether they were accomplished under a loan-and-subsequent-purchase program or a direct-purchase system. Either way the Government was under-writing the farm economy by agreeing to buy agricultural commodities at minimum prices. The minimums established a floor under all prices paid for the commodities.

The legislation hardly had time to go into effect before World War II broke out in Europe in 1939. Two years later the United States was in the war, and suddenly a nation that had been plagued with surplus food production for two decades needed to change its course abruptly to encourage farmers to produce all the food they possibly could get out of their fields. As it did a generation earlier, America once again had to feed a world at war.

The experience of the seven years from 1933 to 1939 that the United States had with farm production controls and farm price guarantees was inconclusive and to some extent disappointing. Farm income did rise, but not until 1941 did it reach the admittedly unsatisfactory $6.8-billion-a-year level of 1929, the predepression high. The 1939 figure was $5.2 billion compared with $2.5 billion in 1932. Production was cut back during the 1930's, but only because of the serious drought. In the South, where production control and price incentive programs had perhaps their fairest trial, cotton acreage began to increase after the initial cutbacks.

The experience showed that at best farm programs could reduce production only at a high cost to the Government. Without attractive price guarantees, farmers would not cut back their production, and even with good guarantees the reductions would not necessarily make a significant dent in surplus production. Farmers were still not convinced that less production was the answer to their income problems.

In 1940, as war in Europe began to raise farm prices and increase the demand for farm commodities, Wallace resigned as Secretary of Agriculture after the Democrats nominated him for Vice-President. Wallace was succeeded as Secretary by Claude R. Wickard, an Indiana farmer who had been in Washington since the early New Deal days helping to run the corn-hog production control programs. In January 1940 Wallace selected Wickard as Undersecretary and in August Wickard took over as Secretary.

Like Wallace, Wickard had lived with the farm problem during the 1920's and had participated in the long campaign for Government aid for agriculture. Wickard was born on an Indiana farm and was a successful farmer when he came to work for the Agricultural Adjustment Administration in Washington in 1933.

Wickard's farm program philosophy was little different from Wallace's, but his problems as Secretary were considerably different. Wallace struggled to increase farm income primarily by reducing production. Wickard hardly was settled in the Secretary's magnificent office overlooking the Mall and the Washington Monument when it became clear that the war in Europe would mean expansion, not contraction, of the American farm economy.

Most of Wickard's five-year tenure as Secretary was devoted first to establishing his supremacy over the nation's food programs after the United States entered World War II in December 1941, and then to getting maximum production from the nation's farms. Although Wickard was not particularly skilled in the fine art of bureaucratic infighting in Washington, he did manage to maintain control over the food programs that Leon Henderson of the War Production Board and others would have liked to take over.

During World War II questions of surpluses and controls became academic. A Government that had been seeking to discourage farm production now wanted food and more food, cotton and more cotton. As long as the war lasted farmers had no reason to fear sudden declines in prices or the loss of markets and the piling up of surpluses. From 1939 to 1945 farm production increased by almost 25 per cent. By 1943 farm prices were more than double their prewar levels.

It would not seem that farmers needed more encouragement to produce all the required food and fiber, but they feared there would be another agricultural depression once the war ended. Congress passed legislation providing for further guarantees, expanding the list of commodities for which prices would be supported until it included practically all crops. Even more important was an amendment to the basic 1938 legislation stating that the Government would underwrite farm prices at no less than 90 per cent of parity as long as the war lasted and for two years after it ended.

During the depression years prices of only a few basic commodities like corn, cotton and tobacco were supported by the Government, and only at 52 to 75 per cent of parity. The prewar guarantees were quite reasonable compared with the 90 per cent wartime and postwar guarantees. A farm program that was modest during the 1930's, when farmers needed help the most, started to get out of hand during World War II, when farmers required no assistance. Farmers quickly discovered that wartime was the best time to get what they wanted from the Government.

After Roosevelt's death in April 1945 his successor, Vice-

President Harry S. Truman, asked Wickard to resign and become head of the Rural Electrification Administration, a post that he accepted and held until Truman left office in 1953.

Wickard had contributed little to farm policy, because the wartime shortage of food had taken care of the surplus problems that Wallace had struggled with for seven years. Wickard was neither a strong man nor a forceful administrator, but he was able with the help of generous agricultural legislation to get the farm production that the nation and its allies so badly needed.

To succeed Wickard, President Truman chose a New Mexico Congressman named Clinton P. Anderson. Before entering Congress the soft-spoken Anderson had been a successful insurance agent, president of Rotary International and an administrator of Federal relief and unemployment compensation programs in his state.

Born in South Dakota, Anderson was educated at Dakota Wesleyan University and the University of Michigan and then went West to New Mexico. Just fifty years old when he entered the Cabinet, Anderson was a big, slow-moving, deliberate and tenacious man who was serving his fifth year in Congress and was chairman of a Special House Committee to Investigate Food Shortages.

When the war ended, farmers found that they would not immediately have to rely on the new price guarantees. Europe desperately needed American food for her recovery. Emergency postwar food relief programs continued to encourage maximum production.

By 1948 Western Europe was beginning to meet most of its own food needs, and Anderson and Truman realized that the high wartime price support programs could not be continued without costly and harmful effects on the farm economy. Anderson drafted a program calling for the gradual reduction of price supports to lower, flexible levels.

The legislation was passed by Congress in 1948, shortly before Anderson resigned as Secretary to run for the Senate from New Mexico. He was elected and is now in his third Senate term.

In the congressional debate over the legislation, the arguments were not over whether the Government should remain as an active force in the farm economy but over how the Government should carry out its role as the guarantor of farm prosperity. The legislation reaffirmed a national policy making the Government responsible for a stable farm economy through price guarantees and production controls.

There seemed to be a consensus among both Republican and Democratic members of Congress that a return to a sliding scale of farm price guarantees was a workable solution to the postwar farm problem.

Had the 1948 legislation been allowed to go into effect, much of the heavy cost of the farm program during the 1950's and 1960's could have been avoided. The whole outlook for farm legislation was changed by Truman's spectacular upset of Thomas E. Dewey in the 1948 presidential election. To the surprise of Democrats and Republicans alike, Truman carried traditional Republican states in the Midwest.

Truman's victory in the Midwest was attributed in large part to another farm bill passed by the Republican-controlled Eightieth Congress shortly before it adjourned in June 1948. Congress cut back a Federal program for the construction of warehouses and bins for the storage of surplus commodities. The Republicans said they wanted to get the storage business out of Government hands and turn it over to private enterprise.

During the campaign Truman charged that the Republicans were trying to sabotage the farm program by failing to provide enough storage space for surpluses. It was an issue farmers easily understood. They knew that without adequate storage facilities they would not be able to take advantage of price guarantees. The Government would not lend money on a commodity unless it was placed in approved warehouses.

Farm production in 1948 was greater than it had ever been before. With this huge production and the decline in European markets, farmers realized that for the first time since the United States had entered the war seven years earlier, the loan and guarantee programs would be needed. As a shortage of storage facilities developed during the fall presidential campaign, partly because of the Republican legislation and partly because of the large crop, farmers became alarmed and showed their displeasure by voting for the Democrats and against the Republicans.

Truman's triumph was interpreted by both Democrats and Republicans to mean that farmers did not want anyone tampering with their subsidies and guarantees.

Immediately after the election Charles F. Brannan, who had succeeded Anderson as Secretary of Agriculture in May 1948, went to work drafting new farm legislation. Brannan was a Colorado lawyer who had spent his working life as an Agriculture Department attorney. Moving up through the Department hierarchy, he had taken over as Secretary when few men wanted the job. No one expected Truman to win in 1948, and when Anderson made known his intention to resign to run for the Senate it looked as if his successor would be a lame-duck chair-warmer until the Republicans took over.

Instead, in January 1949 Brannan, a careful lawyer with a wide understanding of agricultural problems despite the lack of a farm background, was busily at work preparing a new farm program. His thinking was extensively influenced by the National Farmers Union, a farm organization with pronounced liberal leanings which had been influential among Western wheat farmers since its establishment in the early 1900's.

The Brannan Plan, which Truman presented to Congress in the spring of 1949, became the subject of the most heated controversy among farmers and farm groups since the slaughter of the little pigs. It was attacked largely because it provided for direct subsidy payments to farmers.

Under Brannan's proposal consumer demand would have set the market price for perishable commodities. The difference between what farmers were paid for the commodities and what the Government considered a fair price would be made up by direct subsidy payments from the Federal Treasury to farmers. The direct payments would be substituted for the loan and purchase programs that had been the basis of farm policy since 1933.

For commodities like cotton, corn and wheat that could be stored the Brannan Plan would have relied on rigid production controls and high price guarantees. The Brannan Plan envisioned a high cost and high price but low production agricultural economy.

Both the leaders of farm organizations and farmers themselves were fearful of direct handouts from the Government. They preferred the complicated price support system that perserved at least the illusion that prices were made in the marketplace and that farmers were being paid in accordance with what their commodities would bring in the market.

The objections of farmers and their organizations to a direct payment system of subsidies were based on a political fear. Farmers believed, and with some justification, that direct subsidies would be more susceptible to change and annual manipulation in Congress than the indirect subsidies of the price support programs.

Congress turned down the direct-payment features of the Brannan Plan but made some important changes in the 1948 sliding-scale farm legislation. The 1949 law continued the 90 per cent parity formula and postponed the effective date of the sliding-scale plan.

The day of reckoning for farm policy was further postponed by the Korean War, which began in 1950 and was not ended until 1953. Like all wars before it, the Korean conflict bolstered the demand for farm commodities and quickly reduced the surpluses that had begun to accumulate after Europe's postwar food needs were met.

When President Dwight D. Eisenhower assumed office in January 1953, the United States was still following a wartime farm policy. Prices were guaranteed at high levels and there were no controls except over tobacco production. The demands for food resulting from the Korean War had temporarily saved the country from a dangerous surplus, but the war was now over and something had to be done about America's unrealistic farm policies.

Ezra Taft Benson, the man Eisenhower selected for his Secretary of Agriculture, was eager to make some basic changes in Government farm programs. A Mormon who had become one of the ruling Apostles of his church, Benson had been a farmer and a county agricultural agent in his native Utah, where he and his fellow Mormons had demonstrated how cooperation combined with self-help could make agriculture a prosperous and rewarding life.

Benson was not just a farm boy. During the 1940's he had been a lobbyist in Washington for the National Council of Farmer Cooperatives. The new Secretary knew his way around Capitol Hill as well as in the labyrinthine corridors of the huge Agriculture Department buildings.

His view of farm programs was very different from that of his immediate predecessors. Wallace, Wickard, Anderson and Brannan all saw Government guarantees as necessary to modern agriculture. Benson believed that the Government should get out of agriculture. He saw a role for Government in the farm economy only during times of extreme emergency, such as the great depression.

This was an extreme position even for Eisenhower, who wanted to diminish the role of Government in the lives of all Americans. Largely for political reasons the White House persuaded Benson to seek a gradual reduction in the Government's role in agriculture through a system of sliding price supports. This approach had the enthusiastic support of the powerful American Farm Bureau Federation.

In 1954 Congress approved a compromise version of the Eisenhower-Benson program providing for a reduction in price support levels over a period of years. It was the first of a series of compromises adopted by Congress during the 1950's. All of them provided for relatively high price guarantees but inadequate production controls.

The Democrats, who gained control of Congress in the 1954 elections and kept control throughout the rest of the 1950's, would not allow Benson to put his programs into effect. The legislation of the 1950's continued essentially the same programs that had been set up in the 1930's.

The result was a spectacular accumulation of surpluses. During the 1950's the stockpile of surplus farm commodities increased from less than $1.5 billion worth of crops to $10 billion. By 1960 it was costing taxpayers $1 billion a year just to store the surpluses and pay the interest charges on them.

The surpluses piled up even though controls were put into effect on wheat and cotton production in 1954 and continued on these crops throughout the remainder of the decade. Surplus production of cotton and wheat had reached such high levels that Benson had no choice under the farm laws except to put controls into effect, however distasteful they were to him.

The controls could not become effective unless at least two thirds of the affected farmers approved them in a special referendum. Each year when the programs were put to a vote of cotton and wheat farmers, they were approved because along with the rigid restrictions on production farmers were assured a high price for their crops. If the farmers had rejected the controls they could have planted all the cotton and wheat they wanted, but their Government support prices would have dropped sharply. When the choice is between high and low prices, farmers usually take the high price road.

Democrats blamed the buildup of farm surpluses during the 1950's on Benson and his laissez-faire agricultural philosophy. This was unfair. The farm policies of the 1950's were not what Benson wanted. They were an uneasy and tenuous compromise between his no controls, no subsidy beliefs and practical farm politics.

Year after year more and more commodities were produced on fewer and fewer acres. By 1962 the number of harvested acres for all crops totaled only 288 million, the smallest acreage in more than sixty years, but per acre yields were so large that total production remained at or near record levels.

During the 1950's farm technology completely outdistanced farm programs and farm politics. Efforts and exhortations to cut back production were to no avail. Instead, farmers poured on the fertilizer, used better seeds, packed more rows of crops onto an acre, and with the help of expensive machinery discovered constantly more efficient production techniques.

From 1950 to 1962 crop production per acre increased by one third. In the six years from 1957 to 1962 per-acre production jumped 21 per cent. Farm output per man hour invested in agriculture has doubled since 1950. In 1947 the average acre of wheat yielded 17.4 bushels. By 1960 the average acre yield was up to 24.7 bushels. The story was the same in corn, where average yields per acre increased from 36.9 bushels in 1951 to a spectacular 61.8 bushels in 1962.

In 1960 farmers produced the same amount of wheat — 1.3 billion bushels — on nearly 55 million acres as they had on 78 million acres in 1947. Corn plantings fell from more than 71 million acres in 1951 to less than 57 million acres in 1962, while total annual corn production increased in the same period from 2.6 billion bushels to nearly 3.5 billion.

The surpluses that these increases in production created can most easily be understood by comparing the annual carryover of the crops — the amount of a commodity unsold except to the Government and unused at the end of a crop year when new production starts to come in.

In 1947 the wheat carryover was a hardly noticeable 84 million bushels. From 1958 to 1962 the wheat carryovers ranged from a low of 881 million bushels in 1958 to a high of 1.4 billion bushels in 1961. The figure estimated for 1963 was 1.1 billion bushels. These annual carryovers represented about a two-year normal wheat supply for the United States.

The story is the same with the corn carryover. It amounted to 740 million bushels in 1951 and was more than doubled — 1.6 billion bushels — by 1962.

Two innovations in farm policy were tried during the 1950's, but neither had a significant impact on the costs of farm subsidies or on the accumulation of surplus commodities.

The first new approach sought to find outlets for agricultural surpluses in the underdeveloped countries of the world. Approved by Congress in 1954, Public Law 480, as the program was called during its first six years, provided for the sale abroad of surplus farm commodities for local currencies. The United States then loaned to the countries the money it obtained from the sale of the commodities for use in their own economic development projects. Surplus food was being substituted for dollar grants and loans as part of the postwar United States foreign aid program.

Although Public Law 480, which President John F. Kennedy renamed the Food-for-Peace program when he took office in 1961, has been of great assistance to the underdeveloped countries of the world, American farmers have continued to produce surpluses faster than they could even be given away abroad. From 1954 to 1962 more than $9 billion worth of United States surpluses were moved abroad under the program. There are, unfortunately for American farmers, limits on the extent to which food can be distributed without disrupting existing world markets and without discouraging the development of agriculture in the newly independent countries of Asia and Africa as well as in the South American countries.

The other innovation of the 1950's was the soil bank. In an effort to reduce surplus production, Congress approved a program providing for Government payments to farmers who took their land out of production and promised to keep it fallow or to plant trees or grass on it for a specified period of years. Farmers quickly took advantage of the program, but the patterns that have frustrated farm policy makers for so long were again followed. Although the Government paid out more than $2 billion to farmers who deposited 45 million acres of land in the soil bank, total farm production continued to expand.

The soil bank differed from other production cutback measures by requiring some land to be taken out of production for five years. Also, the soil bank was not directly tied into the price control programs.

The unsuccessful soil bank approach to the surplus problem had been abandoned by the time President Kennedy entered the White House, but he expanded the Food-for-Peace program. His Secretary of Agriculture, Orville L. Freeman, also abandoned the low support price, no control, free market approach to the farm problem favored by his predecessor.

Freeman came to the Agriculture Department after serving for six years as Governor of Minnesota. He was a city boy who had spent summers on his grandfather's Minnesota farm but had grown up in Minneapolis. A graduate of the University of Minnesota Law School, Freeman was a lawyer before he entered Democratic politics as a protégé of Senator Hubert H. Humphrey of Minnesota.

Although Freeman knew little about the intricacies of agricultural economics and farm politics, he learned quickly. He also had the politician's instinct for the heart of an issue as well as for compromise.

He surrounded himself with advisers who thought that the problems of overproduction could be solved only through rigid Government controls. Under Freeman the influence of the National Farmers Union was again strong in the Agriculture Department, as it had been when Brannan was Secretary.

Freeman asked Congress to impose stringent controls on production while guaranteeing farmers high prices for their crops. Congress responded as it had during the 1950's when demands were made that it face up to the cost of farm subsidies. Congress compromised.

The Senate and the House enacted legislation requiring farmers to cut back their production of wheat, corn, sorghums and other feed grains before they could be eligible for price support guarantees. Farmers also were given handsome Government payments as a reward for taking land out of production. The acreage restrictions themselves were not nearly so severe as those Freeman and Kennedy had sought.

In 1961 net farm income increased less than $1 billion, to a total of $12.5 billion, but the cost of agricultural subsidies went up by almost the same amount. In 1962 farm income increased only $100 million — to $12.6 billion — although the total annual cost of farm subsidies was $5 billion.

Under the Kennedy programs, surpluses declined somewhat, and Freeman has claimed that the reductions in production that the programs brought about in the first two years of the Kennedy Administration would eventually save taxpayers more than $500 million, largely in handling and storing surplus commodities.

The farm program remained the single largest nondefense

cost of the Federal Government. The Kennedy Administration did not have much more success in its struggle with the farm program and its proliferating subsidies than its predecessors had had since it all began with the little pigs.

During thirty years of Government attempts to solve the farm problems of overproduction and lagging income, the panaceas have changed only slightly. There has been a certain cyclical movement to the efforts to save the farmer. The cycles have moved from rigid controls to gradual attempts to rid the agricultural economy of controls. Never has the consensus in Congress allowed a full swing in either direction on all commodities. Never has Congress seriously considered abandoning the price support system.

Since 1933 the number of farms has drastically declined. Agricultural production has become increasingly concentrated on fewer and fewer but larger and larger farms. The farms have become increasingly specialized. The crop rotation system among prosperous farmers in the Midwest, it has been said, is corn, soybeans, and Miami Beach in the winter. Not only are the farms larger and more specialized; they also represent heavy investments in expensive machinery as well as land and buildings.

During the last ten years contract farming has developed rapidly. Under this system of farming a feed manufacturer, for example, signs a contract with a farmer, who promises to raise chickens to the precise specifications of the manufacturer. The feed and usually the chickens are provided by the feed company. The farmer is guaranteed a fixed price or a percentage of the sale price for the chickens. Much of the poultry now mass-produced on Southern farms is fed and raised under contract farming agreements.

Similar systems are spreading into feeding operations for

hogs and even cattle. Fruits and vegetables have been grown for canneries under contract for many years, but the expansion of the system to poultry, hogs and cattle is a new development in the trend toward specialization in agriculture.

Contract farming has been widely criticized by many farm politicians and farm spokesmen, who argue that the contract system undermines the family farm and turns farmers into little more than employees of feed companies. Contract farming may rob farmers of some of their independence, but the system has assured many farmers of an adequate income by removing from their operations a great deal of the uncertainty about price and market.

The decline in farm population has been one of the most spectacular developments in the American economy during the twentieth century. In 1910 a total of 32 million persons — almost 35 per cent of the population — lived on farms. The number of people on farms remained constant at 32 million for nearly twenty-five years, but by 1933 farm families represented only 25 per cent of the total population. By 1940 farm population had dropped to 30 million, or 23 per cent of all Americans. In the 1950 census only 23 million persons were counted on farms, and they amounted to just 15 per cent of the total population; and by 1961 the number had declined to less than 15 million, a mere 8 per cent of the total United States population of 183 million.

In 1954 there were nearly 4.8 million farms in the United States. Of these, almost 2.7 million, or more than half, had cash sales of less than $2500 a year. By 1959, the year of the last farm census, the number of farms had declined to 3.7 million. Of these, 1.6 million had annual cash sales of less than $2500. Total net farm income declined from more than $15 billion in 1951 to a low of $11.4 billion in 1955. Average income per farm, which stood at $2947 in 1947, was down to $2465 in 1955. In 1962 the figure was $3498, which is over one third less than the per family income of Americans who do not live on farms.

The average size of farms increased from 174 acres in 1940 to 215 acres in 1950 and 307 acres in 1961. The increase in farm assets also reflects the changes that have overtaken the farm economy. In 1950 the average farm had total assets of $17,193, including $1756 for machinery. By 1962 the average farm had assets totaling $47,632, and machinery accounted for $4310 of that figure.

In the 1960's the commercial sector of the farm economy into which nearly all of the $5 billion in subsidies were being poured each year constituted a highly specialized and heavily capitalized but sharply declining number of Americans — the two million plus farmers who were growing 85 per cent of all the food and fiber.

The other 1.6 million farms — the farmers the nation has forgotten — were receiving few of the subsidy benefits. The programs have been geared primarily to the needs of commercial farmers, which the Agriculture Department defines as farms with annual cash sales of at least $2500.

As the farm economy has contracted and drastically changed in character, agricultural subsidy programs have remained virtually unchanged, largely because of political considerations. The politics of the farm subsidy program have now become part of the folklore of American agriculture. The still rurally oriented political forces that control Congress, particularly the House of Representatives, are fearful of the political consequences if farm subsidies should be drastically reduced.

It is now part of conventional farm wisdom to argue that payments totaling billions of dollars a year are necessary to maintain farm prosperity. No one in Congress — or in the Administration — has tried to determine whether such subsidies are needed in a greatly contracted, highly specialized farm economy. Conditions today among the farmers who get nearly all of the subsidy payments are not the conditions of the depression era.

What about the politics of agriculture? What are the political and economic forces that keep the pressures on Washington to help wheelers and dealers like Billie Sol Estes as well as all the other farmers who benefit so handsomely from the farm subsidies?

4

Powerful Peasants

H<small>ENRY</small> L. M<small>ENCKEN</small> once observed that "the vote of a malarious peasant on the lower Eastern Shore counts as much as the votes of twelve Baltimoreans." Farmers and the residents of small towns who depend heavily on the farm economy for their livelihood have been overrepresented in Congress ever since the mass migration from farm to city began late in the nineteenth century. Congressional districts are drawn by state legislatures, most of which failed to reapportion themselves properly for decades. So the congressional districts have also been weighted in favor of rural residents.

Until 1962 Federal and state courts refused to try to solve the apportionment problem, holding that this was a political question to be decided by the legislatures themselves. But in March 1962 the United States Supreme Court ruled that Federal courts have the power to review reapportionment legislation to make certain it provides for fair representation for all citizens of a state. During the first year after this decision fifteen state legislatures reapportioned the seats in one or both of their houses. In all fifteen states the result has been to diminish the influence of rural and small-town voters in the legislatures. So far the most dramatic change has occurred in Georgia, where the county unit system was thrown out by the courts and the stranglehold that rural counties had on the state was broken.

The political revolution that is beginning in the country-side will soon rival in its repercussions the economic changes that have occurred on farms in the last thirty years. It will be another ten years, however, before the complexion of Congress will be changed enough to diminish significantly the rural bias now reflected in so many of the actions of the House of Representatives. Seats in the House are apportioned among the states on the basis of each state's share of the total population only after each decennial census, and the next census will not be taken until 1970.

The forces largely responsible for the perpetuation of farm subsidies over the last thirty years may be making their last stand during the next decade. It is not that there has been monolithic agreement on the details of farm legislation; the debates have often been anything but pro forma affairs. Rather, it is that there has never been any serious disagreement among farm state Senators and Representatives over the need for continuing generous farm subsidies. The arguments have always been over the way to reach the subsidy goal.

As yet few members of the now divided farm bloc act as if they realize that their power in Congress will be diminishing because a state's representation both in Washington and in its own legislature will have to be more carefully based on people instead of a countryside populated with almost as many abandoned farmhouses as there are voters. In arguing for the Kennedy Administration's farm programs, Secretary of Agriculture Orville L. Freeman has frequently warned rural audiences that unless the farm subsidies are brought under control the whole program may collapse in the face of an urban revolt against the costly subsidies. As long as the House of Representatives remains as rurally oriented as it is there is little likelihood of a real revolt breaking out in Congress against the farm programs. The rural, small-town and other pressures for the programs are still too great, despite the continuing exodus from the countryside to the city.

Not only have the farmers and their families gone to the city; the city Congressmen who once supported farm subsidies in exchange for rural votes on labor, housing and other measures of interest to the cities have changed their minds about the efficacy of such arrangements. During the 1930's and even as recently as the early 1950's, city Congressmen backed farm subsidy programs and in return managed to pick up some votes from rural areas for liberal, city-oriented welfare legislation; but increasingly the bargain has been one-sided and of benefit only to the rural legislators. Fewer and fewer rural Representatives have supported welfare and other "city" legislation in recent years, while city Congressmen find farm subsidies harder and harder to explain to housewives faced with high grocery bills at the end of the cash register tape every week in the supermarket.

Each commodity, from milk and honey to soybeans and safflower seeds, has a well-organized lobby behind it, generally with a full-time Washington representative keeping congressional friends advised as to the wishes and wants of the producers of his favorite commodity. A Congressman whose constituency includes many producers of a commodity can be depended upon to champion that crop, however unjustified the farmers' demands for Government assistance may be at times. Among the powerful organizations representing the interests of particular commodities are associations speaking for cattlemen, wheat growers, cotton producers, tobacco growers, beet sugar producers, citrus fruit growers, and even the owners of large colonies of honeybees.

Even more important than the commodity organizations are the three most powerful pressure groups representing general agricultural interests: the conservative American Farm Bureau Federation, which with its membership of 1.6 million farm families claims representation of 60 per cent of the nation's commercial farmers; the liberal National Farmers Union, with 500,000 members, most of whom are Western wheat farmers; and the careful National Grange, with 800,000 members (about half are wives of farmers), much of whose strength is concentrated among dairy farmers in New England and New York State.

An upstart farm lobby is the radical National Farmers Organization, which advocates direct action to force up farm prices. The NFO, a modern version of the Farmers' Holiday Movement of the early 1930's, would withhold commodities from market until processors agreed to pay what farmers consider to be a fair price. No NFO membership figures are published, but it has been estimated that the organization, which was established in 1955, represents well over 100,000 farmers concentrated in the corn- and hog-producing areas of Iowa, Missouri, Minnesota and Illinois.

Except for the NFO, whose headquarters are in a Main Street store in the little southwestern Iowa town of Corning, the major farm organizations maintain high-powered lobbying operations in Washington. Members of the organization staffs move rather freely from lobbying payrolls to key jobs in the Agriculture Department and then back to the pressure groups. Although Farm Bureau lobbyists wrote most of the original New Deal farm legislation, the Farm

Bureau is out of sympathy with the present Democratic Administration. It got along extremely well with the Republicans under Secretary of Agriculture Ezra Taft Benson.

When Orville L. Freeman became Secretary of Agriculture after the Kennedy Administration took over, he was asked at a press conference whether Charles B. Shuman, president of the Farm Bureau, was still sleeping in the Secretary's office. If Shuman were still trying to sleep there, Freeman replied, he wouldn't be getting much rest, because there was so much work going on all the time.

The Farm Bureau has always represented the more prosperous farmers. Its greatest strength has been among the well-to-do cotton farmers of the Old South and the efficient grain, hog, cattle and dairy farmers of the Midwest. Until the mid-1950's, county Farm Bureaus helped to finance the operations of county agents in some states.

Shuman has been president of the Farm Bureau since 1954. He is a farmer from Central Illinois who still operates a farm near the small town of Sullivan. A tireless spokesman, who rolls out country phrases in a flat Midwestern accent, Shuman is a Methodist Sunday school teacher who knows his way around Washington as well as any lobbyist.

The Farmers Union backs the high price support, rigid control programs pushed by the Kennedy Administration. John A. Baker, who used to be the chief lobbyist for the Farmers Union, was appointed Assistant Secretary of Agriculture under Freeman.

The Farmers Union was organized by ten farmers in Point, Texas, in 1902 as the Farmers Educational and Cooperative Union of America. In its early days the organization spread rapidly throughout the South, but today most of its strength is among Western wheat farmers. Stressing the organization of cooperatives and the development of Government credit and price support programs for farmers, the Farmers Union has always been a vigorous advocate of Government programs. It was active in the farm movements of the 1920's as well as in the development of the first Government programs of the 1930's.

Since 1940 James G. Patton, a Colorado farmer, has been president of the Farmers Union. He is a soft-spoken but convincing orator and a shrewd lobbyist in Washington for the views of his organization. Former Secretary of Agriculture Brannan has served as general counsel for the Farmers Union since 1953.

The National Grange tends to be more sympathetic with the Democratic emphasis on farm subsidies than with the Republican approach, but the Grange is no longer much of a power in American farm politics.

The great power and influence of the Farm Bureau has been demonstrated in Washington again and again. Two examples which bridge the period under discussion illustrate the importance of this organization.

First, Roosevelt's allowing the farm organizations, led by Edward O'Neal of the Farm Bureau, to write the kind of farm program that they wanted — special interest groups frequently are able to tailor legislation to their own needs, but seldom are they invited in and given the carte blanche accorded the Farm Bureau and the other agricultural groups thirty years ago.

Second, in 1962 Farm Bureau opposition to the Kennedy Administration's rigid control program succeeded in defeating the legislation by a margin of only five votes in the House of Representatives. The Farm Bureau brought pressure from its state and county organizations, particularly those in the South, to bear on members of Congress who were heavily dependent on Farm Bureau political support as well as on campaign funds raised by local Farm Bureau members. Washington lobbyists for the Farm Bureau also brought to Capitol Hill the officials of their state and local affiliates to help argue the organization's case against the controversial Kennedy legislation. There was nothing illegal or unethical about the way the Farm Bureau helped to defeat the legislation, but the organization's success demonstrated once again its power and influence even thirty years after many persons in Washington had thought that it had reached its peak.

The Agriculture Department itself is also an extremely potent lobbying force in Washington. During the 1962 jockeying on Capitol Hill over farm legislation, Secretary Freeman spent as much time in the offices of Senators and Representatives as he did in his own department. He was explaining the Administration's farm program to any member of Congress who would listen to him, and he also was trying to persuade Congressmen to vote for his program. While the crucial debate in the House of Representatives over the farm program was taking place, Freeman sat in the office of the Speaker of the House, just a few steps off the House floor, carrying on desperate last-minute efforts to get votes for the Administration. On the House floor itself one Congressman charged that there had been offers of new post offices to members who would vote for the Administration's farm legislation. In addition to the Secretary of Agriculture, the Undersecretary, the Assistant Secretaries and the holders of other top appointive jobs in the Department were pressed into service as lobbyists for the legislation.

The Capitol Hill pressure points of the Farm Bureau and the other farm organizations are the Senate and House Agriculture Committees and the agricultural subcommittees of the Senate and House Appropriations Committees. The influence of the farm lobbyists also is frequently brought to bear on such other key spots as the Senate Finance Committee and the House Ways and Means Committee, where tax matters are considered, and on the Labor Committees, where the Farm Bureau supports the kind of controls over unions it opposes for farmers. The Agriculture Committees are the focal points of farm lobbying; here farm legislation is written and amended, and here is carried on the amendment trading among commodity groups through which senators and representatives take care of all special farm interests back home.

Lobbying is not of course necessary to convince the members of the Agriculture Committees and the Agricultural Appropriations subcommittees that the interests of farmers should be carefully cultivated and tended in Congress. The Agriculture Committees are now headed by two Southern gentlemen who look upon farming matters as their special preserve and disdain advice from outsiders. Allen J. Ellender, a Democratic Senator from Louisiana, is chairman of the Senate Agriculture Committee, and Harold D. Cooley, a Democratic Representative from North Carolina, heads the House Committee.

In addition to doing their best to oversee the domestic farm economy, both Ellender and Cooley have maintained an unusually strong personal interest in sugar legislation. Sugar beets are an important crop in the Western states and sugar cane is a crop of some significance in Ellender's own state of Louisiana. The Ellender-Cooley concern over sugar, which is primarily an international problem, apparently is due in large part to their personal desire to run as much of the Government as possible. Sugar production in the United

States and sugar imports to the United States from other countries are carefully regulated by a rigid quota system that must be extended periodically by Congress.

Ellender is a seventy-two-year-old "lawyer and farmer," according to his biography in the *Congressional Directory*. He has spent most of his life in politics and was a political lieutenant of the late Huey P. Long, Governor of Louisiana during the turbulent thirties, who said that he wanted to make every man a king. Long was assassinated by a doctor while serving in the United States Senate, and Ellender was elected in 1936 to succeed him. A short, peppery man, Ellender has served in the Senate since then, rising through the seniority system to the chairmanship of the Agriculture Committee.

Ellender is perhaps best known as an inveterate world traveler, at taxpayers' expense. During nearly every congressional recess in recent years he has embarked on some foreign inspection trip which he has then proceeded to describe in book-length reports prepared and published at the taxpayers' expense. In 1962 he was in Africa, where some countries refused to let him in because he had said Africans were unprepared for self-government. His senatorial career has been undistinguished. In addition to taking an unusual interest in sugar legislation, Ellender has also been particularly concerned with cotton and rice programs, also important to the agricultural economy of Louisiana. Ellender was a vigorous defender of the dictatorial, sugar-producing Trujillo regime that governed the Dominican Republic until it was overthrown in 1961.

Cooley is a sixty-five-year-old, leathery North Carolina lawyer who has served in Congress since 1935. He has been chairman of the House Agriculture Committee since 1949, with the exception of 1953 and 1954, when the Republicans

were in control of Congress. Cooley represents a big tobacco state, and his principal agricultural interest outside of
sugar is tobacco. Tobacco production is rigidly controlled,
but Cooley's tobacco farmers are guaranteed extremely high
price supports by the Government.

A man who is better at maneuvering behind the closed
doors of his committee than at operating in the hurly-
burly of debate on the House floor, Cooley has little influence in the House on matters other than farm programs.
His great interest in sugar legislation and his great friendship for the Trujillo regime have never been satisfactorily
explained either by Cooley or by his many enemies and de-
tractors on Capitol Hill and elsewhere in Washington.

Now and then a brave city Congressman decides to be
adventurous and takes a seat on the House Agriculture
Committee. He quickly finds it is all but impossible for him
to make the voice of the consumer heard amid the babble
of the special farm interests. Democratic Senator Eugene
McCarthy of Minnesota served on the House Agriculture
Committee when he was a Congressman from St. Paul. His
avowed purpose was to speak out for consumers, but he had
little influence on committee deliberations. In 1962 Democratic Representative Benjamin Rosenthal of Brooklyn was
the lone city Congressman on the Committee.

Corn is represented on the House Agriculture Committee
by the gentleman from Iowa. Kansas could be concerned
only with wheat. And there is Mississippi representing the
cotton-planting aristocracy of the Delta. Texas is also concerned with cotton but not nearly so much as with cattle.
Next to oil, there is nothing dearer to a Texas Congressman's heart than a cow. The chairman, as noted above, is a
tobacco man from North Carolina. Also surrounding him

are Congressmen representing the warring dairy farmers of New York and Wisconsin and the battling orange and grapefruit growers of Florida and California. The Senate Agriculture Committee also runs the agricultural spectrum from apples to zoysia grass.

There are the committee members on the dais, or around the table, sitting like roosters in a barnyard. Watching their every gesture, jotting down their every word, are the farm lobbyists who fill the hearing rooms when the committees meet in public session. Sometimes lobbyists even sit in on the closed committee sessions when the Senators or Representatives are supposed to be writing legislation in the public interest rather than for the special interest of a group of farmers. The lobbyists and the members of the Senate and House Committees generally know each other's minds so well that it hardly seems necessary for them to have closed-door confrontations during the amending and writing of legislation. It is always better to be sure by being there and looking over the shoulder of your favorite Senator or Representative.

Nearly ten years ago the farm bloc on Capitol Hill started to come unglued. Since then it has been increasingly difficult for farm state Senators and Representatives to agree on legislation, but to say that the farm bloc has disappeared is to overstate the case considerably.

Disagreements during the last decade among members of the farm bloc have been over such questions as rigid vs. loose production controls, relatively high vs. lower price support guarantees, and efforts to freeze existing production patterns to try to reduce surpluses. In 1962 the South resisted and helped to defeat a tough production control program on corn, sorghums and other food grains. The program would have restricted the expansion of such crops in the South, where dairying and cattle operations are supplanting cotton, tobacco and peanuts as the major agricultural activities. For dairying and cattle farming to be successful, abundant supplies of low-priced corn and other feed crops are necessary. The best way for a farmer to get cheap feed is to grow it himself. Southern farmers feared, with considerable justification, that the proposed feed grain control program would make it difficult for them to produce all the feed they needed and would force them to buy corn and other grains at relatively high prices from Midwestern producers who had surpluses.

Whatever differences over the approach to agricultural legislation may have developed among the members of Congress from the farm states, the Senators and Representatives whose constituencies include large numbers of farmers are in basic agreement on the need for continuing massive assistance to farmers. There is much brave talk on Capitol Hill and on the hustings during congressional campaigns that the Government ought to get out of agriculture. When the talk gets down to votes and alternatives the differences concern the form and amount of aid to agriculture rather than the basic question of assistance or no assistance. Members of Congress from agricultural areas are like farmers. When farmers are confronted with a referendum in which the choice is high prices with controls or low prices without controls, high prices — and high subsidies — usually get the majority of the votes.

During the 1962 congressional campaign two Kansas Representatives, Democrat Floyd Breeding and Republican Bob Dole, ran against each other in a contest widely believed to be a key test between a man who wanted heavy Government involvement in the farm economy (Breeding) and one who did not want such Government interference with farmers (Dole). The districts in western Kansas in the heart of the wheat belt that Breeding and Dole had represented were combined into a single district after the state lost a congressional seat following the 1960 census. Breeding supported the Kennedy Administration's rigid wheat control program. Dole said that he was for less Government in agriculture, but he was never too specific about how he would get the Government out, and he was not against price supports and price guarantees for farmers. Dole won the election.

Dole held out to farmers the prospect of fewer controls but did not say the Government should stop guaranteeing good prices to farmers. This position taken by Dole and so many other rural Congressmen like him follows the present stand of the Farm Bureau. The speeches of Farm Bureau officials bristle with denunciations of the Government and its programs and with impassioned pleas for a return to freedom from all Government interference in the production of farm commodities and in the making of farm prices. The Farm Bureau program also calls for the continuance of farm price supports and the payment of subsidies to farmers who take land out of production under a program which would rely heavily on the retirement of land. At some unspecified time in the future, after the necessary adjustments are made in corn production, controls and guarantees would be gradually ended. No one knows when that Valhalla would be attained, and in the meantime it is likely that the Farm Bureau program would be as expensive as the present agricultural legislation.

Farm prices, it has frequently been said, are made in Washington, and the ultimate shape of farm legislation is generally determined in the Agriculture Committees. Over the last thirty years farm programs have become so complicated and so overlaid with a mystifying jargon of their own that on Capitol Hill few Senators and Representatives other than the members of the Agriculture Committees even pretend to understand the details of agricultural legislation. Even many members of the committees do not understand the details of the programs, but they know their dollar-and-cent values to farmers.

Like most other legislative programs of the last thirty years, farm legislation has originated within the executive branch. The Secretary of Agriculture, the Undersecretary, who is in charge of the day-to-day operations of the Department, the Assistant Secretaries, among whom are divided some of the lesser policy-making and administrative functions, the heads of agencies within the Department, and some of the key departmental career people are continually subjected to pressures both from Capitol Hill and from the farm lobbyists.

The Agriculture Department is the spokesman for and guardian of farmers' interests as they are interpreted by whatever Administration is in power. In the same way, the Commerce Department is charged with looking after the interests of the business community and the Labor Department is concerned with the rights of workers. From time to time the Agriculture Department makes a pass at protecting the interests of consumers.

When the Department's expenditures, which totaled $6.8 billion in the 1963 fiscal year — higher than any other Government activity not connected with the defense program — are criticized as being far too large in light of the dwindling farm economy and population, Department officials seek to show that much of their budget goes to help all Americans.

They cite such programs as the inspection and grading of meat and the distribution of surplus foods to the needy.

When it comes time each year for the Department to justify its requests for funds before the agricultural subcommittees of the House and Senate Appropriations Committees, the emphasis is on what the spending programs will do for farmers. The subcommittees are made up of members of Congress with heavy farm constituencies.

In the development and preparation of farm legislation, the Agriculture Department actively seeks the advice of the farm pressure groups. It is not that any of the farm lobbies hide their lights under a bushel of surplus corn. The seeking of advice is a good public relations device, whether the advice is accepted or ignored. Secretary Freeman has particularly favored the use of advisory committees composed of representatives of all viewpoints in agriculture. The recommendations of the committee members are frequently ignored, however, and opponents of the Freeman farm program have charged that the committees are merely show animals rather than work horses.

The resourceful Washington representatives of the farm organizations, concerned as they are about farm policy, are also intimately familiar with the inner workings of the Agriculture Department. Many of the members of the Farm Bureau staff in Washington are former top officials of the Agriculture Department. They know who on the lower departmental levels makes the decisions to implement existing policies or to determine the direction of proposals and programs newly enacted into law by Congress.

The members of Congress who write farm legislation in the committees and amend it on the floor of the Senate and the House also oversee the administration of the programs by constantly looking over the shoulders of the bureaucrats to make certain the programs are being carried out to give all possible breaks to farmers. Nothing makes a Government administrator jump into action like a letter or a telephone call from a member of Congress or one of his assistants. Wheels that may have been stuck for months suddenly begin to move when the office of a Senator or Representative demands an explanation for the long delay and calls for action. This informal system of congressional oversight is not by any means all bad or venal. Career civil servants who administer complicated Government programs can be as obstinate, as wrong and as unfair as political hacks appointed to Government posts because they had a talent for getting out the votes on election day. Congressional prodding of the bureaucracy can be a useful device for righting governmental wrongs and for maintaining expeditious as well as fair administration of tangled regulations and laws like the farm program.

The pressures on the Agriculture Department from the farm organizations and members of Congress are like the pressures business puts on the Commerce Department and unions on the Labor Department. In the abstract, everyone may be for the fair and impartial administration of the laws, but all of us really prefer a Government that sees the logic of our particular interpretation of legislation and regulations.

There is a significant difference between the role of the Agriculture Department and that of the Labor and Commerce Departments in today's economy. Neither the Labor nor Commerce Department has the direct subsidies that the Agriculture Department has to offer farmers and businessmen storing and handling farm commodities. The relationship between the Agriculture Department and farmers and business is more like the relationship between the Defense Department and Government contractors. Both the Agriculture and the Defense Departments have large sums of money for public disbursement, although of course the $50 billion or more a year at the disposal of the Defense establishment is more than ten times the $5 billion in the Agriculture Department subsidy kitty.

There is still another important aspect to the story of pressure politics in agriculture that is all too seldom discussed but is often as significant as the constant efforts of the farm organizations themselves: the pressures engendered by agricultural business organizations that now have as much of a vested interest in many of the farm programs as do farmers. The businessmen who store surplus commodities do more than half a billion dollars' worth of business each year in crops the Government either owns outright or on which it has loaned money to farmers. The giant chemical companies that produce the new fertilizers want to expand their markets. It is not hard for such companies to decide whether farm production should be rigidly controlled or allowed to be relatively free from Government restrictions. The men who buy and sell corn, wheat, cotton and other crops on the commodity exchanges also have a vested interest in heavy farm production. The more commodities there are, the more trading there will be on the commodity markets. And the processors themselves can exercise a powerful influence over farm legislation. Their interest is in having ample supplies of a commodity available at the lowest possible prices. During the late 1950's, textile manufacturers vigorously opposed an increase in cotton price support levels and the subsequent subsidized sale abroad of

American cotton at lower prices than they themselves had to pay for the same cotton.

An example of the way corporations with a heavy stake in farm legislation try to get key Agriculture Department information was unearthed by a House Government Operations subcommittee headed by Democratic Representative L. H. Fountain of North Carolina which in the summer of 1962 investigated the grain storage activities of Billie Sol Estes. In the files of the Commercial Solvents Corporation of New York, which sold fertilizer to Estes, subcommittee investigators found correspondence from Martin Sorkin, a former career Agriculture Department economist who had been an adviser to Benson. Sorkin left the Department with Benson and joined the legion of private consultants in Washington, most of whom rely on past governmental connections for much of their stock in trade.

Sorkin was retained by Commercial Solvents as a consultant, but correspondence between Sorkin and the corporation found by the subcommittee staff indicated that Commercial Solvents was most interested in getting from Sorkin advance information on Agriculture Department legislative and administrative plans and their probable reception on Capitol Hill. In 1961 the corporation was particularly concerned about proposed farm legislation that would have allowed the Government to make loans to cooperatives for the construction of facilities to store and process agricultural commodities. In one letter Sorkin told Maynard Wheeler, president of Commercial Solvents, how he had sought an interpretation of the proposal from Agriculture Department lawyers. In another, he noted that the House Agriculture Committee had been discussing the objectionable section of the legislation. "Yesterday," he wrote, "they went into Executive Session. As you would expect, I had tipped off several of the Committee members and a personal friend on the Committee staff on the full implications of Section 314 of the proposed Agricultural Act of 1961." In the same letter Sorkin also noted that he was furnishing material on agricultural policy to the Republican National Committee.

Although the interests of businessmen who depend on agricultural commodities to keep their plants operating are generally at considerable variance with the interests of farmers who want high prices for their crops, the businessmen are usually accorded a sympathetic hearing by farm-oriented members of Congress. The processing of farm commodities is often so closely tied to the economy of agricultural areas that a Congressman may find it extremely difficult to balance the interests of the processors against those of the farmers if he is genuinely seeking to determine what are the best interests of the majority of his constituents. Congressmen representing rural districts usually are conservative and business-oriented in their general economic outlook, too. To pick a Southern example, farmers want high prices for their cotton, while textile mills, some of which are located close to the cotton fields, want low-priced cotton.

The men and organizations who deal in grain, from the country elevator operator to the gigantic Chicago Board of Trade, have vast influence over agricultural policy. They are interested in ample supplies of commodities, in the market prices as well as the guaranteed prices for crops, and in Government charges for storing and handling commodities.

The interests represented by small-town businessmen,

bankers, storekeepers and property owners form part of the pressures of farm politics — men who have money invested in small-town enterprises do not want to see farmers leaving the countryside. Agricultural cooperatives also wield a powerful influence over farm policy. These groups include the small rural electric associations as well as such giants as the Land O' Lakes dairying cooperative and the Farmers Union Grain Terminal Association, an offshoot of the Farmers Union itself. All these cooperatives, whether large or small, have a huge economic stake in heavy production and in agricultural policies that keep farmers on the farm. The cooperatives are persuasive political forces, sometimes locally through campaign contributions and at other times nationally through such Washington lobbying organizations as the National Association of Rural Electric Cooperatives and the National Federation of Milk Producers.

Farm politics as it is played today is a curious amalgam of rural and small-town pressures. The men who represent farmers in Congress are generally from small towns or medium-size cities. Their values are usually a mixture of those prevailing in the small towns and countryside of their boyhoods. The values are inherently conservative, except for farm legislation. When it comes to voting on agricultural programs, these men seem always to welcome Government guarantees into their midst. But the rest of the time they publicly frown on Federal assistance.

For all of these reasons, pressures in favor of farm subsidies are enormous. The rural bias that still exists in Congress tends to magnify the demands from farmers and their spokesmen both in and out of Government for Federal assistance. A farm program that first developed out of desperate depression conditions has become so much a part of the nation's economy that few persons are courageous enough to question the program's propriety in the midst of a booming economy, and fewer still have tried to determine what alternatives there might be to the continued heavy subsidization of American agriculture.

Billie Sol Estes not only understood the economics of an American agricultural system largely controlled by Government decisions; he also understood the politics of agriculture. When a key Government decision went against him — a decision that meant the loss of Government cotton acreage allotments worth millions of dollars — he immediately sought redress by appealing to his friends on Capitol Hill and in the Agriculture Department. Estes had no need to know all the history, economics and politics that went into the making of the farm program he learned to manipulate so well for himself. It was there waiting for him. All he had to do was take advantage of it.

5

"A Real Ball"

IT TOOK the officers of the big Commercial Solvents Corporation on sophisticated Madison Avenue in New York City only a few months to realize that they had an unusual customer way out West in the hot, dusty and windblown town of Pecos, Texas. Young Billie Sol Estes was a man who thought perhaps a little too big for his britches, but in less than four months in the spring and summer of 1958 he had demonstrated that he knew how to sell fertilizer. Yet he was slow in paying his bills, was always wanting more credit, and had run up a disturbing $550,000 debt with Commercial Solvents.

In the fall of 1958, Commercial Solvents asked supersalesman Billie Sol "to come in to talk about a past due account on some fertilizer," William S. Leonhardt, vice president and treasurer of the company, recalled in testimony before a Texas court of inquiry in 1962.

Estes, who liked to call himself a farmer and a "poor country boy," flew from Pecos to New York, a calculating rustic armed with a plan worthy of the shrewdest and most ingenious Wall Street financier. Billie Sol was no stranger either to the big town or to its fast-buck ways.

After Estes sat down in the comfortable offices of Commercial Solvents and got a little better acquainted with Leonhardt and some of the other officers of the company, he quickly dispensed with the small talk and unfolded the big deal he had carefully worked out in far-away West Texas.

"In essence," Leonhardt told the court of inquiry, "Mr. Estes said he was expanding his anhydrous ammonia distribution setup in Texas and was going into the Plains area, as I understood it. He was also contemplating, or had made arrangements to buy, a grain storage facility in Plainview, Texas. His proposal was that because of this increased volume that he had . . . he would like to enter into a sales arrangement with Commercial Solvents . . .

"We agreed," Leonhardt went on to testify, "on a sales contract whereby Commercial Solvents would supply Mr. Estes with anhydrous ammonia . . . In consideration of this, Mr. Estes suggested that we enter into a $900,000 loan . . . The loan was to be made up in three parts. The first part covered the past due accounts receivable on anhydrous ammonia, roughly around $550,000. We were also to advance Mr. Estes roughly $225,000 . . . for him to make a down payment on his purchase of a grain elevator that he told us he was going to try to conclude arrangements on." The rest of the loan, about $125,000, was to finance future shipments of fertilizer from Commercial Solvents to Estes.

To both Billie Sol and the company the most important part of the loan was the $225,000 for a down payment on some grain elevators. As collateral for the entire $900,000 loan, Estes agreed to turn over to Commercial Solvents all the money he would receive from the Government for the storage of surplus grain.

"The arrangement was actually very simple," Leonhardt pointed out. "We shipped him anhydrous ammonia and in return, rather than go on waiting for the receipts of proceeds that he got from anhydrous ammonia, we took the grain receipts to pay off the anhydrous ammonia we were shipping him."

The Agriculture Department generally approves such assignments of receipts by grain warehousemen to their creditors. These assignments are usually made to banks or other lenders who help to finance the construction of warehouses. The Estes assignment to a creditor with whom he was doing business every day was unique. Department officials took the position that the way a warehouseman uses his money is not their concern so long as there is nothing illegal about the operation.

To secure its loan still further, Commercial Solvents had Estes turn over to it chattel mortgages on eight hundred 1000-gallon fertilizer tanks and four hundred 500-gallon tanks that Estes said he was buying. Estes also assigned his substantial life insurance policies to Commercial Solvents.

"Our position on all of it was that although we had examined his financial statement, we were unable to obtain an audited statement," Leonhardt said, "so on this statement we felt that the only position we could take was to obtain all the security we could get."

In June 1962 Maynard C. Wheeler, president of Commercial Solvents, told a House Government Operations subcommittee that "such an agreement with Estes was particularly advantageous to the company because it gave the company an opportunity to sell its ammonia in a rapidly expanding and prosperous market."

The Smith-Bawden grain storage operations in Plainview that Estes took over in the fall of 1958 were relatively small — with a capacity of only 2,960,000 bushels. Estes had had no experience in the highly competitive grain storage business, but it was not by whim or accident that he became a grain warehouseman.

He knew that there was an ever-increasing demand for grain storage facilities. Ever since controls had been placed on wheat production in 1954, farmers had been turning to milo, a grain sorghum fed to cattle. If there was one thing most cattle feeders did not need in the 1950's it was more feed; they already had corn running out of their ears.

In 1954 and in succeeding years wheat farmers were given a choice between restricted production with high prices and unrestricted production with low price guarantees. Each year two thirds or more of them chose the high price guarantee program, even though it meant restrictions on their wheat acreage. Once such a program was approved by at least two thirds of the wheat farmers voting in a referendum, no wheat could be marketed without severe penalties unless it was grown in accordance with the Government quota program. The penalties, or fines, on wheat marketed outside the program were so stiff that no farmer could make a profit on such wheat.

If farmers could not grow all the wheat they wanted to, they could put these idle acres into grain sorghums. The price of sorghums was also supported by the Government at a high level that assured a handsome return on the crop, and there were no restrictions on sorghum acreage at that time.

The result was soaring sorghum production throughout the wheat country of the West. In 1953 only 6.3 million acres of sorghums were planted. They yielded an average of 18.4 bushels to the acre, a total crop of 116 million bushels. By 1957 sorghum plantings had increased more than threefold, to 19.7 million acres. Yields had gone up one fourth, to an average of 28.8 bushels to the acre. The farmers were learning the benefits of anhydrous ammonia fertilizer in the desert soil of the West. Total 1957 sorghum production was 568 million bushels, almost five times the 1953 figure. In 1962 sorghum production dropped back to 487 million bushels because Government restrictions had reduced total sorghum plantings to 11.3 million acres. Each heavily fertilized acre yielded an average of 43 bushels in 1962, or well over twice the 1953 figure of 18.4 bushels. Meanwhile, the annual carryover of sorghums (the surplus) increased from a negligible 7 million bushels in 1953 to a still not troublesome 79 million bushels in 1957 to a totally unrealistic and unneeded 690 million bushels in 1962.

Grain sorghums are not as good a feed for cattle as is corn. The expansion in sorghums production came when corn was in surplus, too, so there was no need for sorghums in the glutted feed grain markets of the late 1950's. This was particularly true in West Texas, where Estes went into the grain storage business. This dry country was not suitable for the extensive cattle-feeding operations needed to consume all the sorghums being substituted for wheat. In West Texas the grazing of cattle in fields of grass is big business, but sorghums and corn are fed cattle only after they come in off the range and are placed on "feeder" lots for "finishing" into choice beefsteaks. These feeder operations are generally carried out in the Midwest rather than in such places as the far reaches of West Texas.

Within six months after Estes returned home from New York with the Commercial Solvents agreement in his pocket, his fertilizer sales techniques were the talk of Texas. Glenn R. Lester, a Plainview fertilizer dealer, later told one of the courts of inquiry how Estes operated. Lester was a partner in the fertilizer company that Estes purchased and he continued in the firm as manager for Estes. To get business, Lester said, Billie Sol sold fertilizer at cut-rate prices.

"Now what were the mechanics of the price cuts when they would come?" Lester was asked by Texas Attorney General Will Wilson. "After you got instructions from Billie Sol Estes that you were going to put into effect a price cut, how did you go about doing it?"

"As a rule, to use his terminology," Lester answered, "we'd just surround them and hit them. What he meant by that was that we'd get on the telephone and notify all of our dealers at a certain day and not to begin before and not to let the word out. But on a certain day, a certain morning, we'd start booking ammonia. And we'd contact everybody that we could. And, by night, we would have a lot of it in."

James Potts was a fertilizer dealer in Amarillo, Texas, who quickly felt the effects of the Estes price-cutting operations.

"When you say that your sales dropped down to about ten to twenty per cent of what they had been in prior years," Potts was asked, "what in your opinion brought this about, why the drop?"

"It was very clear," Potts said. "However, we couldn't do anything about it. Mr. Estes and his associated dealers, or whatever association there might be, were selling fertilizer for less than we could buy it, and so we couldn't ask our farmers to pay more, that is, our customers. We disguised our men as farmers, and went to their storage and picked it up, and paid $60 a ton for it, because we could not buy it for that price."

Weldon Bradley of Dimmitt, Texas, one of the many fertilizer dealers who were run out of business by Estes, told of meeting Billie Sol in an office of one of the Estes fertilizer operations.

"I told him that I had been wanting to meet him," Bradley recalled. "I wanted to see what kind of a fellow — what kind of a man looked like that could upset this thing like he had. And he says, 'Are you beginning to feel me?' And I said, 'Not only that,' I says, 'I have just stopped.' And he kind of had a big laugh out of that . . . He said he didn't want to hurt me. He wanted to sell me ammonia, and fix it so I would have a margin on it so that I could meet anybody's price. And he made me feel pretty good."

N. J. Cain, who supervised the Southern Farm Supply Association's fertilizer operations in Amarillo, also ran into Billie Sol's buzz saw.

"The situation deteriorated," Cain said, "until in the fall of 1959 Commercial Solvents ammonia sold cheaper than we could buy it as a distributor, which put us in a very unfavorable position with our dealers as you can well imagine . . . It was in their marked tank cars, it was advertised on the radio, and it made it look like we were either paying too much for ammonia or that we were robbing the public . . . We spent many a night holding a series of meetings with the farmers . . . We protested rather vigorously to Commercial Solvents on these tactics . . . that their ammonia was being sold cheaper than we could buy it."

Cain said that the protests did no good. He said that "the best" he could get out of Clyde Marshall, the company's sales manager, was that "he was a very busy man from New York, he didn't have time to listen to rumors, they would offer us no relief whatsoever." Cain was angry because his company had been buying fertilizer from Commercial Solvents, too. Late in 1959, after getting nowhere with his protests, Cain decided his best course would be to stop doing business with Commercial Solvents.

Estes also had in his contract with Commercial Solvents what treasurer Leonhardt called "a normal competitive type clause . . . where he could buy from other people if we failed to meet the terms." Attorney General Wilson described the clause as providing that "if he secured more favorable terms from some other company, he had to first give you the opportunity of selling at the same terms." Leonhardt concurred with Wilson's interpretation of the clause.

James A. Oates of Plainview, a salesman for the Monsanto Chemical Company, which also makes anhydrous ammonia, told how Estes tried to use the "normal competitive type clause."

"A few months later," Oates recalled, "he did contact me regarding the price of ammonia on the Plains, and asked me if I would be interested in making $5000 for a few minutes' work. And I said, 'Well, I don't know, what's the proposition?' And he said, 'I would like for you to set the price of one load of ammonia to one of your customers at a figure which I would give you at the time that I tell you to do this, and for this little chore, I would put $5000 in the bank in your account today.' "

"What reply did you make to that?" Oates was asked.

"I told him that I wouldn't be interested in it at all."

"What was his purpose? Did he say?"

"He said," Oates replied, "that he had sold quite a number of tons, if I remember correctly, something around 10,000 tons of ammonia, at a discount price, and that he had a contract with his company at that time, which, if some major competitor should break the price below that, they would back him up. In other words, he would make the difference between what he had sold already in advance and the price that he told me to set this one load on."

Billie Sol's business boomed while the sales of other fertilizer dealers in West Texas declined. They were unable to compete with a man who was selling anhydrous ammonia fertilizer for as low as $40 a ton. Until Estes began his widespread price-cutting activities the retail price for fertilizer in the area was $110 a ton, or nearly three times his rock-bottom price.

"His account in 1959 built up very rapidly," Leonhardt testified, "to an open balance . . . around $3.5 million. It was during this fast buildup period that we became more concerned about it and that's why we requested a revised agreement and we requested additional collateral be given to us. We were most concerned over this fast buildup by Mr. Estes from a financial standpoint. We requested, in addition to the usual type of chattel mortgages that we were able to obtain, additional types of securities such as assignment of accounts receivable covering anhydrous ammonia sales, chattel mortgages on any inventory of anhydrous ammonia. We were trying in every way so far as we were concerned at Commercial Solvents to protect exposure that we had through accounts receivable . . . In 1959 we obtained the additional security and felt that we were fairly well protected."

"In the meantime," Attorney General Wilson went on to ask, "you were familiar with the fact that he was acquiring rapidly additional grain elevators?"

"My knowledge of it," Leonhardt said, "was strictly through the increase in the receipts from the grain elevators through Commodity Credit because we could tell by the number of bushels that he certainly was acquiring more facilities."

"Now," fertilizer manager Lester was asked, "did you talk to farmers about inviting them to store grain in his elevators?"

"We did."

"And your sales force for anhydrous ammonia was generally used to try to persuade the farmers to store their grain in the elevators?"

"I wouldn't say it was generally used to try to persuade them," Lester replied, "but when we had this sale last winter, we were asked to suggest to the farmers that we'd appreciate their grain business, too."

Lloyd Stone, who was Lester's partner in one of the fertilizer businesses that Estes bought, was considerably more positive than Lester in his testimony about the close ties between Billie Sol's fertilizer and grain operations. Like Lester, Stone stayed with the company after it was taken over by Estes.

"Did your salesmen talk to the farmers about storing their grain?" Stone was asked.

"Yes," he answered. "I think that was a normal practice . . . that when we sold a man fertilizer we wanted all of his business. We wanted his grain business as well as his fertilizer business. Of course, the fertilizer business was calculated to make more grain, and being more grain, then we'd have opportunity to get more for our storage."

"Is it a fact," Wilson then asked, "that a cheaper price on anhydrous ammonia actually increased the total production of grain in the area here?"

"Yes, sir," Stone quickly replied. "I think up until the time that ammonia got so cheap that the average production, probably, of Hale County was some 4000 pounds per acre, and that also with hybrids considered. But with the increased use of fertilizer, and most people used twice as much as they had ever used before because they were buying it at a price that they could afford to do that, and in the process Hale County this last year probably averaged 6000 pounds to the acre. A 2000-pound increase per acre multiplied by the number of acres in the county would be tremendous."

"So that one of the effects of his cutting the price of ammonia was to drive up the per acre production?"

"Right."

"And, of course, that also means more grain to be stored, doesn't it?"

"That is right."

"And more storage fees?"

"That's right."

"Now," Stone was asked, "what did Billie Sol Estes say to you about how to go about building the business and expanding it?"

"Billie Sol," Stone remembered, "always used analogies, and he said, 'Now, we can go in here and work real hard for fifteen years and build a business, or we can come in and' — as he said it — 'if we hit them, it will all fly up in the air, and when it falls down then we'll grab our part of it.'"

Grain man Frank Farriss told of another method used by Estes to fill his expanding chain of grain warehouses.

"Mr. Estes," Farriss testified, "operating as United Grain, and Allied Grain, along with other people, were offering free storage up until March 31, at which time the Commodity Credit would take charge of the grain . . . which means in effect he [the farmer] will get that much more money in his Government loan."

Robert Wilson, who was in the grain storage business in Plainview, also told about free storage.

"Did you," Wilson was asked, "in 1956 receive some notice from the Commodity Credit on the subject of the free storage, offering free storage for limited periods?"

"Yes, sir," Wilson replied. "In '56 we gave some free storage due to competition, and we were notified it didn't comply with the rules and regulations of uniform grain storage, and to discontinue the practice."

"Now then, was Estes one of your competitors?"

"Yes, sir."

"Did he start this free storage business again?"

"In '59, I think in October, why, it was started again."

"And then state whether or not Commodity Credit stopped it then."

"It wasn't stopped."

At one point Estes was so anxious to get more grain storage facilities that he offered to buy out a warehouseman at a price that amounted to twice the cost of building new facilities. The offer was made to Harry Igo, the owner of the Plainsman Elevators in Plainview.

"He told me he would give me 50 cents a bushel for my grain storage," Igo testified, "and then replacement value for my ammonia storage."

"What can grain storage be built for?" Igo was asked.

"About 25 cents," he replied, "for the type that most of us have today."

"Now, why did he make that offer, Mr. Igo?"

"I suppose he wanted us out of his way."

"What were the terms of the offer?"

"He was to pay me 10 per cent cash and then the balance in 30 days. And then he had a noncompete clause in there that provided I wouldn't go back into business anywhere in the United States or the world or any planet in outer space that was now existing or any that would be discovered."

"How did you feel about that?"

"I said, 'Billie, you don't love me like I thought you did, so I just believe I'll keep it.' "

"In view of this space travel and the moon . . . trip, you thought you might want to go into business in outer space somewhere?"

"Well, yes, you couldn't never tell."

Billie Sol's grain warehousing operations and fertilizer business grew hand in hand, as they had been designed to do in his 1958 agreement with Commercial Solvents. In 1959 he added four warehouses with a total storage capacity of 9,040,000 bushels to his original facilities at Plainview, which could hold 2,960,000 bushels. In 1960 seven more warehouse operations, with a combined capacity of 14,642,-000 bushels, were added to his storage empire. The next year was by far his biggest. From January 1961 through February 1962 Estes purchased warehouse facilities with a capacity of 27,436,504 bushels. By the end of February 1962 he had a total of twenty-two separate warehouse operations with enough space to store 54,078,504 bushels of surplus Government grain.

The payments made to Estes by the Government rose as rapidly as did his storage capacity. In 1959 Estes got $776,-801 in Government grain storage receipts, all of which went directly to Commercial Solvents to pay for his fertilizer purchases. In 1960 the figure rose to $2,423,929, and in 1961 it went up again, to $3,536,229. For the first three months of 1962 the Government payments totaled $911,514. His total "take" from the Government for the storage of surplus grain amounted to $7,648,474 in four years.

Estes sold fertilizer even faster than he bought and built grain warehouses. Commercial Solvents allowed him to buy nearly $11.4 million worth of anhydrous ammonia from 1958 to 1962. Of the $7.6 million that Commercial Solvents got from the Government's Commodity Credit Corporation through its assignment arrangement with Estes, $6.4 million was applied against his anhydrous ammonia bill, leaving $5 million in outstanding debts at the time of his arrest. The other $1.2 million of the $7.6 million in total grain receipts was given to Estes by the company to help him pay for the purchase of additional storage facilities.

It was easy for Estes to expand his grain storage operations as rapidly as he did. Government farm programs, with their high price guarantees, were encouraging farmers to get as much out of each acre of land as they could. The fertilizer sold by Estes at cut-rate prices was helping the farmers to expand their production of the grain sorghums that Estes was then storing in his elevators and warehouses.

Anyone owning warehouses meeting Government specifications can store grain for the Agriculture Department. Many warehousemen obtain grain when it is placed in their facilities by farmers to get a Government loan. Of the thirty-three million bushels of Government grain in the Estes elevators at the time of his arrest, all but three million bushels had been placed there by farmers. The farmers redeem their loans only if market prices for their grain are higher than the Government-guaranteed support prices. Most of the grain put under loan is never redeemed, because the Government guarantees become the market prices. When grain is placed directly in warehouses by the Government, or is moved from one warehouse to another, the grain is allocated among eligible warehousemen by a committee of Agriculture Department officials. These officials have denied that political favoritism plays any part in their decisions, but other Department officials have acknowledged that efforts are often made by members of Congress to put pressure on the Department to get grain into facilities owned by warehousemen who have friends on Capitol Hill.

Each warehouseman had to post a bond before he could store Government grain. The amount of the bond was determined by such factors as the size of the warehouse facilities and the net worth of the owner of the warehouses. In Estes' case his bond was gradually increased from $200,000 in 1959 to $700,000 a year later. Then, early in 1961, an Agriculture Department official recommended that the bond be raised to $1 million in view of the further expansion in the Estes warehouse operations. This determination was made by Carl J. Miller, who as chief of the United States Warehouse Act Branch of the Agriculture Department was charged with establishing the size of individual bonds for grain storage operations. Miller informed Estes of his decision, and also told him that a current financial statement certified by an independent auditor would be required. A week after Billie Sol received this request from Miller, he unexpectedly showed up in Miller's Washington office.

"He took up a great deal of time," Miller recalled in testimony before the House Government Operations subcommittee, "telling me about his humble beginnings and his early life and the struggle that he had had from a poor boy to what he was now, which was obviously a millionaire. He told me about working his way north with combine crews during the harvest time, from Texas on up to the Canadian border. He told me how he had gotten into the cotton-growing business by buying cheap land near Pecos, finding that water was available for irrigation, that this land when irrigated would produce two bales of high-quality cotton per acre, which he sold for as much as 50 cents a pound and it didn't take long to pay for the land and the irrigation wells.

"He told me," Miller continued, "about his philosophy of life, how you win by losing, you multiply by dividing, you increase by diminishing. He said that the idea of the word 'surplus' of anything was wrong. Surplus grain — there was no such thing. It was merely a matter of working out a method of getting our abundance into the stomachs of hungry people around the world, and he was about to solve that problem by going over to India and doing something which I told him a good many people had failed to do. He said that the ability to raise food in this country in abundance was a God-given gift and if we didn't use that gift to the full, that gift would be taken away from us . . . He mentioned his church work and the number of people, young people, whom he was helping through school . . . that he was a lay preacher . . .

"I described him forever after," Miller said, "as the most unusual person I had ever met."

Miller told Estes that he still needed to submit an audited financial statement if he intended to keep the bond on his grain warehouses at $700,000. Within a few weeks Miller received a statement signed by Winn P. Jackson, a certified public accountant. Jackson declared that the net worth of Estes as of December 31, 1961, was $13,734,954.75. This figure was well above the $2,250,000 net worth that Agriculture Department regulations required for the owner of storage facilities of the magnitude of the Estes operations.

Miller accepted the accountant's statement without seeking to verify it and left the Estes bond at $700,000. He should have done some checking. In May 1962 Jackson admitted to the House Government Operations subcommittee that Estes had paid him six thousand dollars for certifying a financial statement which Estes himself had prepared and which Jackson had never tried to check. When asked whether the financial report that he signed "would be something that you would rely on as an accounting of a man's interests and his net worth," Jackson replied, "As an accountant I would file it in the wastebasket as far as depending on it for anything."

Jackson told the subcommittee that he met Estes in the summer of 1960, when he did some research for him on the depreciation of grain storage warehouses for tax purposes. Estes paid him only fifteen dollars for the report, Jackson said. He did not hear from Estes again until early in 1961, when Estes telephoned him at his Lubbock, Texas, office and asked whether he would be " 'interested in doing whatever work I might need . . . on the basis of $500 a month retainer.'

"I said 'Yes,' " Jackson recalled, "because naturally I felt I would never have a client like that, you know, probably again, and that my ship really had come in. So I managed to squeak out a 'Yes.' "

A few days later Jackson got a letter from Estes saying, " 'I am going to send you, or I am sending you, a financial statement and would you please put it on your stationery.' " Jackson said that Estes told him over the telephone, " 'It's all right, there is nothing wrong with it. You know it's right to the penny.'

"Everybody thought that he was such a Christian gentleman and, with his wide reputation," Jackson testified, "I made the mistake of believing him."

When asked by a subcommittee member whether he could not have said, "This is an unaudited balance sheet prepared from figures prepared by Mr. Estes," Jackson answered: "I could have said a lot of things. I have rewritten it in my sleep or laying awake nights. Since February or March I have rewritten it a dozen times already."

Shortly after sending back to Estes his own figures with the letter in February 1961, Jackson said he received a check for six thousand dollars from Estes. The money was supposed to be an advance payment for Jackson's first year of work, at the rate of five hundred dollars a month, but Jackson said that he had done no other work for Estes since then.

"Now we've got this agricultural program wrapped up in a real ball," a confident Billie Sol Estes told a startled Dallas lawyer named Frank Cain. "I want to tell you," Billie Sol went on to say, "that we've got such control over this that if they elected so-called conservatives every election it would take eight years to get us out of control."

Cain had gone out to Pecos to talk to Estes early in March 1962. Cain represented the Pacific Finance Corporation of Los Angeles, which had asked him to check on reports that mortgages purchased by the company were on nonexistent fertilizer tanks. Cain not only discovered a great deal about the fertilizer tank deals (a story which will be told later); he also learned a lot about the Estes grain storage and fertilizer sales operations.

A shrewd, likable and talkative lawyer in his fifties, Cain made two hurried trips to Pecos to see what Pacific Finance could salvage from its entanglement with Estes. Billie Sol's grain storage operations were of great concern to Cain because they seemed to be the most profitable part of his business empire.

"I felt I could get on the inside of this man," Cain told a court of inquiry in Dallas. "I felt that I could talk his language. As he put it, he said I could talk his language. I won him over pretty well."

Cain said that Estes assured him he could keep his grain storage facilities full. Estes indicated to Cain that he had enough connections in Washington to do so. At one point, Cain said, Estes "pulled out of his pocket a gold-plated laminated card . . . that certified him as a hundred-thousand-dollar sustaining member of the national Democratic Party. And I said," Cain continued in his testimony, " 'Now listen, there's one thing that is bothering me. You remember . . . the other day when you said, 'I've got a commitment for forty thousand dollars.' I said, 'Now that was a payoff, wasn't it?' And he said, 'Yes.' I said, 'Well now — let me ask you this: Have you got to keep up these kind of payoffs to keep these grain storage — storage tanks, or these terminals full?' And he said, 'Oh, yeah, I have to do that.' . . . And I said, 'Well now, just how much money are we talking about like that? Just how much money will it take for these payoffs?' He said, 'A hundred thousand to two hundred thousand dollars a year.' "

Estes went on to say, according to Cain's testimony, " 'You know the way I get these farmers over a barrel in this thing . . . I control over a hundred farmers out here . . . You know I sell this ammonia . . . I cut the prices down so that . . . I've got a corner on this market just like I said I was going to get . . . Some of these farmers are going to have to deal with me . . . From the farmers' standpoint we will get the grain in there and from the Government's standpoint we will keep it there.' "

After this conversation, which occurred in the Estes offices on the outskirts of Pecos, Billie Sol took Cain downtown to his hotel. On the way they stopped at a funeral home that Estes had just built.

"He showed me all inside his funeral home," Cain said. "I says, 'Are you making any money out of this?' and he says, 'Oh, no, this is just one more way of getting these farmers over . . . You see I bury everybody around here . . . whether they've got anything or don't have anything.' And he said on any kind of terms. And he said, 'Then, of course, I've just got me another farmer on the hook.' "

In his testimony both before the court of inquiry and before the House Government Operations subcommittee, Cain described a breakfast on a Sunday morning in March 1962 in the Estes home in Pecos. Seated around the dining room table were Estes, his wife, their five children, Maynard C. Wheeler, president of Commercial Solvents, his wife and Cain.

"I nibbled on a couple of hot cakes and drank a cup of coffee," Cain told the House subcommittee. "We were not at the table more than fifteen minutes and the ladies excused themselves and Mr. Estes, Mr. Wheeler and I retired to the living room. Just as we were sitting down, Mr. Estes, in a joking manner, said, 'They' (meaning Commercial Solvents) 'want to put me in business in Brazil.' There was no comment from Mr. Wheeler."

The conversation turned to other matters, and then, Cain continued: "Mr. Wheeler said Billie Sol had called him about an assignment which he had prepared and filed of record that indicated Billie was transferring several millions of dollars to the Bank of Switzerland, and he (Wheeler) thought he had better come out and talk with Billie . . .

Mr. Wheeler said that if matters got too bad for Billie Sol, that Solvents could use him as a consultant in Switzerland. Mr. Estes immediately said, 'I think Brazil would be better.'

"Mr. Wheeler explained generally Commercial Solvents operations, and said they were closely associated with many people in the United States Department of Agriculture, and there was no reason why they could not take over all of Mr. Estes' enterprises, and operate them as good as he could . . . Estes, on several occasions during the conference, said he was prepared to turn all his operations over to Commercial Solvents Corporation. Mr. Estes remarked that Commercial Solvents had sent him $400,000 in cash only a few days before. I could tell from the facial expressions of Mr. Wheeler that he did not like the remark."

Cain told the court of inquiry that Estes also discussed "the Bank of Switzerland and the number system and so forth, of which Estes had a very, very complete knowledge." Swiss bank accounts can be camouflaged through numbers assigned to them. Such accounts are frequently used by persons who wish to hide their financial operations. Before the court of inquiry, Cain also quoted Estes as saying to him and Wheeler, "You know Mr. Wheeler has been just like a father to me; he put me in the ammonia business."

When he testified before the House subcommittee Wheeler denied most of the statements that Cain had made, but Wheeler did confirm that Commercial Solvents had loaned $400,000 to Estes in February 1962.

"Except as I shall presently relate," Wheeler said, "I deny emphatically that I ever made the statements attributed to me by Cain, and I also deny that there were made in my presence the statements attributed to me by Cain to himself and Estes. As part of the small talk, it is entirely possible that

Estes again might have told of having filed the document concerning the Swiss bank to give the rival newspaper an opportunity to spend six months investigating."

Wheeler told the subcommittee that Estes said he had filed a document, presumably with the Reeves County clerk in Pecos, "indicating a loan of $4.5 million to him from a Swiss bank . . . as a joke to give the Pecos *Enterprise* people something to investigate . . . He told me he had not borrowed money from Switzerland, and that the name of the bank he had given on the document had been pulled out of the air." Estes had started his own newspaper, the Pecos *Daily News*, in August 1961, and it was engaged in a bitter fight for advertising and circulation with the long-established Pecos *Independent and Enterprise*.

"But I deny saying, or hearing anything said," Wheeler continued, "concerning any number system in Switzerland, or using Estes as a consultant in Switzerland or putting Estes into business in Brazil . . . I deny making any statement concerning our desire, intention or ability to 'step in and take the place of Billie.' Moreover, there was no mention in my presence of my having put Estes in the ammonia business, no mention of the grain storage facilities, 'grain tanks,' or keeping them filled; nor was there any mention of the Department of Agriculture. Except for Secretary Freeman, I did not know the name of any officer or employee of the Department of Agriculture, and I deny mentioning the name of any officer or employee of the Department, or of any individual who could bring influence to bear on the Department or any other branch of Government. I did not and do not know of any such individual."

In May 1962, Texas Attorney General Wilson filed an antitrust suit in the District Court of Potter County in

Amarillo which charged that in 1958 Estes put into effect a plan to control the West Texas market for the sale and distribution of anhydrous ammonia. To do this, Wilson said, Estes sold ammonia below cost to try to drive his competition out of business.

In Texas the Attorney General is primarily responsible for the enforcement of the state's antitrust laws. The laws were enacted in the 1890's and were among the earliest legislation in this country dealing with bigness in industry and monopolistic business practices. The legislation grew out of one of the early farm protest movements. The southern branch of the Farmers' Alliance movement began in Texas, and one of its principal goals was regulation of the trusts.

To gather information that he deems necessary for the enforcement of the state antitrust laws, the Texas Attorney General has the authority to convene courts of inquiry. They are presided over by state judges. Witnesses are questioned by the Attorney General and his assistants under proceedings similar to those followed in congressional committee investigations.

In his antitrust suit Wilson charged that Estes hoped to capture the West Texas fertilizer market in three years. "The basic tactic Estes planned to, and in fact did, use to effectuate his scheme," Wilson said, "was to shatter the market by selling anhydrous ammonia below cost at tremendous financial losses to himself and the defendant co-conspirators, and to 'pick up the pieces' and put together a near monopoly through which the retail price of anhydrous ammonia could be controlled.

"On occasions," Wilson noted, "Estes would direct that the price be dropped in a specified area for the purpose of injuring or eliminating certain competitors. On other occasions Estes would engineer a general decrease in price . . .

Estes on various occasions approached competing dealers and gave them the alternative ultimatum to sell to him or be driven completely out of business. If the dealer refused to sell or cooperate, Estes endeavored to make good the threat."

When he filed the antitrust suit, Wilson stated: "We feel that Commercial Solvents was an active party in the scheme to sell fertilizer below cost to drive out competition. As such, they are a proper defendant in this antitrust case."

In his testimony before the House Government Operations subcommittee Wheeler, president of Commercial Solvents, emphatically stated: "The relationship between Estes and the company was that of customer and supplier — and no more. The customer wanted credit and CSC was willing to accommodate its customer so long as the credit was adequately covered by collateral. The list of collateral that CSC obtained from Estes indicates how prudent the corporation was in demanding security as a condition of continuing business relations."

Commercial Solvents treasurer Leonhardt told a court of inquiry that the cost of manufacturing anhydrous ammonia ranged from thirty to thirty-five dollars a ton. The fertilizer was made at a plant in Louisiana. The wholesale price Estes was charged for the fertilizer was generally around ninety dollars a ton, nearly three times the manufacturing cost.

"Throughout this whole transaction, Mr. Leonhardt," Wilson asked, "the money you were getting from Estes more than covered your cost of operation, did it not? The cost to you of the ammonia you were selling him?"

"Yes, sir," Leonhardt replied.

"So that," Wilson continued, "in extending this line of credit under these circumstances, the risk you took was in risking your profits in the transaction?"

"After a certain point," Leonhardt conceded. "In other

words, as the account was building up over the years, we saw to it that at this stage of the game the grain receipts had built up to a point where we were more relaxed on credit today than we were a year ago."

Although Estes still owed Commercial Solvents $5 million at the time of the collapse of his operations, the company had already received $6.4 million in grain storage payments which it applied to his fertilizer account. Its total fertilizer sales to Estes amounted to $11.4 million. Its receipts thus came to more than half of total sales, but the cost of manufacturing the fertilizer was, according to Leonhardt, only about one third of the wholesale price charged Estes. So Commercial Solvents apparently did not lose any money in its dealings with Estes. If we accept Leonhardt's figures, the company even made some money on the deal, despite the $5 million still owed it by Estes at the time of his arrest! In April 1963 Wheeler told a Commercial Solvents stockholders meeting in Baltimore the company expected to recover an additional $3.7 million under the terms of an agreement for the liquidation of Estes' assets. At that time Wheeler estimated the company's losses on the Estes account at $5,626,850.

Two former Agriculture Department officials, Walter C. Berger, who helped to set grain storage policies in the Eisenhower Administration, and James K. McConnell, an Assistant Secretary of Agriculture under Ezra Taft Benson, served as consultants to Commercial Solvents during the period that the company maintained its unusual business relations with Estes. Berger was also a member of the board of directors of Commercial Solvents. In discussing the tasks performed for the company by Berger and McConnell, Wheeler told the House subcommittee that neither man, or anyone else working for Commercial Solvents, sought or obtained special favors for the company or for Estes from the Agriculture Department.

Commercial Solvents is a medium-size chemical company, established in 1919, which extracts products for industry and agriculture from natural gas and grain starches. Sales of the company have never exceeded $100 million in a single year, and in 1962 it ranked twenty-fifth among general chemical firms. It had seventeen thousand stockholders in 1962, when its balance sheet showed a net worth of more than $48 million. Anhydrous ammonia accounted for 5 per cent of its sales. Estes had been by far its largest dealer in anhydrous ammonia.

In less than three years Estes leaped over more than eight thousand rivals to become one of the nation's largest operators of warehouses for the storage of surplus Government-owned grain. This was no easy achievement, even for an entrepreneur like Billie Sol. The storage of surplus crops was a $500-million-a-year business. Competition for the surpluses was fierce because the Federal payments to warehousemen were so generous. Many warehousemen were able to make a profit of 100 per cent or more on their Government business.

Billie Sol's swift climb to the heights of the lucrative grain storage business was all the more remarkable because he did it with little risking of his own money. Loans from Commercial Solvents and other sources financed much of his rapid expansion as a Government grain warehouseman.

In 1961 alone, the last full year of the Estes operations, the Government paid out nearly $3.5 million for storing grain with him. Only eight other operators of Government grain storage facilities got more money from the Agriculture Department in 1961 than did the Estes enterprises.

The C–G–F Grain Company of Texas, Kansas, Missouri and Nebraska was the largest operator of Government grain facilities. C–G–F received nearly $25 million from the Agriculture Department for the grain that it stored in 1961. Seventy-four companies each received $500,000 or more for storing Government grain in 1961. They got $148 million of the $500 million that the Government spent for handling and storing surplus crops that year. Most of the storage costs went for wheat, corn, sorghums and other feed grains.

It cost another $500 million to pay the interest in 1961 on Government bonds that had to be sold to finance the storage program. All agricultural subsidies and price support activities amounted to more than $5 billion in 1961. So the $1 billion cost of handling, storing and financing the costly farm surpluses came to one fifth of the total agricultural subsidy expenditures. This $5 billion went to maintain the income of the two million commercial farmers who benefited from the programs. Looking at these billions in another way, the Government was spending an average of about $2500 per farm to bolster the income of the nation's two million commercial farmers, while per farm income for all of the 3.7 million farmers amounted to only $3498.

The costly grain storage program is by far the most dramatic example of what has happened to agricultural subsidies because of the failure to adjust programs designed for depression years to the needs of the highly scientific, heavily mechanized and on the whole quite prosperous commercial agriculture of today. Henry A. Wallace and the other advocates of the Government price support and loan and storage programs of the 1930's envisioned a system under which crops would be stored only until their prices were right. Farmers would then redeem their loans and take most of the crops out of storage. What was left could be kept in the "ever-normal granary" to be available during lean years. Wallace failed to reckon with the vast mechanical and scientific changes that would overtake agriculture. The productivity of American farmers is now so great that even the drought of the late 1950's in the Western states failed to result in a significant reduction in surplus production.

Instead of being a service to farmers and an assurance to Americans of an always abundant supply of food, the storage programs have become a bonanza for warehousemen.

Although Secretary of Agriculture Freeman vigorously denied that Estes received any favoritism in his remarkable climb to the top of the grain storage business, the story of the Estes storage operations is still important because it showed one spectacular way in which the farm program had gone wrong.

The only indictment arising out of the Estes storage operations charged Billie Sol with filing a false financial statement to keep his bond at $700,000. Neither House nor Senate investigators found any evidence that Estes was paying off Federal employees to get Government grain, but the Agriculture Department withdrew the grain from his warehouses after his arrest.

Estes was not the first farmer or businessman to realize huge profits from Government subsidy programs; nor is it likely that he was the last to cash in on the programs. Many others did so before him and many more will do so in the future unless farm production is brought into line with domestic and international demand and farmers are no longer encouraged to produce commodities that are wanted by no one except warehousemen.

6

Subsidies, Everyone?

THE FARM PROGRAM has flourished in an American economy that oozes with Federal subsidies. Governments have always subsidized and protected favored or powerful groups. The subsidies and protections are proclaimed to be in the public interest, and frequently they do serve a useful purpose. Sometimes, however, the subsidies merely constitute a sop to an influential group or industry. Frequently, too, a subsidy that was justified when it was first put into effect outlives its usefulness. By then the subsidy has become so entrenched in the economy and so many people come to depend upon it that it is extremely difficult to cut off.

To many a group or special interest benefiting from particular laws or programs a subsidy is what the other fellow is getting from the Government. A 1960 House Agriculture Committee report issued to try to justify the huge Government outlays for farmers observed:

There is one concept of subsidy which extends to all persons and enterprises whose economic positions are improved, or whose purposes are advanced, as the result of Government action. This embraces industries whose profits would be less without protection of the tariff laws and the many other statutes that soften the full force of competition in a private enterprise economy; and this broad definition likewise encompasses all working people whose earnings are greater because of minimum wage, collective bargaining and immigration laws.

It is pointed out, by those favoring this definition, that the economic benefits accruing to industry and labor, from Government policies, are paid for — as are the costs of the farm program — by the general consuming and taxpaying public.

Thus virtually all of the population would seem to be in a subsidy recipient posture and, moreover, almost all are participating in the payment of the costs. It is certain that the total population feels the economic impact of the subsidy programs for industry, labor and agriculture.

Less self-serving than the House Agriculture Committee's definition was one used by Robert L. Hubbell, a fiscal economist for the Bureau of the Budget, in discussing concealed subsidies in the Federal budget. Writing in the September 1957 issue of the *National Tax Journal*, Hubbell defined a subsidy as:

. . . a governmental financial device which enables sellers to get more money or buyers to get more goods and services than would be the case if the affected commercial transactions had occurred without Government intervention. The financial device may involve (1) direct or indirect payments in cash or kind, (2) provision of goods or services for prices or fees which do not reflect full competitive market value or (3) lower taxes which are exceptions to general tax rates.

In a study entitled *Subsidy and Subsidy-like Programs of the U.S. Government* which he made for the Joint Economic Committee of the Senate and House in 1960, Julius W. Allen of the Legislative Reference Service of the Library of Congress indicated his general agreement with Hubbell's definition and then noted:

It is often remarked that bachelors and childless couples subsidize children's education through the taxes they pay. Even contributing to the support of a son-in-law is considered a subsidy by some, who may conceivably be motivated in part by envy. However, broadening the meaning of subsidy to include this type of nongovernmental assistance may well be considered to involve a *reductio ad absurdum.*

Tariffs are the oldest Federal subsidy. They constitute a tax on foreign goods. The purpose of the tariff — or tax — is to protect American producers from foreign competition. Such protection amounts to a subsidy to the American manufacturers. One of the first laws enacted by the First Congress in 1789 was a tariff act. Assistance to shipbuilders, owners and operators was included in the first tariff legislation. The law put into effect a tax on tonnage that favored American ships and provided for a 10 per cent reduction in customs duties for goods imported to the United States in ships owned by Americans. Tariffs still protect both large and small American industries, and maritime subsidies remain a part of every Federal budget.

During the nineteenth century railroads got more aid from the Federal Government than any other industry. For twenty-one years, beginning in 1850, the Government gave land to railroads to encourage their westward expansion. The grants generally took the pattern of alternate one-mile-square sections of land along the right-of-way of the railroads being built in the West. From 1862 to 1866 more than 100 million acres were handed over to the railroads. The total land obtained by railroads through state as well as Federal grants amounted to 183 million acres. The value of the land and other assistance to the railroads during the period of their westward expansion totaled nearly $1.3 billion, a huge figure in the American economy of a century ago.

But it was not until the New Deal days of the 1930's that

subsidy programs costing hundreds of millions or even billions of dollars a year came to be first a hotly disputed and then a generally accepted part of Federal budgets. The Puritan ethic, which holds that everyone must be self-reliant, meant that both industries and individuals preferred indirect or hidden subsidies to open handouts that all taxpayers could see and more easily condemn. The tariff, the grandfather of them all, was also the first of the disguised subsidies.

The 1960 subsidy study prepared for the Joint Economic Committee took seven pages to list "the sweeping, amorphous . . . subsidy programs." The report estimated that in the 1961 fiscal year measurable subsidy payments amounted to nearly $7.5 billion, of which $4.7 billion, or well over half, went for Federal farm programs.

The ten broad categories into which the report divided subsidies ranged from direct payments to farmers and businessmen and special tax benefits for specific economic groups to indirect aid to groups and industries, programs with incidental effects similar to those of subsidies, Government services offered free or at less than cost, lending, loan guarantee and insurance programs, and Federal aid payments to state and local governments and to individuals.

Direct payments to business included mail subsidies to airlines and shipping companies above the actual cost of carrying the mail and the partial financing of plants by the Government to generate electricity from atomic fuels. In addition to the farm price support, loan and purchase programs, the report also listed such other direct aids to farmers as payments for carrying out good conservation practices, irrigation and flood control work, and subsidies to domestic sugar producers. Among the special tax benefits cited were depletion allowances for the oil, mineral and other extractive industries, accelerated depreciation allowances for defense facilities, and the deductions that borrowers, the elderly, the blind and the sick can make in figuring their income taxes.

Indirect Government subsidies included the benefits that the trucking industry obtained from the construction of highways, for which the industry has generally not paid its fair share through gasoline taxes, assistance to airlines through Federal aid in the construction of airports, and the aid that business has received under the purchase restrictions of the Buy American Act. Government programs with incidental subsidy-like benefits involved all defense and other Federal contracts, special provisions in the contracts favoring small businesses and depressed areas, the disposal of surplus property, the stockpiling of minerals and other strategic materials, and the purchase of silver. Practically every department and agency of the Government provides services free or at below their cost. There are crop reports from the Agriculture Department, weather forecasts from the Commerce Department, employment and business statistics from both the Labor and Commerce Departments, scientific and industrial research reports from nearly all Departments, and postal services to magazine and newspaper publishers, to businessmen who use the mails for advertising, and to farmers and other persons living on rural free delivery routes. None of these services to special groups pays its way.

Government lending and loan guarantee programs aid people who want to buy homes, contractors who want to build them, farmers who want to expand their land holdings, and businessmen who cannot get financing from banks or other private sources. A veteran who wants to buy a home or go into business gets even greater subsidies than someone who was not in the armed forces. Federal insurance programs protect farmers against crop failures, and banks and their depositors against embezzlers. The social security program uses an insurance system to help the old and the disabled. The unemployment compensation program makes sure that a man has some income when he is thrown out of work.

The Federal Government also makes large payments each year to the states to carry out such programs as agricultural research, highway construction, special aids for health, education and welfare, and assistance in the planning and rebuilding of cities.

From this list [the Joint Economic Committee report noted], a further problem suggests itself. It is in many cases impossible to determine the incidence of these subsidy and subsidy-like programs. The school lunch program subsidizes the farmer by helping cut back on farm supplies, but clearly also subsidizes the recipients of this food and their parents. The second-class postage rates are far from covering the costs of carrying the magazines and newspapers within this class, but the benefit of the subsidy is shared among publishers, advertisers, subscribers and other readers.

The clearly identifiable subsidy payments listed in the Joint Economic Committee report increased from $1.9 billion in the 1951 fiscal year to nearly $7.5 billion in 1960. "The most important element in the increase as shown," the report pointed out, "is the increase in net current expenses for agriculture and the increases in inventory accumulations." Net current agricultural subsidy expenses were listed at nearly $3.6 billion for 1960. The net additions to the Commodity Credit Corporation's huge inventory of agricultural commodities took another $1.1 billion out of the Agriculture Department budget, making total farm subsidy expenditure $4.7 billion for that year.

Totaling the costs of Government programs over several years can of course lead to meaningless and largely irrelevant statistics. It is still useful to note that of the $17.7 billions spent by the Government on farm subsidies from 1932 to 1959 only $2.2 billion was spent during the depression years of the 1930's. A total of $3.4 billion was spent in the 1940's. More than $12 billion, or over two thirds of the total amount expended since 1932, was spent during the 1950's. The decade of the fifties was also the period of the greatest migration from farm to city. At the end of a decade when farm population was at an all-time low and there were only 3.7 million farms left in the United States, farm subsidy payments were at a record high level of $4.7 billion, which by 1962 had increased to $5 billion.

Farm subsidies cannot be considered and evaluated in isolation from the many other Government subsidy programs. From 1946 through 1959, for example, the total postal deficit amounted to $7 billion. Nearly all of the deficit was caused by the failure of magazines and newspapers that benefit from second-class mailing privileges and businessmen who avail themselves of cheap, third-class mail rates to pay for the postal services they use. Yet even this subsidy is little more than half of what it cost the Government to support a dwindling number of farmers in the 1950's.

Much of the defense program, which has been costing more than $50 billion a year, constitutes subsidies to businessmen holding defense contracts and to their employees. The businessmen and the leaders of the unions representing their employees combine with members of Congress from the districts and the states where the defense industries are located to prevent or to postpone the cancellation of contracts for equipment that changing defense needs has made obsolete. But the exact amount of subsidy in the defense program is difficult to determine, while the farm subsidies just sit there, sticking up like a grain elevator on a flat Texas horizon.

Yet, because so many members of Congress represent states and districts that have a tremendous vested interest in the farm programs as they have operated since the end of World War II, few Senators and Representatives raise questions about the billions of dollars that have been pouring into the countryside, the small towns and the big commodity dealers in the cities. Even when the Senate Investigations subcommittee headed by Democratic Senator John L. McClellan of Arkansas spent most of the summer of 1962 holding lengthy hearings on the Billie Sol Estes cotton transactions, the two Republican members of the subcommittee seemed to be holding back the kind of politically tinged criticism expected from the opposition in a scandal of such dimensions. The Republicans were Senator Karl E. Mundt of South Dakota, who had thrived in the past on investigations both as a member of the House and as a Senator, and Senator Carl T. Curtis of Nebraska. At times during the hearings both Mundt and Curtis seemed far more concerned with the problems of the farmers and the even more important grain dealers back home. The grain dealers are the men who help to finance the elections of so many Senators and Representatives from rural areas.

The cost of farm subsidies has been in dispute for many years. The Agriculture Department and the farm organizations try to minimize the costs by claiming that most of the Department's budget benefits all Americans and not just farmers.

In 1963 the Bureau of the Budget included in its analysis of Federal spending a summary of "current expenditures for aids and special services," a bureaucratic euphemism for subsidies. This summary showed that actual expenditures in the 1962 fiscal year for these aids and special services totaled $17.6 billion. Agriculture accounted for just over $5 billion of the aids and special services. The $5 billion represented about three fourths of the total fiscal 1962 Agriculture Department budget of $6.8 billion.

Veterans' benefits were slightly higher than the farm subsidies, topping them by $41 million. The cost of aids and special services to business totaled $1.7 billion. The big items here were more than $700 million for the postal deficit, almost $400 million for the Federal Aviation Agency, $200 million for Coast Guard navigational aids, and $186 million for ship operating subsidies.

Labor accounted for only $361 million in aids and special services, nearly all of which went into emergency Federal unemployment compensation payments. Federal payments to people on relief amounted to $2.4 billion. Another $2.7 billion was spent on special international services, principally military and economic foreign aid.

Nearly $2.7 billion, or more than half, of the agricultural expenditures were for price support and related programs. The other big farm subsidy expenditure was nearly $1.5 billion for the sale of surpluses for foreign currencies under the Food-for-Peace program. Most of the foreign money thus obtained is in turn loaned to the countries for economic development projects. The money is of no use to the United States and constitutes a net loss to the Federal Government. Secretary Freeman and farm spokesmen on Capitol Hill argue that the cost of the Food-for-Peace program should not be charged off as part of the farm subsidy program because the donations benefit American foreign policy. If the farm surpluses were not available, however, it is unlikely that the United States would have a Food-for-Peace program of the magnitude of the present effort.

The rest of the $5 billion in farm subsidies is accounted for by such programs as direct payments to wool and sugar beet producers, milk programs, and subsidies to make possible the sale abroad of wheat for dollars.

The estimated figures for aids and special services for the 1963 and 1964 fiscal years were about the same as the actual figures for 1962. The agricultural estimates for both 1963 and 1964 were $4.9 billion, compared with a total Agriculture Department estimated budget of $7.5 billion in 1963 and $6.6 billion in 1964. The total aids and special services figures for all groups are estimated at $18.3 billion for 1963 and $18.4 billion in 1964.

In commenting on its classification of programs under the aids and special services category the Budget Bureau noted:

This category contains expenditures which provide — mainly in the year in which the outlays are made — aids or special services to certain groups. In addition to such items as losses on farm programs, maritime subsidies, veterans pensions and grants to foreign nations for economic and military assistance, the category includes (a) administrative and other operating expenses attributable to most of the investment-type programs discussed previously, and (b) the costs of maintaining the physical assets related to some of these investment-type programs.

This classification only reflects part of the Federal Government's aid to special groups since it is by definition limited to current expenses. It does not cover, for example, subsidies for the construction of private merchant ships which are classified as additions to private assets. Similarly, outlays for which the Federal Government receives assets or collateral (as the acquisition of farm commodities by the Commodity Credit Corporation) are treated as additions to Federal assets, although realized losses on such assets are included in this category. Some Government aids are indirect and are excluded from this classification because they are not reflected in expenditures or cannot be readily measured. Examples of such indirect benefits include low interest rates on some loans and certain preferential tax treatments.

Although the category deals essentially with expenditures of a direct aid or service character, some of the outlays included contribute indirectly to the Nation's future development. Among these are grants for slum clearance and urban renewal, and contributions to local authorities for low-rent public housing.

In 1960 a special subcommittee of the Senate Agriculture Committee investigated the grain storage operations of the Commodity Credit Corporation, which is the Government agency that handles the storage programs. Although the subcommittee, whose chairman was Democratic Senator Stuart Symington of Missouri, was designed in large measure to be a political instrument to embarrass the Eisenhower Administration, the hearings and the subcommittee's subsequent report constituted one of the few efforts before the Billie Sol Estes investigations of 1962 to get out into the open some of the facts of the costly storage programs.

The subcommittee report noted that from 1953 to 1960 the Agriculture Department spent more than $2.3 billion to store and handle surplus commodities. Ninety per cent of the storage costs went for Government-owned grain that the Agriculture Department was piling up in private facilities operated by eight thousand warehousemen throughout the country. From 1952 to 1960 the value of commodities pledged for outstanding loans to farmers and of commodities owned outright by the Commodity Credit Corporation increased from less than $1.5 billion to more than $10.4 billion. Storage, handling and transportation costs and Government interest expenses charged to price support inventory and loan operations went up from less than $149 million in 1952 to more than $1 billion in 1960. For grains alone the storage and handling costs rose from under $66 million in 1952 to $587 million in 1960, or from $268,000 a day in 1951 to more than $1.2 million a day in 1959.

Despite the tremendous expansion of the grain storage business, the subcommittee noted that "no comprehensive survey of warehousemen's operating costs had ever been made in order to provide a firm basis for determining the reasonableness of the rates and the impact of price trends reflected in cost indices on such rates." As the subcommittee report also noted, the Agriculture Department initiated a cost study only after the Senate investigation got under way. Before the investigation was completed the Department put into effect a 19 per cent reduction in storage rates that the Senate subcommittee estimated would save taxpayers $85 million to $100 million a year. Included in the evidence presented to the subcommittee on the costs of storing grain was a report by the General Accounting Office showing that net profits per bushel of wheat stored in fifty-seven commercial warehouses in Kansas, Minnesota, Mississippi, Nebraska, North Dakota, Oklahoma, South Dakota and Texas ranged from 84 to 265 per cent of the estimated storage costs. Richard Phillips, professor of agricultural economics at Iowa State University and a recognized authority on the marketing of grain and feed, told the subcommittee that a survey he made of forty-four country elevators in Iowa revealed an average profit of 74 per cent on the handling and storage of Government grain. Other testimony showed that operators of the warehouses paid bonuses to farmers to get them to store grain under the Government loan program in their facilities.

The subcommittee also cited Standard and Poor's financial report on the Archer-Daniels-Midland Company, a publicly held corporation that has been one of the large operators of facilities for the storage of Government grain. For the year ending June 30, 1958, the company had net sales and operating revenues of more than $225 million and grain storage and handling revenues from the Agriculture Department of $6.9 million. "In 1957 and 1958," Standard and Poor's noted, "grain operations accounted for four per cent of the combined sales and revenues, and 24 per cent of the gross profit (after depreciation)."

Representatives of the grain trade who appeared before the Symington subcommittee bitterly criticized the Agriculture Department for lowering its grain storage rates and maintained that even higher rates were needed. Frank A. Theis, president of the Terminal Elevator Grain Merchants Association of Kansas City, said that "instead of standing up for its policies, the Department this year has fled in panic before the verbal guns of Congress, and has tried to clothe their sellout of the grain industry in the respectable garb of a 'comprehensive cost study.' "

The Symington subcommittee also investigated the Government's use of two large storage bins owned by Cargill, Inc., in Savage, Minnesota. Officials of the Agriculture Department in Washington ordered the use of the facilities for the storage of surplus grain, despite protests from Department officials stationed in Minnesota that grain kept in the bins for long periods of time would deteriorate because it could not be properly handled and maintained in good condition in such large warehouses.

The subcommittee reported that

. . . in late 1958 and early 1959 the storing warehouseman [Cargill] and the Commodity office in Minneapolis became fearful of this grain going out of condition, and it became necessary for the Commodity office to empty the elevator and dispose of the stored wheat. CCC, therefore, began to take steps to sell some six million bushels of wheat, and did, eventually, dispose of it, selling some 4,836,630 bushels to the storing warehouseman, Cargill, Inc. A report by the Internal Audit Division of the Department of Agriculture . . . was critical of this transaction. It stated that while the storing warehouseman had agreed with the Government to keep sufficient open space so as to make room to efficiently turn the grain for conditioning . . . that the condition of the grain, which necessitated its disposal, "resulted in lack of turning and conditioning."

The Agriculture Department auditors also discovered that Cargill bought the grain from the Government at prices ranging up to 16 cents a bushel below market prices and then applied for and received export subsidies of $1.5 million for the resale of the wheat to foreign countries. The export subsidy was from 54 to 60 cents a bushel. This meant that wheat the Government had sold because it was considered substandard was marketed abroad by Cargill for substantially more than the world wheat price. The Government pays subsidies on wheat sold abroad so that the foreign market price is competitive with wheat from other countries. The wheat Cargill obtained at a bargain price obviously was not in nearly so bad a condition as someone in the Government thought it to be. What is more, as the Symington subcommittee report went on to say, "Two million bushels of this wheat were sold to Tradex International, South America, a Panamanian corporation, which, Cargill informed the subcommittee, was a South American corporation owned by certain stockholders of Cargill."

The subcommittee report concluded that in operating the grain storage program the Agriculture Department had disregarded "sound business procedures" and had been guilty of "mismanagement of the taxpayers' dollars." The report went on to note:

The insistence of the Department on continuation of an absolute uniform rate for grain storage throughout the country is, in the opinion of the subcommittee, a serious mistake. It can only allow some persons to continue receiving exorbitant profits from the storage of Government grain, while others performing a needed service to the farmers and communities of this Nation are denied a chance to make any profit at all.

In the same year — 1960 — that the Symington subcommittee issued its report, another group of congressional investigators, the Intergovernmental Relations subcommittee of the House Government Operations Committee, also issued a report on the serious shortcomings of the agricultural subsidy programs enriching middlemen at the expense of taxpayers. This same subcommittee, whose chairman was Democratic Representative L. H. Fountain of North Carolina, in 1962 investigated the Estes grain operations.

Fountain's 1960 report summed up questionable Agriculture Department subsidy operations going back to 1955 to what the Congressman called the "cheese deals." "In this instance," Fountain said, "although the farmers received no benefit, the Administration simply gave away more than $2 million to business firms and charged it to the farm program. The deal supposedly involved purchases and resales of cheese which never left the warehouses in which it was stored."

Turning to the much bigger grain storage programs, Fountain said:

Non-conventional facilities such as Army buildings, hangars, oil tanks, coal bunkers and lumber sheds have been and are being used for storage of Government grain under contract with private firms at the same rates paid for conventional space instead of directly using Government-owned or acquired facilities at much lower cost. In one case of this kind, a warehouseman grossed nearly 2 million in payments for storing wheat in buildings rented from the Air Force for $29,000. . . .

A really monumental storage fiasco occurred when a top Washington official approved storage of 37 million bushels of Government wheat in tents under contract with a commercial warehouseman, after the operation had been turned down by his subordinates as too risky. Much of the wheat spoiled and became unfit for human consumption, resulting in a multimillion-dollar Government claim against the warehouseman. Instead of moving immediately to collect the Government claim, Department of Agriculture officials first waived the Government's prior rights to most of the warehouseman's assets in favor of a group of banks which had loaned him large sums of money on long-term unsecured notes, and then advanced $2½ million in impounded storage payments. Thereafter, disregarding prior complaints about the poor quality of wheat exported from the United States, the Department actually paid export subsidies on the unfit wheat. The cost to the taxpayers for such export subsidies at 75 cents per bushel or more was millions of dollars; the cost in lost markets from damage to the reputation of United States wheat abroad cannot be calculated.

Another particularly shoddy chapter in the storage story concerns favored treatment for a small group of West Coast firms and individuals at the expense of the taxpayers. In the Pacific Northwest, 25 million bushels of wheat were removed from Government ships where it was being stored at a cost of two cents per bushel per year while Government wheat remained stored in substandard private facilities where the cost was eight times as much. The Department of Agriculture's own auditors vigorously protested this wasteful action, but their protests were ignored at a cost to the public of millions of dollars annually.

Fountain noted, too, that when it came to the buying and selling of surplus farm commodities, one Government agency frequently did not know what another agency was doing:

The International Cooperation Administration paid $58 per ton to have 7000 tons of rice shipped to West Africa, even though the rice had just been sold by the Department of Agriculture for $38 per ton. Dry milk purchased by a dairy firm from the Agriculture Department for less than ten cents per pound was immediately resold to the Army for 34 cents per pound. As a result of the subcommittee's investigation of the rice and dry milk deals in 1958, a total of more than $100,000 has been recovered. . . . [In 1959] the ICA paid as much as 79 cents per pound . . . to finance exportation of butter to Vietnam which had been sold by the Department of Agriculture for only 39 cents per pound.

Finally, Fountain cited serious conflicts of interest that his subcommittee found in the late 1950's:

The former manager of the West Coast office of the Department of Agriculture was recently convicted on conflict of interest charges, after he realized a profit of $83,000 without any investment on a Government grain storage deal . . . Until a few weeks ago, the person who decided which West Coast warehouse would receive Government grain for storage was the wife of the traffic manager of a grain firm receiving millions of dollars annually in Government storage payments. Washington officials took no action to correct this situation until several months after they learned of it. A former State ASC [Agricultural Stabilization Committee] Chairman, with the full knowledge and apparent approval of his superiors, operated a commercial warehouse storing Government grain during his service as a Department of Agriculture employee. During this time, he greatly increased the size of his warehouse operation, obtaining three Government loans from the Small Business Administration for the purpose.

Not all the abuses of the farm programs that have been brought to the attention of members of Congress have involved the storage of surplus commodities. Since the middle 1950's, when surpluses began piling up and the farm program started to get out of hand, Republican Senator John J. Williams of Delaware has been seeking to alert the

Senate to the dangers of such costly programs. A former feed dealer representing a small state where poultry producers and dairy farmers depend heavily on grain purchased from the Midwest, Williams knows how important cheap and abundant feed is to his farmer-constituents. So his crusade against high price supports and rigid Government restrictions on production is not altogether altruistic. Whatever his motives may be, Senator Williams has succeeded in calling attention to some of the most glaring inconsistencies of the farm program. He has been particularly critical of large Government payments to big corporate farming operations.

In 1959 Williams presented to the Senate an analysis of the soil bank program which showed that two years earlier the Government had paid out in price support loans a total of nearly $3.5 million to ten of the nation's largest producers of cotton, wheat and rice. The largest payment, $1,167,-502.35, went for cotton loans taken out by a British-owned corporation, the Delta and Pine Land Company, whose operations are centered in Scott, Mississippi. Williams went on to point out that the same ten companies received additional payments of more than $557,000 under the soil bank program for taking land out of production. The Delta and Pine Land Company's share of the soil bank payments was $20,761.20. Thus, Williams concluded, "these same corporations and individuals who were receiving substantial Government support on crops produced were at the same time also receiving thousands of dollars for not producing crops on other land which they owned or controlled.

A year earlier, in 1958, Williams had told the Senate the incredible story "wherein," to use the Senator's words, "the owner of one of the country's richest racing stables has been found to be on the Government relief rolls. The official records show that Rex Ellsworth and his brother, owners of the Ellsworth Ranch, Seligman, Arizona, and owners of the race horse Swaps, were upon their application approved as eligible to receive over two million pounds of subsidized feed under the Emergency Drought Relief Program. Under this program the Government contributed a $1.50 per hundredweight subsidy, which subsidy was authorized by Congress on the basis that it was to assist needy and bona fide farmers to maintain their basic herds of livestock, and the definition of livestock eligible under this program definitely did not include race horses. Most of these payments to Mr. Ellsworth were made in 1957. When an inquiry was made they were stopped, but before they were stopped they had received total Government subsidies amounting to $28,914, with $26,049 of this amount representing subsidy feed payments and $2865 free hay — all paid for by the American taxpayers."

In a review of large Government payments made to cotton producers, Williams placed in the *Congressional Record* in 1960 a list of corporations and individuals receiving more than $100,000 in loans on 1958 cotton crops. Included in the list was Anderson Clayton and Company of Houston, the world's largest cotton brokers. The company received $707,-907.61 in loans on 1958 cotton crops. In 1958, as in 1957, the largest cotton loan went to the Delta and Pine Land Company. This British corporation got $1,212,699.80 from the United States Government in loans on its 1958 cotton crop.

"Why," Williams asked the Senate, "should this wholly-owned British corporation receive more assistance in the form of price support loans on its 1958 cotton crop than did all the farmers of the great State of Pennsylvania on all the crops they produced? Why should our taxpayers support this British-owned corporation in its farming operations here in America? Remember all this is being done under legislation enacted in the name of our small farmers."

Early in 1960 and again in 1961 Williams attacked the soil bank program in speeches on the Senate floor. His 1960 speech concerned a report by the General Accounting Office. "Based upon this report," Williams said, "twenty-three million acres have been contracted for under the conservation reserve program. Of this amount 5,400,000 acres, or 23 per cent of the estimated total, either had been devoted to hay and pasture, had been idle or summer fallowed, or had a history of continuous crop failure. Payments on this land alone would amount to $54 million annually, or about $270 million over the average life of the contract [five years]. These are payments being made to remove from agricultural production land which was never intended to be and more than likely never would have been in annual production anyway."

Williams then told the Senate about a North Dakota farmer who in July 1956 bought 280 acres of land, 139 acres of which were in crops, for $5000. Three years later the farmer put into the soil bank, under a five-year contract, most of the 139 acres planted to crops. During the five-year period, Williams pointed out, the farmer would receive a total of $6400 from the Government, or $1400 more than he paid for the entire farm in 1956.

The Senator also discussed another North Dakota case involving a man and his father who circumvented soil bank regulations by dividing a farm among themselves and the man's four children, whose ages ranged from ten to fourteen, so that the family could receive a total of $165,000 in soil bank payments. The father was to get $50,000, the grandfather $50,000, three of the children another $50,000, and the fourth child $15,000. "Not only are these payments excessive," commented Williams, "but here we have three children under the age of twelve being paid $50,000 not to farm."

In 1961 Williams told the Senate how "the soil bank program has again been turned into a racket." He cited the case of a man who bought a 6960-acre ranch in Colorado for $139,200. Through complicated arrangements for subleasing the land, 3879 acres of it were placed in the soil bank. Over a ten-year period these acres would be eligible for soil bank payments totaling $271,000, or $131,800 more than the purchaser paid for the land.

In 1961 and in 1962 Williams turned his critical attention to the Kennedy Administration's farm programs. The feed-grain program required farmers to take land out of production before they could receive price support guarantees for their corn, sorghums and other feed grains. Williams pointed out that under this program the Government paid farmers up to $50 an acre to retire land from production, but some land was "retired" that apparently never was intended for corn.

"In 1961," Williams told the Senate, "the Department of Agriculture had contracted to pay the American farmers around $680 million to retire 20 million acres of corn-producing land from production; but based upon their own figures, while they paid $680 million to retire this 20 million acreage from corn production, the 1961 corn acreage actually only received a reduction in 15,379,000 acres. Thus they paid approximately $150 million to retire 4.5 million phantom acres of cropland."

Williams also noted that under the feed-grain program eight "farmers" received more than $50,000 each, with the

Farmers Investment Company of Tucson, Arizona, getting the largest payment, $94,092.30. Nine "farmers" got from $40,000 to $50,000. In this group were the Northern Trust Company of Chicago, which received $41,253, and the Louisiana State Penitentiary, which got $45,414. "Under the Kennedy-Freeman farm program as recommended in 1962 to the Congress," Williams noted, "these payments not only would have continued but it would have been mandatory that the farmers participate, even under the threat of fines and the penitentiary for noncompliance. This raises a most interesting question — just how would Secretary Freeman put a penitentiary in the penitentiary for noncompliance?"

Other recipients of subsidies under the 1961 feed-grain program included the Reynolds Metals Company ($12,984), the Ford Motor Company ($5,394), the University of Illinois ($6,598), St. Benedict's College of Atchison, Kansas ($11,575), the Waterloo Municipal Airport of Waterloo, Iowa ($5,846), and the Kearney Municipal Airport of Kearney, Nebraska ($6,707).

"Even," Williams added, "the city of St. Louis, Missouri, was classified as a 'farmer' under the 1961 Kennedy-Freeman feed-grain program and collected $12,203, and a motel" (Sand and Sage Motel, Inc.) "in Dimmitt, Texas, was listed as a 'farmer' and collected $9,409."

Williams's old friend the British-owned Delta and Pine Land Company was also on the 1961 feed-grain subsidy list, for $11,409. So was Billie Sol Estes. "The wonder boy from Texas . . . qualified as a farmer," said Williams, "and collected $22,875.24 from the Department of Agriculture under the 1961 Kennedy-Freeman feed-grain program."

In a 1962 Senate speech Williams pointed out that final figures showed in 1961 the Government spent a total of $1.1 billion to get American farmers to retire 53.6 million acres of land from production. Nearly $782 million of this amount, or more than two thirds of the total, was paid to farmers who cut back their corn and sorghum production. The rest, more than $336 million, went to farmers who had placed acres in the soil bank conservation reserve program.

"After paying out over $1 billion to the American farmers for reducing their acreage during 1961," Williams went on to say, "the Department of Agriculture then paid the American farmers another $208,182,000 to subsidize the purchase of additional lime, fertilizer, etc., and for certain soil conservation practices. This subsidized lime and fertilizer was made available for the announced purpose of increasing the productivity on the remaining acreage.

"Now, the United States Government itself is the largest owner of agriculture crop and grazing land in America, but instead of just keeping its own agriculture land out of production it leased it to the American farmers for the purpose of producing more crops and more livestock. During 1961 the record shows that the Government leased 4,881,395 acres of farmland to the American farmers for agriculture production at an average of less than $3 per acre, or a total annual rental of $13,327,953.

"Thus we find that on the New Frontier Secretary Freeman was paying an average of over $20 per acre to retire 53 million acres of cropland from production while at the same time the Government was leasing 4,881,000 acres of its own cropland back to the farmers at an average of less than $3 per acre . . .

"But this does not represent all of the confusion on the Potomac. During 1961 the Government spent millions under the Bureau of Reclamation to irrigate and bring into production an additional 113,700 acres of cropland. Under these reclamation projects full or supplemental service was furnished to this acreage at a cost to the taxpayers ranging from a low of $159 per acre up to a high of $1227 per acre. Under numerous other reclamation projects, some of which have already been authorized and some of which are still being approved, millions will be spent to irrigate and bring into full production thousands more acres of farmland."

There is indeed, as Senator Williams and others have noted, confusion on the Potomac over farm programs. One program seeks to reduce surpluses by retiring land from the cultivation of crops, while another subsidizes the pouring of fertilizer on the remaining cropland under the guise of promoting good soil practices. As the Agriculture Department implores Congress to pass legislation to reduce farm production, the Interior Department's powerful Bureau of Reclamation is lobbying on Capitol Hill for the authorization of expensive irrigation projects to bring more land into production in the arid West.

"For fifteen years Congress has procrastinated," Senator Williams told the Senate one day in August 1962, during the height of the congressional investigations of the Billie Sol Estes manipulations of the farm program. "Billions of dollars have been poured down the drain under the guise of helping the American farmers, and today we have a multi-billion-dollar inventory in the Government warehouses which hangs as a ceiling over the prices of all agricultural commodities.

"Furthermore," Williams added, "this program which is flaunted as being of great assistance to the small farmer is a farce. During these fifteen years more small farmers have closed their operations than ever before in the history of our country.

"I recognize," the Senator went on to say, "that all of this change cannot be charged to the support program, however, since with the mechanization of our farms with modern equipment, farming operations of necessity have become large business, but under the farm program, as it has been approved by Congress over these years, this trend from the small farm has been accelerated . . .

"These high-support programs could have been repealed outright fifteen years ago without any disastrous effect to the farmers. We had no inventories. They could have been repealed on many subsequent dates at which time the inventories were not excessive, but now the inventories are there. No responsible person is suggesting that they be dumped on the market or destroyed. They cannot be dumped on the world market without creating international complications or chaos. Nor can they be dumped on our domestic market without a complete demoralization of prices."

While Congress has procrastinated the farm subsidies have become so entrenched in the American economy that it sometimes seems as if they can never be brought into line with reality. Meanwhile, operators like Billie Sol Estes have looked upon the subsidy programs as avenues to riches. Not only did Estes use the grain storage program to build up his fertilizer business; he also saw unprecedented opportunities in the cotton program. Cotton production is rigidly controlled by the Government, and the Federal cotton-planting permits, or acreage allotments, are more valuable to cotton farmers today than slaves were before the Civil War. This was why Billie Sol Estes expended large amounts of money and energy for a period of more than two years to get additional acreage allotments. For Billie Sol Estes, cotton allotments were not a dry, bureaucratic subject; rather, his efforts to get more and more allotments were tinged with mystery, with intrigue, and finally with politics at the highest levels in the Agriculture Department.

7

In the Land of Cotton

HENRY H. MARSHALL had been working hard all through the spring of 1961. The new feed-grain subsidy program had kept him and his aides in the Texas office of the United States Agriculture Department extremely busy. There were mounds of paperwork and rounds of conferences from one end of the state to the other. There had also been some nagging cotton acreage allotment problems in West Texas that were still on Marshall's mind. By early June the feed-grain program was in hand, and it was with some relief as well as anticipation that Marshall set off on a Saturday morning for a restful day on his fifteen-hundred-acre ranch near Franklin, Texas. A day in the rolling, quiet East Texas countryside that Marshall loved so well obviously would do him good.

Marshall's wife made sandwiches for his lunch and he drove off from his modest home at Bryan, Texas, in his Chevrolet pickup truck. At Marshall's side were a rifle and his ten-year-old son Donald. Marshall dropped Donald off at the home of Mrs. Marshall's brother, L. M. Owens, in Franklin, a thirty-mile drive from Bryan. Donald had been looking forward to spending the day with his favorite uncle. Later in the day Owens and Donald were going to a nearby town to attend a big homecoming celebration. Marshall planned to pick the boy up late in the afternoon on the way back home to Bryan.

After letting Donald off at his uncle's house, Marshall stopped in Franklin to pay some bills and then drove on to his ranch, less than eight miles away. There were cattle to be checked on, fences to be examined and a barn to be looked over. Marshall would have no trouble keeping himself busy until four o'clock, when he planned to meet Donald at L. M.'s house in Franklin.

Donald and his uncle were an hour late in returning from the homecoming celebration, and they were surprised when they did not find Marshall waiting for them at home. Shortly after five Mrs. Marshall telephoned Owens to ask what time her husband and son would be home. When she learned that Marshall had not yet returned from his ranch, she became worried and suggested to Owens that he go out and see what was keeping Henry. He had suffered a heart attack a few years earlier, and although he had made a good recovery, his health was of concern to his wife.

Owens and a friend got into a car and headed for the ranch. They searched more than an hour for Marshall before they found him, sprawled near his truck in a patch of grass along a lonely lane on the ranch. When Owens first caught sight of Marshall he thought his brother-in-law had had another heart attack; but as he ran up to Marshall, Owens saw blood and some discarded .22 cartridges on the ground beside him. Marshall was dead, but he had not died from a heart attack.

Five shots from the .22 bolt-action rifle had been fired into Marshall's left side. Lined up neatly on the seat of the truck were Marshall's unopened paper sack of sandwiches, his wallet, and a safety razor blade still in its paper package.

Sheriff Howard Stegall of Robertson County was called

to investigate Marshall's death. Justice of the Peace Lee Farmer of Franklin, who was the county coroner, also was asked to look into the case. Both Stegall and Farmer concluded that the fifty-one-year-old Marshall had taken his own life, and Farmer issued a verdict of suicide.

Neither Marshall's wife nor his brother Robert could believe that Marshall had died by his own hand. They wondered how a man could shoot himself five times in the side with a bolt-action rifle that had to be pumped after each shot to eject a cartridge.

Despite his heart attack, he was in good health for a man of his age. In his twenty-five years with the Agriculture Department he had frequently been praised by his superiors as a dedicated public servant. Marshall was not an outgoing man, but he had shown no signs of despondency. During the last few months of his life his work had been hard and tiring, but he had had the satisfaction of knowing that a difficult job had been well done.

At the time of his death Marshall was concerned about some cotton allotments Billie Sol Estes had obtained the previous winter. Some of Marshall's Agriculture Department colleagues thought he was planning to ask his superiors in Washington to order an investigation of the Estes allotments. Washington was notified of the strange circumstances of Marshall's death, but the Agriculture Department made no investigation of its own to see if the suicide verdict could be substantiated.

A month after Marshall's death the Department did ask its investigators to look into the cotton allotments that had been troubling him. The request for the investigation was made by I. H. Lloyd, who succeeded Marshall as head of the production adjustment and marketing quotas section in Texas of the Department's Agricultural Stabilization and

Conservation Service. This is the agency that administers the multibillion-dollar farm subsidy programs. In the same month the investigation was ordered, Estes was appointed to the Department's National Cotton Advisory Committee as a reward for his political work and contributions on behalf of the Democrats in 1960.

As the months passed, the mysterious circumstances of Marshall's death receded into the background. Late in October 1961, the Department investigators completed their report on the Estes allotments. It contained several references to Marshall, but in noting his death said only that it had been ruled a suicide.

It was not until early in May 1962, eleven months after Marshall had died, that the nation suddenly became aware of him and the strange way in which he had died. At a crowded press conference in his office in Washington, Secretary of Agriculture Orville L. Freeman was being closely questioned about the Estes case. The hard-pressed Secretary answered some questions in a straightforward manner, dodged direct replies to others, and admitted that he did not know the answers to still other questions. Near the end of the hour-long session with the press Freeman noted that it would be easier to unravel the mysteries of the Estes cotton allotment transactions if Marshall were alive and able to tell of the key role he apparently played in the case.

Freeman's reference to Marshall's critical importance to the Estes case led to the convening of a grand jury in Robertson County to investigate the death of Henry Harvey Marshall, an Agriculture Department employee who had faithfully served his Government for a quarter of a century and who in death had become better known than any living Department official except Freeman himself. The Texas Rangers also moved in on the Marshall case.

Newspaper, magazine, television and radio reporters from throughout the United States converged on the tiny town of Franklin in May 1962, as they had swarmed into Pecos a few weeks earlier when Billie Sol Estes had burst into the headlines. Marshall's body was taken from the grave and an exhaustive autopsy was performed by a group of medical examiners headed by Dr. Joseph A. Jachimczyk, a well-known Houston pathologist. For reasons that no one seemed to be able to explain adequately, there had been no autopsy at the time of Marshall's death eleven months earlier.

As Billie Sol Estes and more than a score of other witnesses appeared before the secret grand jury sessions to tell what if anything they knew about Marshall and his death, Dr. Jachimczyk and his aides painstakingly examined tissue and other matter from Marshall's body. The pathologist concluded that the cause of Marshall's death could have been suicide but more likely was homicide. At the end of a month of testimony and deliberations the grand jury decided only that "the evidence is inconclusive to substantiate a definite decision at this time or to override any decision heretofore made."

The Texas Rangers continued their investigation. In July, Homer Garrison, Jr., director of the Texas Department of Public Safety, sent a detailed report on their findings to Senator John L. McClellan, whose Senate Investigations subcommittee was then in the midst of its hearings on the Estes cotton allotments. Garrison noted that a considerable amount of carbon monoxide had been found in Marshall's lungs, that he had "received a serious brain injury and cut over his left eye," that his hands were severely bruised, that "there was blood on both sides and the rear of the pickup truck nearby," and that the truck had been dented on the right side on the day Marshall died. The dent, Garrison added, "was caused by some type of instrument other than a human hand or head, indicating the possibility of a struggle on the opposite side of the vehicle from where the body was found."

Could Marshall have shot himself five times with a long, bolt-action .22 rifle? Garrison's report continued:

Investigation revealed that it was difficult for Mr. Marshall to straighten out his right arm, due to prior injury; therefore it would have been necessary for him to pull the trigger with his left hand. It would have been necessary for Mr. Marshall to have had sufficient control of his equilibrium to have fired five bullets into the front of his left abdomen with a .22 caliber bolt-action rifle, taking it down each time and ejecting the shell. The five bullets passing through his body traveled at substantially the same angle, giving further indication that he would have had to have good control of his faculties. From the direction of travel of the bullets, Mr. Marshall would have had to hold the butt of the gun in an upward position, causing the bullets to range downward, which would have been even more difficult.

Under the circumstances above mentioned, it would have been impossible for him to have shot himself first for the following reasons: (1) There was no blood present on the ground other than where the body was found. (2) Autopsy reveals that three of the bullet wounds were incapacitating. (3) Autopsy report also reveals that he died quickly from internal hemorrhaging. It is a conclusion that it would have been impossible for him to have first fired the shots with such accuracy under the influence of carbon monoxide, then committed the other acts herein detailed and return to the spot where he died.

In addition to the above, an extensive investigation was conducted to determine whether Mr. Marshall could have had a motive for committing suicide. None could be found. All reports indicate Mr. Marshall was an honest Government employee and that his demeanor immediately preceding and on the day of his death gave no indication that he was a man contemplating taking his own life.

This investigation has resulted in our conclusion that Mr. Marshall's death could not have been the result of suicide; therefore, this Department's continuing investigation will be based on the theory that he was murdered.

After reading the report from the Texas Rangers, McClellan ordered a .22 bolt-action rifle to be brought, unloaded, into the marble-walled Senate Caucus Room where the subcommittee was holding its hearings. McClellan picked up the rifle, stretched his arms to their full length, and pointed the barrel of the rifle at his left side to show how difficult it would have been for Marshall to kill himself in this awkward manner. "I don't think it takes many deductions to reach the irrevocable conclusion that no man committed suicide with a weapon like this," McClellan declared.

If Marshall was murdered, who killed him? And why? Did his death have anything to do with the Estes cotton allotment case?

The fall and winter months were the slack season for an entomologist like Glenn L. Blake. He was a highly intelligent, restless and aggressive young man who had found that even an entomologist's life could be exciting when he was working for Billie Sol Estes.

One day in October 1960, Billie Sol called Blake into his office. Like Estes, Blake was a self-assured Texan who talked glibly but convincingly and favored carefully tailored dark suits and handsome alligator shoes.

"He wanted to know if I wanted to go on the road for him, travel," Blake said in recalling the conversation in testimony before the Senate Investigations subcommittee in July 1962. "I told him yes, I would. We were in our slack season again. He told me what I was supposed to do."

After receiving his instructions from Billie Sol, Blake

took an airplane from Pecos and flew to Temple in East Texas, where he met Billie Sol's brother Bobby Frank, who filled him in on the details.

"That was in connection with what particular type of work?" subcommittee counsel Donald F. O'Donnell asked Blake.

"I was selling land," Blake replied.

"You were selling land to displaced farmers and having the farmers transfer their full cotton allotments to Billie Sol Estes?"

"Right."

"Where did you operate?"

"East Texas and Oklahoma," Blake answered. "I went to Temple, Texas, and met Bobby Frank and then he elaborated on the deal . . . He told me how we worked it. We have a sales contract to sell them land and they would have four years, you know, for payment and there would be no down payment. If the farmer didn't want to pay for that after the first year, he had a year to think it over, and if he didn't want to pay for it, he could reconvey it back to Billie Sol with no loss to him at all. The interest on note, money and everything would be null and void. And we drew up a lease agreement for four years where Billie Sol Estes would lease acres from the farmers for four years for fifty dollars an acre."

"Can you tell us exactly how you operated?" O'Donnell asked.

"The contracts . . . were printed, they were a form," Blake replied. "All you had to do was fill in the blanks. So, when I would approach someone that had been displaced, I would sit down and go over the contract with him which brought out the whole thing. That is, usually, I would tell him what was in the contract."

Before long Blake was supervising a crew of four men who were seeking out "displaced" farmers not only in East Texas and Oklahoma but also in Georgia and Alabama. A displaced farmer was a man with a cotton allotment but with no land on which to plant cotton. In every cotton-producing state there is usually a "pool" of unused cotton allotments. Each allotment is owned by an individual farmer. Some of the allotments are not used because farmers to whom they have been granted decided not to plant cotton for a year or two. Other allotments are not used because farmers have lost their land under eminent domain proceedings to such Government projects as military bases, highways and reservoirs.

Cotton allotments are Government permits to plant cotton. When a farm with an allotment is sold the allotment goes with it. It is illegal to sell an allotment as such. Under only one special set of circumstances can allotments be transferred from one piece of land to another: when a farmer loses his cotton land through Government eminent domain condemnation proceedings. If he does not find new land for his allotment within three years of the condemnation proceedings, the allotment is placed in a pool for redistribution among the remaining cotton farmers in his state.

A displaced farmer can transfer his allotment to any land where cotton can be grown. He need not operate the new farm himself. He can lease it to someone else, but the displaced farmer must be the owner of the land or must be buying it.

In West Texas land without an allotment is worth fifty to one hundred dollars an acre, while land with an allotment sells for up to three hundred dollars an acre on the few occasions when it is placed on the market. Billie Sol Estes and all the other large cotton farmers in West Texas and elsewhere in the nation were constantly on the watch for land with allotments that they could buy or lease. Estes had good reason for spending considerable amounts of money to pay salesmen to get displaced farmers with cotton allotments to buy his land in West Texas and then lease it back to him for the production of cotton.

The plan Estes followed to obtain more cotton acreage did not originate with him. It was developed by other cotton farmers and their lawyers in West Texas as well as in bordering New Mexico. Government price guarantees for cotton were established at a high level so that cotton farmers in the Southeast could make a good profit on their small acreages. For the highly efficient farmers on large, irrigated acreages in the Southwest, the high price guarantees were a windfall. It was no surprise that they developed ways to get allotments moved to the Southwest through land sale and lease-back arrangements, but it remained for Estes to turn the plan into a multimillion-dollar operation.

On the surface it looked like a good arrangement for all concerned. The displaced farmers were not using their valuable allotments. It seemed profitable to buy irrigated land where up to three times as much cotton could be produced on an acre as in regions that depended on unpredictable rainfall. The terms were good. No down payment was required and the first payment did not have to be made for a year. In the meantime, Estes was paying fifty dollars an acre annually to lease the land for cotton production. If after a year the displaced farmer decided he wanted to drop the whole transaction he would not be liable for interest or additional payments. The land would belong to Estes once again. Billie Sol also would have the cotton allotment because it would remain with the land, but the displaced farmer had not been using the allotment until Billie Sol's agent came by, and in a single year it would bring him the pure gravy of fifty dollars an acre in lease payments.

"Did you," counsel O'Donnell asked salesman Blake, "ever indicate to anyone that they should not pay on their first installment so the land could revert to Billie Sol Estes?"

"Run that by again," the puzzled Blake said, and O'Donnell obliged by running the question by Blake for the second time.

"I don't remember stating anything like that," Blake finally replied.

"Did you ever sell Mr. Bell in Texas?" O'Donnell then asked him.

"Yes, I did."

"Mr. Bell's testimony was exactly to that effect," O'Donnell reminded Blake.

"Well, I don't remember it," Blake said, "but I will put it this way: I think Mr. Bell is a very honest man, and if he said I said it, I did. I will just put it that way."

"If, in fact," O'Donnell asked, "you made this statement, were you not trying to buy pooled cotton allotments?"

"No," Blake maintained, "I wasn't trying to buy cotton allotments. I have been approached and people asked me if I would buy their cotton allotments and I told them then, and everyone I dealt with, I was not buying cotton acres, I was selling land, and I explained the whole deal to them."

Blake stuck to his story, even after the Senate subcommittee confronted him with a huge chart showing that the land the displaced farmers were supposed to be buying was in mile-long strips sometimes only forty feet wide. The strips made up irrigated fields obviously designed to be operated as a single farm.

It may have been perfectly clear to Blake what he was

trying to do, but the sales he and his crew were making were being questioned by Agriculture Department county employees in West Texas, by Henry Marshall and other employees at the Department's state headquarters at College Station, Texas, and by administrators in Washington. Marshall was particularly concerned because any transfer of cotton acreage allotments to Texas had to be approved by his office. As a veteran Agriculture Department employee who had grown up with the complexities of the farm programs, Marshall was regarded throughout Texas as the state's No. 1 authority on the intricacies of the subsidies. One of Estes' lawyers, John P. Dennison, talked with Marshall at least on one occasion about the acreage allotment transfers, but like every other aspect of the Estes case that touched Marshall there is disagreement over what Marshall told Dennison.

Two conflicting memoranda about the allotment transfers were issued in Washington in 1960, one in October and the other in December. The October memorandum said that "any attempt to read intent into these transactions is not administratively feasible," and that "so long as the interested parties certify . . . that no side agreements are involved in a transaction and the documentation supports a bona fide real transaction which does not specify or imply, directly or indirectly, the sale or transfer of allotments, the case should be accepted at face value."

This memorandum was signed by R. B. Bridgforth, Acting Deputy Administrator of Production Adjustment for the Commodity Stabilization Service. The memorandum was prepared after Washington received queries from Texas concerning the transfer of allotments by displaced farmers in a manner similar to the plan being used by Blake and the other Estes agents.

The memorandum, which seemed to sanction the Estes deals, fell into Billie Sol's hands. He had copies of it made and they were used to help clinch deals with doubting farmers who expressed concern about the legality of the transactions.

The December memorandum dealt with a sample Estes contract that had been sent to Washington by Department officials in Texas. After examining the contract Department lawyers concluded that it constituted an illegal scheme and device to sell cotton allotments and that no contracts of that sort should be approved. H. L. Manwaring, who had succeeded Bridgforth and was now Deputy Administrator for Production Adjustment, signed the December memorandum.

Early in January 1961, Agriculture Department officials from Washington went down to Dallas to discuss the transfer of cotton allotments by displaced farmers with Department officials from Texas as well as Oklahoma and New Mexico. At that meeting it was agreed that the displaced farmer who was seeking to transfer his allotment would have to appear before the Agricultural Stabilization and Conservation Service committee in the county to which he was trying to move his allotment to satisfy the three farmers who make up the committee that he was actually buying land rather than trying to sell his allotment. Only elderly people who could not easily travel and persons who could not leave their jobs were exempted from this new requirement.

In February, at a meeting in Fort Stockton, Texas, Marshall explained the personal appearance provision and other parts of the allotment-transfer regulations to county committeemen and office managers of the county agricultural committees in West Texas. At that point both Marshall and his superiors in Washington thought they had the situation well in hand and would be able to prevent any questionable transfers.

None of the meetings and regulations slowed down Blake and his sales force. New men were added to the crew in January and February. April would soon be here and it would be time once again to start planting cotton in West Texas. If more valuable allotments were to be transferred to West Texas for Estes to lease in 1961, not a moment must be lost.

Among the newly recruited salesmen was Doug Younger, another Estes entomologist. He was sent out to Alabama, where he seemed to be particularly good at finding people with unused allotments who were unable to travel and thus could be exempted from the onerous personal appearance regulation.

One day in March 1961, Younger wrote jubilantly from the Town Terrace Motel in Bufala, Alabama, to Bobby Frank Estes and to Blake. "Here," Younger began, "is a contract I feel like framing. Sure spent some long hours with Mrs. Credille before I got her to sign, but, as you can see, it was well worth it. Mrs. Credille here is a widow lady about 75 years of age. This is the kind we like to sign up, huh?"

In another letter from Bufala, Younger told Bobby Frank about an equally good contract: "Mrs. Stanley is a widow lady 72 years old. She will be easy for an affidavit." The affidavit would state that Mrs. Stanley was too old to travel to Pecos to appear before the county committee. Younger also signed up a woman whom he described as "a lady about 40 years old and in good health." Then he added, "We shouldn't have too much trouble getting an affidavit as she is teaching school."

From East Texas, meanwhile, Blake had shifted his head-quarters to a town in Oklahoma. Blake set up his new sales shop in the Western Motel in Bufaula, Oklahoma (not to be confused with Bufala, Alabama), because a nearby reservoir project had flooded much cotton land in the area.

Among the Oklahoma farmers with whom Blake dealt was Swan August Sandstrum of McIntosh County. He was a big man with a wind-burned face, a heavy Scandinavian accent and a healthy skepticism for get-rich-quick schemes.

Sandstrum told the Senate Investigations subcommittee that he thought there was something "feeshy" about the proposal Blake put to him, but that Blake "recommended this man Sol Estes very highly . . . and stated that he was a very successful businessman and he stressed the point that he belonged to the church."

Despite his misgivings about a deal that at one point he said he had considered "ridiculous," Sandstrum agreed to sign a contract purporting to be for the purchase of land in West Texas which Estes would then lease from him. Sandstrum told the subcommittee he had an allotment of 8.1 acres, for which he received $418 from Estes.

"Yes," Sandstrum said, "I finally did sign for him, but I had my fingers crossed all the time, thinking it would never go through."

"Thinking it would never go through?" Senator McClellan asked.

"Yes," Sandstrum replied, "and I was surprised when it did."

"Did you get to keep the $418?"

"I did."

"You are still surprised you got it?"

"I still got it."

"Did you ever at any time in the course of this matter

consider owning that land in Texas?" McClellan went on to ask.

"No, sir," Sandstrum quickly replied.

"You realized at the time, or you thought at the time, they were simply buying this eight acres of cotton allotment?"

"That is right."

"And that is what you were selling?"

"That is right."

Another Estes agent who worked the Oklahoma territory was Parnell E. Biggerstaff, a short, chubby and jolly man who good-naturedly referred to Senators as "you boys" and "you fellows" when he told the subcommittee about his short career as an Estes land agent.

Biggerstaff enlisted the cooperation of two veteran Agriculture Department employees in McIntosh County, Louis N. Dumas and Arthur D. Stone. They helped to direct him to farmers who had been displaced from their land and had cotton allotments they were not using.

Biggerstaff said that Dumas told him when they talked in the Western Motel in Bufaula in January 1961: "We are not going to make no deal. We are going to go ahead and help you and give you what information you need. When we are done, then your boss can show us his appreciation."

Dumas and Stone proved to be quite helpful. With their aid Biggerstaff succeeded in transferring 328 acres of cotton allotments from McIntosh County to Estes' use in Pecos and Reeves Counties in West Texas.

"Sometime when we were getting close to winding up all the 1961 allotment transfers," Biggerstaff recalled in his Senate testimony, "Mr. Blake was in Bufaula on some occasion, I don't recollect what he was there for . . . But in this particular case, I told him, I said, 'With these boys, we didn't make no deal with them, but I do know that they are expecting something, and I feel obligated.' "

Biggerstaff also recalled that he had told Dumas and Stone, "I will see if I can't get you boys something for your trouble," whereupon Dumas replied, "Well, be sure it is cash. Don't bring no check."

Later in the spring of 1961 Biggerstaff was back in Pecos when the question of compensating Dumas and Stone for their trouble came up again. According to Biggerstaff, Bobby Frank Estes decided the two helpful Agriculture Department employees should be given five dollars for every cotton allotment acre they told Biggerstaff about which was successfully transferred to West Texas. Accordingly, $1640.80 in bills and change was placed in a brown envelope and handed to Biggerstaff for delivery to his two friends in Oklahoma.

"Then they were discussing among themselves what account they would charge it to," Biggerstaff remembered, "and Bobby Frank said, 'Well, if it was cotton-picking time, we could just charge it to cotton-picking, but it is a little too early for cotton-picking.' "

The expenditure was charged to the Estes commission account, Biggerstaff tossed the money in a box in the trunk of his car and on his next trip to Bufaula laid the envelope on Dumas' desk. "Here is something for you boys," Biggerstaff recalled saying.

Dumas and Stone first denied both to FBI agents and to Senate investigators that they had received money from Estes through Biggerstaff. When the two men, both of whom were in their fifties, appeared before the Senate subcommittee they seemed to be on the verge of tears. Coatless but wearing clean white shirts, they looked like two farmers ready to go into town on a Saturday afternoon. Under the glare of television lights they sat at the witness table and in barely audible voices admitted they had accepted the money. Dumas and Stone maintained that they gave Biggerstaff information available to anyone, but they acknowledged that they had failed to report their $820.40 payments on their income tax forms. Only minutes before Dumas and Stone testified they were fired by Secretary of Agriculture Freeman.

Senator McClellan seemed to express the sentiments of everyone in the Senate Caucus Room who had heard Dumas and Stone testify when he said:

"Gentlemen, the Chair wishes to observe that while I think you realize and everyone now knows that you made a mistake, I do not believe you are bad people. I think you have kind of become the victims of a bigger scheme, an overall scheme, to get rich quick and promote an interest that possibly is inimical to the best interest and welfare of our country.

"You have been caught in this trap. I guess in a sense you have no one to blame but yourselves. But I do hope, and I think surely there will be taken into account by any others and by any who may judge you in this connection — there will be taken into account the fact that you came here and before this committee you have told the whole truth."

By the time Dumas and Stone had received their "something" from Biggerstaff, Estes had added through the land sale and lease-back arrangements a total of 3123 acres of cotton allotments to the 1749 acres he had previously been granted by the Agriculture Department. The transfer of allotments from East Texas, Oklahoma and Georgia was approved by the Reeves and Pecos county agricultural committees as well as by the Texas office of the Agriculture Department. Only in Alabama did Agriculture Department officials refuse to allow unused allotments to be transferred to West Texas and leased by Estes. There were 116 successful transactions involving as many farmers. In each case the contracts were identical.

"With this contract," staff investigator Paul E. Kamerick told the Senate subcommittee, "it seems clear that neither buyer nor seller was in good faith and neither of them could truly consider this a real change of ownership. The allotments therefore should not have been transferred. It seems clear that both Estes and the displaced owners must have understood, as many of the producers say they did, that the first payment would not be made and that both the land and the allotment would ultimately end up in Estes' possession. I might note parenthetically that all this land Estes purported to be selling was encumbered and Estes knew he was not passing clear title even though he was purporting to do so by granting warranty deeds to the buyers."

Kamerick also noted that at the Agriculture Department meeting in Dallas which was called in January 1961 to discuss cotton allotment transfer problems, "it was clear in everyone's mind, according to those in attendance, that the key to the legitimacy of transfer of pooled . . . cotton allotments was the good faith of the transfer of ownership of the land. Most of those in attendance at this meeting have stated to us that they believed at the time that they had stopped the Estes-type transfer. As a matter of fact, almost all of the approvals by the county and state offices in Texas occurred after this date. It is very difficult to attribute this entirely to organizational breakdown; it is difficult not to suspect bad faith.

"If," Kamerick asked, "the Washington headquarters adequately instructed the state office, then why were these transfers not stopped? If the state office adequately instructed the county office, then why did the county offices approve them? If the county offices continued to approve these transfers in violation of instructions, then why did the state office not stop them? And if the state office did not stop the transfers, then why did the departmental headquarters in Washington not step in and call a halt? Inefficiency is probably part of the answer, but it is inconceivable that it is the complete answer."

Senator McClellan noted several times during the course of the Senate hearings on the Estes cotton allotments that questions such as those raised by Kamerick would have been easier to answer if Henry Marshall had been alive. According to the testimony of men who worked with Marshall, he was concerned about the cotton allotment transfers but felt that he was powerless to stop them once they had been approved by the county agricultural committees. Marshall felt that he had carefully spelled out the rules under which the committees could approve the transfer of the allotments, and by their approval the committees had attested to their legality.

The Department investigators who began looking into the Estes cotton allotment case in the summer of 1961 spent most of their time interviewing farmers who supposedly were buying land from Estes. Fifty-one of the 116 farmers involved in the allotment transfers were questioned. "Only five of these producers," the Department report, which was completed in October 1961, noted, "maintained that they were actually purchasing the land, intended to meet their annual payments and considered themselves to be bona fide owners of the land to which the allotment was transferred."

Estes himself learned about the investigation before it was completed and a report was filed. As soon as he found out through his Agriculture Department friends in Texas that the report was likely to be highly critical of his operations and probably would declare them illegal, Estes flew to Washington in October with lawyer Dennison.

The closer they got to Washington the angrier Estes became. As his friends well knew, he had a terrible temper. Dennison's efforts to calm Estes did no good. With Dennison at his heels Estes stormed into the office of Wilson C. Tucker, who was assistant director of the Agriculture Department's Cotton Division. The startled Tucker had never been confronted with anything like this in his long bureaucratic experience.

"Without any preliminary conversation," Tucker told the Senate subcommittee, "Mr. Estes immediately made the statement that this business of them being investigated regarding pooled cotton allotments had to be stopped, as they had not done anything wrong, and their reputation and that of many of their friends was at stake, and that something had to be done immediately.

"Mr. Estes made some very general statements concerning the use of his personal airplane in helping in behalf of the Kennedy-Johnson campaign (summer and fall of 1960) and mentioned his close association with important people in Texas (mentioned Yarborough in particular) and stated that if this thing were not stopped (meaning the investigation) that before night he would have a group consisting of about thirty-eight people, including lawyers and accountants, who would fly into Washington and would set up offices here in Washington and buy space in newspapers and magazines and go to New York and appear on television and embarrass the Administration and the Department because of their attempted efforts to smear his reputation.

"Mr. Estes stated that he didn't want to have to do this. Mr. Estes stated that this pooled allotment matter had caused the death of one person and then asked me if I knew Henry Marshall. I stated that I did and no further mention was made of Mr. Marshall during our conversation."

Tucker went on to tell the Senators that "three or four times Mr. Estes reached into his briefcase and pulled out what appeared to be letters and would start to show them to me and would put them back in his briefcase, and at one time mentioned that I didn't need to see the letter or paper. He did permit me to glance quickly at one letter which I believe was from the national Democratic headquarters in Washington, and at the bottom of the letter was a pen note stating something like this: 'Check mailed . . . day,' and from a quick glance I believe it was $1,000 but may have been $10,000 or some other amount. I was not given time to really see what was written."

Tucker said that he told Estes he should talk to "persons having to do with administration of the program at a higher level." Then Tucker arranged an appointment for him with Emery E. (Red) Jacobs, deputy administrator for state and county operations of the Agricultural Stabilization and Conservation Service. Tucker said that he did not know it at the time, but Red and Billie Sol were old friends. Jacobs was an Oklahoma Democrat who had first worked for the Agriculture Department in the 1930's. He had been active in the Democratic-oriented National Farmers Union and had the strong political backing of the late Democratic Senator Robert S. Kerr of Oklahoma. Jacobs was an old hand at farm politics and had met Estes during the 1960 Democratic presidential campaign. Since then they had become fast friends.

Estes and Dennison talked with Jacobs the next day and

Estes repeated the complaints and threats that he had made to Tucker. Jacobs tried to reassure Estes by telling him that he was certain the Department investigation would be fair.

A week later Jacobs and Estes met again in Dallas, where they were both attending an Agriculture Department meeting. When their official business was concluded they decided to go shopping in the fashionable and expensive Neiman-Marcus department store.

Details of the shopping trip were not revealed until April 1962, when Neiman-Marcus salesmen told of fitting out Jacobs with $1311 worth of clothing, including two $245 suits and two pairs of $135 alligator shoes. The salesmen testified before a Texas court of inquiry, and their testimony led Secretary of Agriculture Freeman to request — and get — Jacobs' resignation.

In his testimony before the Senate subcommittee Jacobs said he paid for the clothing with $1311 in cash out of his own pocket. Jacobs denied that Estes had offered to buy him clothing or that he had been given the money by Estes. All he ever got from Estes, Jacobs added, was a five-pound bag of pecans and a box of cigars.

Jacobs' Government job paid him $16,500 a year. He told the subcommittee that he also had some income from an Oklahoma farm that brought him another $5000 or so a year. In seeking to explain the large amount of cash he said he generally carried with him, Jacobs noted that as a poor farm boy growing up in Eastern Oklahoma he seldom had more than a dollar a year to spend.

"It made you feel good to put your hand in your pocket and feel some money, didn't it?" Senator McClellan asked, and Jacobs said that it did.

The Senators remained skeptical of Jacobs' story. Why was a man paying $245 for suits, $195 for a sport coat, $65 for slacks, $135 for shoes, $22.50 for shirts, $15 for belts and $15 for ties? Why was he buying so much clothing at one time, and at a store in a city so far from his home and office in Washington? Jacobs acknowledged that he had never before bought so much clothing at one time, but he said that at the time of these purchases he had not bought a winter suit in five years and had only one suit that would fit him.

While Estes and Jacobs were shopping and while Estes was becoming increasingly worried about the outcome of the Agriculture Department investigation, the report was being completed. After ten days of review by Department officials, Horace D. Godfrey, administrator of the Agricultural Stabilization and Conservation Service, decided on November 14, 1961, that the 1962 allotments on the 3123 acres in question should be withheld and that action on the use of the allotments in 1961 should be given further consideration. By the time of this meeting, in the middle of November, the 1961 cotton had already been picked. All the Department could do at that point was to levy marketing penalties, or fines, against Estes for growing more cotton than he was legally entitled to raise.

A month later, on December 15, John C. Bagwell, General Counsel for the Department, issued an opinion in which he ruled that the Estes transactions constituted a scheme or device to transfer allotments to a person other than the displaced owner of them. Bagwell recommended that the 1961 allotments be canceled. A week later Undersecretary of Agriculture Charles S. Murphy concurred in Bagwell's finding and ordered the cancellation of the allotments.

In reviewing the Estes case in testimony before the McClellan subcommittee, Secretary Freeman noted:

"I cannot escape the conclusion that these transfers should never have been approved in the first instance, and that they would not have been approved if it had not been for the very confused situation that prevailed in 1960 and 1961, a situation which was unknown to me until after I had studied the investigation which the Department instituted . . . However, as Secretary of Agriculture it was my responsibility. If there had been in existence and operation early in 1961, when most of these transfers were initially approved, an adequate, effective and specifically outlined system of communication and supervision from the Washington office, and if the county committees had been fully and completely informed of their responsibilities and had carried out these responsibilities faithfully, I believe all of this could have been avoided."

Freeman also said that "up to this point of the cancellation of the allotment transfers I believe that any fair-minded appraisal of the Department's actions will conclude that they were taken as promptly and decisively as a careful review of a complicated and difficult situation would permit."

On the same day that Murphy canceled the questionable allotments he decided to reappoint Estes to the Cotton Advisory Committee, despite an adverse recommendation from the Department's personnel office. The chief of the Review and Adjudication Division of the office had noted that an analysis of the investigation of Estes' cotton allotment activities was "derogatory in nature." In explaining to the Senate subcommittee his decision to reappoint Estes, Murphy stated: "The controversy did not suggest criminal conduct on Estes' part. The penalty for excess planting was a civil monetary penalty for excess marketing. Many growers overplant and pay such a penalty and are then free to market the cotton. The planting of excess cotton by Estes was not a crime and the penalties assessed against him are not criminal fines." Murphy also knew that Estes was an important contributor to Democratic campaign funds.

Murphy conceded to the subcommittee that "in retrospect, it would have been wiser not to have kept Estes on the Advisory Committee. Back in December when he was generally regarded as a man of good reputation even though he was about to be penalized for overplanting cotton, my decision was based solely on what I believed was right. No one tried to bring any pressure of any kind. There was no favoritism."

In his testimony on the Estes appointment to the Advisory Committee Freeman was a bit more candid than was Murphy. "Unfortunately, although this decision was made in good faith," Freeman said, "it was a mistake, a fact demonstrated even more clearly by subsequent events."

A few days after he decided to keep Estes on the prestigious and influential Cotton Advisory Committee, Murphy again made a decision in Estes' favor. When Estes received word in Pecos shortly after January 1, 1962, that his allotments had been canceled he was understandably disturbed. He telephoned his great and good friends Senator Yarborough and Representative Rutherford. They were ready to help Estes, who had always been ready with his checkbook to help finance their political campaigns. Rutherford arranged for Estes to meet with Murphy in his office on Saturday, January 6. Both Yarborough and Rutherford were at the meeting. Although Murphy had ruled only two weeks earlier that the disputed allotments should be canceled, he decided after the confrontation in his office with Estes and his powerful congressional friends to give Billie Sol one more chance to prove that the allotments had been legitimately transferred to land that he was selling to displaced farmers.

"I believe that the meeting of January 6 and the actions taken as a result of it were of benefit to the United States," Murphy maintained. "I think it was right to develop something that benefited the United States as this did. I think it was right to give anyone — including Billie Sol Estes — a fair chance to prove his case."

Murphy was a skilled lawyer who knew his way around the capital. As a draftsman in the Senate's Office of Legislative Counsel, he met Harry S. Truman during the 1930's. When Truman became President in 1945 after the death of Franklin D. Roosevelt, Murphy moved to the White House, where he served first as an administrative assistant to the President and then as his Special Counsel. During the Eisenhower Administration, Murphy practiced law in Washington. In January 1961 President Kennedy appointed Murphy Undersecretary of Agriculture, with the strong political backing of Vice President Lyndon B. Johnson.

Not only did Murphy personally inform Estes with a telephone call to his Washington hotel room of the decision to give him another chance to prove the legitimacy of the allotment deals; the Undersecretary also agreed to dispatch more investigators to Texas to take yet another look at the allotment transactions. He did this even though an exhaustive 140-page report on the case had already been prepared and was the basis for his original decision to cancel the allotments.

One of the men who was sent to Texas in January was Thomas H. Miller, who was acting director of the Southwest Regional Office of the Agricultural Stabilization and Conservation Service. He told the McClellan subcommittee that his superior, Red Jacobs, asked him "to send me a report containing every justification that you can find to permit the retention of these allotments." Miller also said that Jacobs told him Murphy would be "amicable, agreeable or even desirous of permitting the retention of these allotments."

Miller did write a favorable report, which he sent to Jacobs, but it never got out of Jacobs' office. Jacobs denied to the subcommittee that he had ordered Miller to write a favorable report or that Murphy had asked that such a report be made. Murphy also denied making such a request.

In his reconstruction of the January meeting in Murphy's office, Jacobs said it was decided then that marketing penalties would not be assessed against Estes for his illegal 1961 cotton plantings because his actions had been taken in good faith and had been based on decisions made by the state and county committees in Texas which approved the allotment transfers. Other participants in the meeting denied Jacobs' statements about the marketing penalties.

Estes must have been satisfied with the results of the meeting in Murphy's office. A few days later he sent a $1500 check to Rutherford, who belatedly acknowledged receipt of the money, which he described as a campaign contribution. (Rutherford was defeated when he ran for reelection in November 1962 largely because of his close relations with Estes.) Although Yarborough did not receive any money from Estes after the January meeting, he said that he had gotten more than $7000 from Estes since he began running for office in Texas in 1952. Some of the money, Yarborough added, was used to help finance radio and tele-

vision programs on which he reported to the people of
Texas on his stewardship as a Senator.

In January 1962 Estes not only cashed in on some old
political friendships; he also made at least one new friend
among the influential Republican members of Congress.
The new acquaintance was Representative H. Carl Andersen of Minnesota, who had been in Congress for twenty-
four years and was the ranking Republican member of the
Agricultural Appropriations subcommittee of the House
Appropriations Committee.

An Agricultural Department employee named William E.
Morris was responsible for introducing Andersen as well as
Assistant Secretary of Agriculture James T. Ralph, who
was his boss, to Estes. Morris had been a man about political
Washington for many years. He once was an administrative
assistant to Congressman Andersen. When hired by Assistant Secretary Ralph as his administrative aide early in 1961,
Morris had already had several years of experience in the
Agriculture Department. He knew how political friendships and connections got things done in the Department
and on Capitol Hill.

Morris told a House Government Operations subcommittee in June 1962 that he first met Estes in March 1961 at an
Agriculture Department conference in Dallas. It was the
beginning of a fast friendship. At another Department
meeting in Dallas in September 1961 Estes took Morris and
Ralph on a shopping trip to his favorite store, Neiman-
Marcus. Estes had already bought Morris a $100 cowboy
hat when Morris visited him earlier in the year at his home
in Pecos. During the trip to Neiman-Marcus, Ralph later
told the House subcommittee, Estes offered to buy him

some expensive clothing, but he said he refused to accept Billie Sol's generous offer. Neiman-Marcus salesmen told a Texas court of inquiry that Ralph was fitted for clothing. Secretary of Agriculture Freeman asked Ralph to resign as Assistant Secretary in February 1962 because of policy differences. Ralph was in training to become an American agricultural attaché in Manila when his name came up in the court of inquiry testimony. He was discharged from the Department in May 1962 after FBI agents learned that he had used Estes' telephone credit card to make personal calls. Ralph said that he used the card at Morris's suggestion.

To Morris, Billie Sol Estes seemed to be the finest man in the world. After visiting Estes in March 1961 at his home in Pecos, where he was given the $100 hat as well as the use of his plane, Morris wrote to Estes:

I meet a lot of people, but if you will forgive the frankness I do believe you are the most remarkable man I ever met. Having read carefully the literature you handed me and from my reflections upon our discussions, I count the meeting among the major events of my years.

You are rendering yeoman service to American agriculture but more importantly you are rendering Christian service to the people of your acquaintance. I only wish your example could be laid before others that they might benefit as I have.

Though my own means are limited and my family responsibilities are considerable, I resolve to try harder in the future to share my material blessing with my fellow men. If it be your purpose to sow in others the seeds of compassion, this you have accomplished.

Our paths will probably not cross again, but I want you to know that I am deeply grateful for the opportunity which was mine. Upon mature reflection, I honestly believe that if I could afford to do so I might some day walk in your door and say that I have come to help bring some of your idealistic dreams into practical doing.

Thanks again, Billie, for the insight you gave me and I hope you make a billion dollars because I know the good you could do with it.

Estes seemed to appreciate the kind words Morris had for him. At Christmastime 1961, Billie Sol sent two hundred-dollar money orders to Morris and two more to Ralph. Both Morris and Ralph told the House subcommittee that the money orders embarrassed them, that they did not at first know what to do with them, but that they finally sent them to the Democratic National Committee as campaign contributions. They neglected to keep any record of the transactions.

Billie Sol seemed to like hundred-dollar transactions. "All he had usually was hundred-dollar bills, rolls of hundred-dollar bills," Morris told the House subcommittee. "I had to pay cab fares for him. He would try to give me a hundred-dollar bill to reimburse me for five dollars' worth of telephone calls."

Estes called on Congressman Andersen one day early in January 1962 after Morris had written to Billie Sol:

You recall we have discussed the wisdom of a "good" Republican contact in Congress. We considered H. Carl Andersen . . .

Talking to him yesterday he made a suggestion I commend to you. He and his brother have a new coal mine in Washington just outside Seattle. They are a coal mining family of Danes and this will be the most modern mine possible . . . The mine is in production and more capital is required to be able to bid on big State, Federal, and other contracts. Most of the stock is owned by the Andersen family.

They have authorized the sale of some additional stock . . . If you would like to buy the stock he suggests you send the check care of me made out to: Treasurer, Coal, Inc. for the number of shares of stock ($100 per share) and I would hand him the check in exchange for his letter to you confirming the commitment to repurchase at your option.

He is really in a bind right now, is good about standing by his commitments and his friends, and this could be a good investment. Let me know your decision right away. It means nothing to me personally — you judge what it might be worth from your standpoint.

When Estes came by Andersen's office, according to a statement that the Congressman issued in April 1962, they talked about Billie Sol's friendship with Vice President Johnson, Yarborough, Rutherford and Morris, Billie Sol's membership on the Cotton Advisory Committee, and then about the coal mine. "That day," Andersen said in his statement, "I sold to him fifteen shares at a par value of one hundred dollars per share for which he later sent me his check. He informed me also that he would be interested in securing more stock whenever available in this very promising enterprise."

Two months later Andersen and Morris flew to Pecos, where Andersen sold Estes another twenty-five shares, again at a hundred dollars per share, making Estes' total investment in the Andersen coal venture four thousand dollars. Estes was arrested just five days later. There was a lot of Government traffic in and out of Pecos that March. Red Jacobs came down one night to speak to a Chamber of Commerce dinner. Unknown to the other Washington visitors, FBI agents were by then also frequent visitors to Pecos and to the Estes offices there. Andersen never delivered the stock to Estes until June 1962, two months after the full ramifications of the Estes operations were revealed.

Also in June, Andersen got up in the House and pleaded with his old friends to "come and say hello to H. Carl Andersen — come shake my hand. I've done nothing to be ashamed of." His Republican colleagues had ostracized him after his involvement with Estes became known. Republi-

cans had no interest in making the Estes scandal a biparti-
san affair.

"I just happened to be walking by the wall down there
when it tumbled on me," Andersen told his colleagues in
an impassioned, forty-minute speech.

After he had finished, many members of the House came
up to him, spoke a few words and shook his hand. In the
Republican primary in Minnesota in September, Andersen
failed to win enough votes for renomination. Politicians
of both parties agreed that Andersen's link with Estes defeated him.

While Estes was cultivating the friendship of a promi-
nent Republican Congressman by buying stock from him,
while the Pecos *Independent* was publishing a series of
articles in February and March of 1962 raising questions
about the Estes fertilizer tank transactions, and while Commercial Solvents Corporation was making an emergency
loan of four hundred thousand dollars to Estes, the Agriculture Department was still giving Billie Sol more time to
prove that he had obtained the questionable cotton allotments in a legitimate manner. Department lawyers even
went so far as to draw up a special "Seller's Certification of
Bona Fide Sale of Land" for the Estes transactions. The
certificates were never filled out. Nor was the cancellation
of the 1961 allotments reinstated. Through January, February and March the case dragged on, with no effort by the
Agriculture Department to bring it to a close. Ever since
Estes had brought to bear on Undersecretary Murphy the
influence of his political friends in Texas, the Department
had slowed down its efforts to terminate the case and penal-
ize him.

It was not until after Estes was arrested on March 29,

1962, in connection with his fertilizer tank deals that his case was brought to Freeman's attention. As the Secretary later remembered it at his hectic press conference in May 1962 when he publicly discussed the Estes case for the first time, he and General Counsel Bagwell initially talked about Billie Sol's cotton allotment problems early in April while riding in the Secretary's black Cadillac limousine the few short blocks from the Agriculture Department to the White House for a meeting with President Kennedy on farm legislation. After their brief limousine conversation Freeman suggested to Bagwell that he prepare a memorandum on the cotton allotment question. On April 11 — two weeks after Estes' arrest and a week after his first indictment — Bagwell delivered the memo to Freeman. It reviewed the Estes case, listed alternative actions that could be taken, and then carefully noted the political interest in Estes' welfare.

Vice President Johnson [Bagwell wrote] requested information on behalf of a representative of Billie Sol Estes with respect to the requirement under Amendment 11 to the regulations that the displaced owner had to appear in person before the county committee . . . Congressman Carl Albert inquired about transfer of pooled allotments . . . Congressman Poage of Texas discussed transfers of pooled allotments with the General Counsel . . .

Bagwell also noted that Senator Yarborough and Congressman Rutherford had met with Estes and his lawyer in Undersecretary Murphy's office in January to discuss the cotton allotment questions. When the Bagwell memorandum was put into the record of the Senate Investigations subcommittee's hearings, both Chairman McClellan and Republican Senator Karl E. Mundt of South Dakota indicated that they felt it was part of a last-minute effort to try to "bail out" Estes. Bagwell denied this. He said that he was merely setting down some of the facts of the Estes matter to serve as a basis for further discussion of the case with Freeman.

The Secretary acted quickly. Within a week he put in motion Department machinery that led to the levying of a fine on Estes of $544,162.71. Meanwhile, the Texas courts of inquiry were beginning to reveal the full ramifications of the Estes case. In quick succession Jacobs was asked by Freeman to resign, Morris was fired, and no one in the Agriculture Department seemed to know where the backlash of the first major scandal of the Kennedy Administration would strike next.

One day the case leaped out of the Agriculture Department and struck down an Assistant Secretary of Labor, Jerry T. Holleman. A former president of the Texas State AFL–CIO, Holleman was a well-known labor leader who had been appointed an Assistant Secretary of Labor as a reward for his work for the Kennedy-Johnson ticket in 1960. Holleman was another old Estes friend. Among other Labor Department duties he was given the job of supervising programs that regulated the importation of Mexican laborers to work in the Southwest on farms like Billie Sol's. Although Holleman's new Government job paid him twenty thousand dollars a year, which seemed to be an adequate salary, he once complained to Estes that he was unable to live on his salary because of all the social obligations his position required of him. Estes was sympathetic, and sent his old and now influential friend a thousand dollars to help with the high cost of his living and entertaining. When this gift was revealed shortly after the Estes case broke into the open, Secretary of Labor Arthur J. Goldberg requested and promptly received Holleman's resignation.

In the middle of May, President Kennedy told a press conference that seventy-six FBI agents were on Estes' "tail." Not only that, but the McClellan subcommittee and a House Government Operations subcommittee were investigating Estes, and state and Federal indictments were being returned against him.

Not all the investigations that the Estes case brought about were efforts to look into Billie Sol's past. In June, Senator Mundt and Republican Senator Carl T. Curtis of Nebraska hurriedly called a press conference to charge that the Agriculture Department was trying to intimidate them as members of the Senate Investigations subcommittee by reviewing their correspondence with the Department over the last ten years. "It is most unusual and reprehensible," said Mundt and Curtis in a joint statement, "that the two Republican members of the Investigating Committee were singled out by name in an effort to try to find some correspondence which might be twisted or distorted to create implications not substantiated by the facts. This raises the serious question as to what the Secretary of Agriculture has to hide and why such tactics of desperation are resorted to in an effort to impede or intimidate the complete investigation."

Thomas R. Hughes, Secretary Freeman's administrative assistant, admitted that he had ordered the search of the Mundt and Curtis files. Said Hughes blandly: "About one month ago I decided that it would be of benefit to review the correspondence between the Department of Agriculture and Senators Mundt and Curtis. The purpose I had in mind in undertaking to review this correspondence was to examine the position of the two Senators and the experience of the Department in connection with two programs.

The first of these was the rapid amortization on grain elevator construction and the second was the effective and economical storage of grain . . . I felt that this material would be useful to Secretary Freeman in connection with his appearance before the subcommittee."

That last sentence, Mundt commented, was "the most intriguing of all." Thus did the politics of Capitol Hill and the Agriculture Department swirl about the Estes cotton allotment case. The Senate investigation of the allotments was not only a fascinating reconstruction of an important phase of the Estes operations; even more significant was the light that the investigation threw on the inner recesses of that mysterious and forbidding congeries of agencies and bureaus which make up the vast, one-hundred-and-two-year-old Agriculture Department.

As Senator McClellan and other members of the subcommittee patiently tried to thread their way through the maze that is the Agriculture Department, they became confused and at times disgusted with the way in which the Department operated, or failed to operate. Senator McClellan acted as if he wanted to pick up the Department and give it a good shaking. There was little question among the investigating Senators that the Department needed a careful overhaul. At times they wondered out loud how any man or group of men could run such an unwieldy collection of agencies and bureaus. Yet none of the Senators seemed to know what should be done with this classic example of big, ponderous and often immovable bureaucracy.

8

Bureaucracy Unbounded

"THE ESTES CASE," Secretary Freeman declared at the beginning of the 1962 Senate investigation of his Department's relations with Estes, "is but an exterior symptom of the underlying sickness of the farm program in this country — a sickness that is begging for a cure."

Six months later, in January 1963, Freeman flew down to Palm Beach, Florida, to report to a vacationing President Kennedy that "we can, and are, turning the Billie Sol Estes affair into a plus by using it to speed an effective management reorganization of the Department to increase efficiency and lower administrative costs."

The extensive Senate and House hearings on the Estes case and the courts of inquiry in Texas uncovered some efforts to corrupt Agriculture Department officials, but graft and corruption were not the real issues. The investigations showed rather that the five-billion-dollar farm subsidy program has been badly administered in a highly political atmosphere. The hearings also called into question Big Government itself, whether it be the farm program, defense contracts, highway funds, rivers and harbors projects or other large Federal spending programs.

Testimony before the Senate and House subcommittees investigating the Estes case showed that often the best way to get action out of a sprawling, cumbersome Government is through pressure and influence exerted by a member of Congress.

In the Estes case two key decisions were made by Under-secretary Murphy. The first was made after Estes, Congressman Rutherford, Senator Yarborough and their aides met with Murphy. At this meeting, in January 1962, Murphy agreed to give Estes still another chance to prove the legitimacy of his cotton allotment transfers, despite the preponderance of decisions and evidence to the contrary already amassed by Agriculture Department investigators and officials. Shortly afterwards the Undersecretary got a call from one of Vice-President Johnson's aides who inquired about the status of the Estes case.

Although the Senators failed to question Murphy about the political pressures involved in visits, calls and letters from members of Congress, no one who followed the Estes case doubted the presence of those pressures. Rutherford, Yarborough and Johnson's aides denied that they sought improper treatment for Estes, but overt requests for favors are seldom necessary. Everyone who understands Washington knows how the "system" works.

The search of Agriculture Department files for letters from Senator Mundt and Senator Curtis ordered by a Freeman aide was a bit of byplay involving the "system." Neither Mundt nor Curtis pressed his demand that the letters be made public. The reasons were obvious. There is no department, bureau or agency in Washington that could not produce damaging correspondence from a member of Congress seeking special treatment for a constituent.

As mentioned earlier, the "system" is not without its positive side. Some of the Agriculture Department officials who testified on the Estes case displayed a shocking arrogance.

Others did not know what they were doing. Congressional pressure can constitute a useful check on the actions of incompetent officials, who can so easily hide behind the protective wall of the civil service system. Too often, however, as in the Estes case, the pressures come from a Senator or Representative acting on behalf of a big campaign contributor neither the member of Congress nor a top political appointee dares offend. Not only did Estes make substantial contributions to the political campaign funds of both Rutherford and Yarborough; he also was an important contributor to the Democratic National Committee. Furthermore, when a highly political Secretary of Agriculture like Freeman is desperately seeking votes in Congress for a controversial farm program, as was the case in both 1961 and 1962, neither the Secretary nor his top aides are likely to overlook an opportunity to give every possible break to the favorite constituents of important Senators and Representatives. The help to an influential constituent is likely to be remembered when it comes time to vote on legislation sought by the obliging Secretary or administrator.

The second key decision in the Estes case made by Undersecretary Murphy seemed to have been as tinged with politics as the first. This was the decision to reappoint Estes to the National Cotton Advisory Committee despite an unfavorable report on him from the Agriculture Department's personnel office. The report was based on Billie Sol's cotton shenanigans. When Murphy decided to give Estes another term on the Cotton Committee he was aware that the Pecos wheeler-dealer was originally placed on the committee largely because he had the strong political backing of Senator Yarborough. Murphy also undoubtedly knew that Estes was a big contributor to the Democratic Party's hundred-dollar-a-plate fund-raising dinners. Murphy's official explanation for keeping Estes on the Advisory Committee was that he did not want to embarrass Billie Sol by not reappointing him while the cotton allotment case was still under consideration and open to appeal.

Seldom has the curtain which discreetly covers the inner workings of a department and the relationships between a department and members of Congress been lifted the way it was in the Estes case. The hearings provided a hardly reassuring look inside Congress and inside the Agriculture Department. Such revelations usually result in a tightening of operations within the spotlighted department. Such reforms have a way, however, of collapsing under the weight of new political pressures. Members of Congress do not change their ways. The requests for special favors continue to come even into scandal-ridden departments and agencies. Nor is the day likely to arrive soon when political administrators suddenly become simon-pure and turn down all requests from Senators and Representatives to help their constituents.

The requests for special attention to the problems of campaign contributors and other constituents may act as a check on the Executive Branch. Flagrantly bad administration also can be remedied through a congressional investigation, or even by the mere threat of public hearings on Capitol Hill. But who checks on the members of Congress and the propriety of their calls, their memos and their personal visits to Department heads and administrators on behalf of favorite constituents?

The problems of sloppy administration which were revealed by the Estes case are infinitely easier to deal with than the far broader and far more difficult questions of political favoritism. Before the congressional hearings were over Secretary Freeman had taken steps to improve the administration of his huge and unwieldy Department.

In the Estes case, cotton allotment transfers were approved at state and county levels in Texas because a Department memorandum prepared in Washington which held that such transfers were illegal never reached the appropriate officials. There was no follow-up by Department officials in Washington to make certain that the proper instructions penetrated to the county level, where policy affects the livelihood of every farmer.

Sloppy administration was also a key factor in Estes' rise as a Government grain storage warehouseman. Within three years Estes became the ninth largest warehouseman for surplus Government grain, mostly by realizing that Government price support programs were encouraging excess production of grain that would have to be stored somewhere. He also knew that there was a shortage of storage facilities.

Agriculture Department officials failed, however, to question the unusual tie-in between Estes' grain operations and Commercial Solvents Corporation, the big New York chemical company that supplied Estes with fertilizer. The Department also accepted Estes' financial statements without checking them, despite warnings from Federal officials in Texas that his net worth probably was not what he claimed it to be. The financial statements relied on by the Department in determining the size of his warehouse bond turned out to have been faked.

Even when instructions from Washington do filter to the county levels, so much paper flows from the capital to the country that Agriculture Department officials at the state and county levels cheerfully conceded during the hearings they did not have time to keep up with all the directives. Besides, one of the harassed officials told the Senate subcommittee, many of the directives are written in such confusing language that only lawyers can understand them. Department handbooks containing all the rules and regulations with which state and county Department officials are supposed to be familiar are as fat as the Washington telephone book.

Despite all the memos and instructions to which departments of the Federal Government are addicted, the Senate subcommittee found no records of the key Agriculture Department meetings involving the Estes case. Revelations such as that prompted Senator McClellan to exclaim in the midst of a particularly maddening day of testimony: "What kind of a railroad are we running here?"

Senate investigator Kamerick summed up the problem this way in his testimony to the subcommittee: "It has become increasingly apparent during the investigation of the Billie Sol Estes case that this subcommittee may wish to consider recommending a major reorganization of the Department of Agriculture. Even if the efforts of the employees were most strenuous, even if their decisions were the wisest, even then the many programs of the Department involving expenditures this year in the area of $7.1 billion would still lose effectiveness without a proper organizational framework in which to operate . . . It appears that over the century of its existence programs have been added piecemeal to the Department and they have been administered piecemeal. A system which permits inefficiency encourages dishonesty and some of the facts we have developed are hard to explain merely on the basis of inefficiency."

Kamerick went on to note that Department officials failed to keep minutes or other records of meetings involving the Estes case, that documents pertaining to the case were difficult to find because the Department had no central repository for records and that "material concerning Estes was located and furnished to us by sixteen different offices in the Department's Washington headquarters.

"The structural weakness of the Department of Agriculture is further demonstrated," Kamerick added, "by a breakdown of communications between the Department and the subordinate organizations at the state and county levels. Some instructions issued by the Department apparently either do not reach the subordinate organizations or are disregarded if they do reach them. There is no method of receipt or follow-up to make certain that such instructions actually reach their destination. In some areas of activity the subordinate organizations of the Department are almost autonomous. There is a similar lack of communications between agencies within the Department of Agriculture in Washington. Within the Department there are eleven internal audit groups including one attached to the Office of the Secretary. Each of these groups reports to the head of its own agency. These audit groups have no authority and little interest in anything that transpires outside their own narrow assignment."

In the Estes case, Kamerick noted, while the Investigation Division of the Agricultural Stabilization and Conservation Service was in the midst of its investigation of the cotton allotment transactions in September 1961, the Internal Audit Division of the Agricultural Marketing Service was beginning an investigation of reports that Estes' financial position was not what he had represented it to be in getting his expanding chain of warehouses approved for the storage of Government grain.

"Neither investigative group was aware of the inquiry being conducted by the other until February 1962," Kamerick went on to point out, "and the parallel investigations were not coordinated at any time."

In his summation of the Senate hearings, Senator McClellan said: "The testimony presented before this subcommittee reveals indecision and complacency which is a matter of concern for this subcommittee and which should be a matter of even graver concern for the Department of Agriculture. There was demonstrated an obvious loss of effectiveness between instructions given at the departmental level and execution of these instructions at the operating level. There was also demonstrated a similar loss of effectiveness on the part of the Department of a follow-up to insure the execution of these instructions."

McClellan cited only one of many examples: "At a time when operating officials in Washington were seeking certain documents unsuccessfully, at that very moment, other units of the Department already possessed two copies of this same document being sought and a third copy of the document was available in Congressman Albert's office and had been seen by Agriculture Department officials. The lack of organization is apparent . . . There exists in the Department such a diffusion of responsibility that it is impossible to fix appropriate blame or credit in connection with many actions taken." The documents discussed by McClellan were copies of the land sale contracts used by Estes in his cotton allotment transactions.

The Agriculture Department has become so big during the last thirty years that succeeding Secretaries of Agriculture have found it increasingly difficult to exercise effective control over the Department's activities. With a budget ranging from six to seven billion dollars a year, the Agriculture

Department has more than one hundred thousand employees. In addition to the Undersecretary there are three Assistant Secretaries reporting directly to the Secretary. There are sixteen separate agencies within the Department, varying in size and independence from the large and free-wheeling Forest Service and Extension Service to the politically sensitive Agricultural Stabilization and Conservation Service, which runs the subsidy programs, and the small Office of Agricultural Economics, which is expected to come up with the right facts and figures to support whatever farm program is currently in vogue. Other departmental agencies are concerned with research, experimental work, cooperatives, soil conservation, marketing, trading on the commodity exchanges, storage and sale of surplus crops, crop insurance, foreign agricultural problems, economic research, statistics, industrial development in rural areas, loans for the construction and improvement of farm homes, and rural electrification loans.

The Department is too large and its operations are too diffuse for a Secretary of Agriculture to keep abreast of all its activities. As an administrator, the Secretary is further handicapped because he must devote so much of his time to propaganda and lobbying. During his first two years as Secretary, Freeman was on the road much of the time, arguing that agriculture was the great American success story, that farmers were grossly underpaid, and that food was the nation's biggest bargain. When farm legislation or Agriculture Department appropriations requests reached critical stages in Congress, Freeman spent practically all of his time on Capitol Hill.

As the chief lobbyist and drumbeater for the Kennedy farm program, Freeman had little time left for overseeing the day-to-day activities of the Agriculture Department. He was not even aware of the explosive Estes case until late in March 1962. By then the case was about to burst into a national scandal and it was too late for Freeman or anyone else to head off the repercussions that were soon to shake the Department from the Secretary's office all the way to the county committees in West Texas.

Undersecretary Murphy was supposed to have been minding the store while Freeman was lobbying and speaking. "I serve," Murphy told the Senate subcommittee, "as general No. 2 man in the Department and have a general supervisory function for all of its activities and agencies. This includes, of course, not only . . . the activities of the Agricultural Stabilization and Conservation Service . . . but . . . the activities of the other fifteen operating agencies of the Department . . . My second major duty is the direct supervision of the Foreign Agricultural Service — there being no Assistant Secretary to whom this function is assigned at present. This includes responsibility for the Department's activities in maintaining and expanding sales of U.S. agricultural commodities in foreign markets and includes the administration of a major part of the Food-for-Peace program under Public Law 480."

Murphy went on to list nine other major functions of his office. He is chairman of the Department's Budget Committee and president of its Commodity Credit Corporation, which buys surplus commodities and disposes of them. He establishes support prices and acreage allotments for tobacco, rice, peanuts, cotton, wheat, corn and other commodities. He also helps to set policies for the storage and disposal of farm surpluses and for the purchase and allocation of commodities for the school lunch program and for distribution to needy Americans. He coordinates and reviews departmental staff work on major legislative proposals. (In a single year, he noted, eight hundred reports on legislation come across his desk.) He is a member, and usually acts as chairman, of the Department's Program Review Board, supervises the Department's extensive civil defense activities (which involve the stockpiling of surplus commodities for use in emergencies), and reviews several hundred marketing orders and amendments each year before they are issued. These orders control the marketing of milk, fresh fruits and vegetables and other perishable commodities to help support the prices that farmers get for them. Murphy is also the Department's representative on the Trade Policy Committee, which is a Cabinet group responsible for making recommendations to the President on foreign trade problems. "Finally," Murphy said with an audible sigh, "I serve as Acting Secretary in the absence of the Secretary.

"I cannot give detailed study to all of the decisions that must be made," Murphy added. "Many decisions, some of great importance, must be made every day. While the responsibility is mine, and I accept it fully, I must rely on information, briefing and assistance from other Department officials whose specialized field of concentration enables them to examine special problems more thoroughly."

In concluding his testimony before the McClellan subcommittee, Murphy observed that "the Estes case has emphasized the extreme complexities and difficulties in administering programs involving millions of farmers. It has brought to light some faults in both communication and administration, shortcomings that have developed over many years. It has caused the Department to accelerate its efforts to achieve administrative improvements."

"Would you say," McClellan asked Murphy, "that the functions and responsibilities of the Department of Agriculture have so expanded, have become so involved and cumbersome, that under the present organization and setup and method of operation it is in many respects . . . unmanageable?"

"Congress," Murphy replied, "has for one hundred years now been assigning one function after another to the Department of Agriculture. I think literally nobody in the world really comprehends the scope, variety and complexity of the jobs that have been assigned to the Department of Agriculture . . . I think it is almost miraculous . . . that the Department works as well as it does and discharges all these functions as well as it does."

McClellan then commented that the subcommittee's investigation indicated a "lack of direction, lack of discipline, so to speak, lack of people willing to make a decision and take responsibility" in the Department.

Senator Mundt told Murphy that "what the Department of Agriculture desperately needs is a Charlie Wilson or a Bob McNamara, a real executive from the standpoint of business administration, who can handle all the intricate jobs of internal auditing, reporting, record keeping, files, business management, which would be handled in private affairs in a multibillion-dollar corporation, which the Department of Agriculture actually has become.

"You have people down there," Mundt added, "who, on their credentials, appear to be experts in peanuts, rice, cotton and everything else except business management."

"We don't have a Bob McNamara or Charlie Wilson," Murphy conceded. "The Department operates through the separate agencies, which have a very large degree of autonomy. It seems to me that the machinery provided for supervision by the Secretary or his office is not as strong as it should be . . .

"I think," Murphy went on to say, "the problem here

is not in terms of personnel, but in terms of organization and the degree of autonomy and independence that the various agencies have . . . If you have a good administrator, and thank goodness we have some good administrators, this works pretty well. It does, however, leave the Secretary, I think, to a considerable extent, to the mercy of chance as to whether or not the administrator is a good administrator, and the Secretary does not have as much machinery as he should have to be able to centralize and fix responsibility . . ."

"Can you name," Mundt asked, "any $500 million corporation in America — we won't go to a multibillion-dollar one like the Department of Agriculture — can you name any corporation that even has a half million dollars which is content to run its operation by having each department head to be an autonomous director, and hopes they get a good one, and that is the end of management control? I think you have to have someone in the Department knocking the department heads together; someone has to step in there."

The Agricultural Stabilization and Conservation Service, which was the focus of the Senate investigation, is the direct descendant of the original Agricultural Adjustment Administration of the earliest New Deal days. The AAA was set up in 1933 largely because there was no existing agency within the Department that was considered politically reliable for the difficult job of controlling production and handing out Government payments to farmers. The Extension Service had worked closely with farmers for more than twenty years, but it was an extremely conservative agency not trusted by the New Dealers. So the AAA became a powerful political as well as economic arm of the Agriculture Department, reaching into every county and touching the activities of almost every farm.

The AAA and its successor agencies evolved over three decades into a curious two-headed organization. At the Washington and state levels the administrators and their advisory committees were intensely political. This was as true during the Eisenhower Administration as in the Roosevelt and Truman years and now. Washington officials of the ASCS and its predecessor agencies often have come right out of the politics-ridden farm lobby organizations and frequently have had little or no experience in managing a large enterprise like the ASCS. Appointments generally have been dictated by political consideration. Horace D. Godfrey, administrator of the agency during the Estes affair, came to Washington after twenty-five years of work with the Agriculture Department in North Carolina, the home state of Chairman Cooley of the House Agriculture Committee. Godfrey had Cooley's strong support for the Administrator's job. Deputy Administrator Red Jacobs' principal qualifications were political.

The committees directing ASCS activities on the state level are even more politically oriented than the top officials in Washington. The Secretary of Agriculture appoints the members of the state committees only after careful consultation with the leaders of his political party in each state and with the state's congressional delegation from his party. Appointments to state committees are choice political plums. Successful farmers who are big contributors to political campaigns and other faithful party members from the countryside are rewarded with appointment to the committees. The trip to West Texas on which former Agriculture Department aide William E. Morris first met Estes was for the purpose of checking on political nominees for the state ASCS committee.

In December 1962 an eight-man study committee headed by A. Lars Nelson, an Overseer of the National Grange and Master of the Washington State Grange, stated in a report to Secretary Freeman on Agriculture Department state and county operations that members of the state committees should be appointed without political considerations. The study committee had been set up by Freeman in the summer of 1962 after the state and county operations had been called into question by the Estes case.

The committee [the report said] was disturbed by evidence that some partisan appointments of State committeemen and farmer fieldmen had a tendency to undermine morale in the committee system. Such political appointments also tend to discourage participation by farmers who object to the political onus. We recommend, therefore, that appointments to State committees be made without respect to party affiliation.

Farmer fieldmen operate under the state offices and serve as area officials within a state. They work with the county committees to carry the subsidy and the acreage control programs down to individual farms.

At a press conference shortly after the report was issued, Freeman avoided a direct answer to a question about his future policies in relation to appointments to state committees. The Secretary's reluctance to give a direct answer was understandable, in view of the political repercussions that would follow on Capitol Hill if he decided to divorce the state committees from politics.

The study group found that the elected county and community farmer committees constituted a basically sound system, even though they frequently included farmers opposed to the subsidy and control programs. The committee system was established in 1933 because Henry A. Wallace and his principal advisers felt that this would be the best way to explain the controversial new programs to farmers and to persuade them to use the programs. The study group's report said:

There are two feasible alternatives to the present dependence on committees for administration of farm programs: 1. An administrative structure with line of command running from the Secretary to appointed state and county officials who exercise all of the authority now vested in state, county and community committees. 2. A structure with line of command running through the state to the county, but with quasi-judicial and limited policy-making authority placed in state and county boards composed of experienced farmers. We gave considerable thought to each of these alternatives, and we rejected them in favor of the present committee system.

The report noted that "there is a great unevenness in the quality of men who have been attracted to serve on the community and county committees" and that in many areas "farmers do not take advantage of their right to vote for community committeemen. Often," the study group added, "the most able men are not elected to serve and those elected refuse to take their jobs seriously."

To upgrade the committees, the report recommended three-year rather than one-year terms for committeemen, with only one man elected each year. Two other proposed reforms provided for a three-term limitation of service by one man on a committee and an age ceiling of seventy years to assure participation by active farmers. Secretary Freeman promised to ask Congress to approve legislation making the recommended changes in the committee election procedures.

Finally [the report said], the committee was concerned about the volume and the detailed character of instructions and regulations prepared to guide and control both state and county committees. We believe they are unnecessarily complex and impose too many restrictions on the committees. We contend that the attraction of better men to committee service will justify granting greater discretionary authority to county committees. Thus, they will more effectively adapt farm programs to local conditions.

The study group also recommended that steps be taken "to give the Secretary of Agriculture and the Administrator of ASCS greater assurance that they can intervene effectively with state and county committees to forestall embarrassing errors, and to correct unwholesome situations which have occurred."

Freeman has simplified instructions and established a direct chain of authority from his office to the county level, so that the Secretary would know when an Estes case is developing in a far-off county.

Two members of the study group sharply dissented from its findings. They were former Secretary of Agriculture Brannan and Morton Grodzins, a professor of political science at the University of Chicago. Both Brannan and Grodzins noted a sample survey of county and community committeemen which indicated more than a fourth of them were not in sympathy with the farm program they were elected to administer. There are nearly one hundred thousand county and community committeemen throughout the country. Brannan said in his dissent from the committee report:

In my firm opinion it is unrealistic to ask the Secretary of Agriculture to direct and manage programs of the current magnitude of the farm price stabilization programs by and through a field organization in which one "employee" out of four is not in sympathy with the program that employee has the responsibility to carry out in his county . . . No private business executive would be asked to operate under such conditions . . .

The democratically-elected Congress, usually after another very laborious democratic process, adopts the programs. The executive branch of Government, the President and chief officer of which was also democratically elected, prepared and issued the regulations to implement the programs authorized by the Congress. But one-fourth of the persons who have been elected by another local democratic process to put the programs in force and effect in a particular political subdivision are not in sympathy with and many are openly opposed to the programs. This is, indeed, a unique administrative instrumentality . . . In fact, if this is a sound administrative mechanism for a Federal program which is expending vast sums of public money, why is it not equally applicable to Federal programs which collect that money? Many a taxpayer should welcome the opportunity to elect the I.R.S. [Internal Revenue Service] agent for his community.

Brannan, who as Secretary of Agriculture under President Truman had considerable experience with the county committee system, recommended that the Secretary be given authority to choose committeemen from a panel elected by farmers. This approach would give the Secretary greater authority to make certain that the farm programs are carried out the way Congress intended them to operate, but political considerations that would be inherent in making such selections from county panels could result in problems as difficult as those caused by the present elective system.

Political scientist Grodzins was even more outspoken than was Brannan in his comments on the shortcomings of the county and community committee systems. Wrote Grodzins:

I believe that a good deal of the cant about the committees as proud local democracies and as efficient administrative arms is evidence of a general unwillingness to recognize the committees as, primarily, program sales units. And doubts about the committees as purveyors of justice are fortified: since they must spawn *gemütlichkeit*, justice is harder born . . . I believe a prudent Secretary of Agriculture would, while improving the system, look to its eventual demise . . . There seems to me great merit in the Department's turning to a system by which it shares its responsibilities for ASC programs with the duly constituted system of local governments. This would end the Department's current game of charades with local democracy.

Of the county committee system, Grodzins also noted that

in a rural community . . . powerful people have a great opportunity to punish their local opponents with a wide range of economic, social and political weapons. The linkage in many counties between political (or farm) organizations and ASC committees is also prejudicial to justice. Where this relationship exists it at least implies that the dominant organization in the county can prevent certain people from holding membership in the committee; at most, it means that the organization consistently receives for its adherents special consideration in committee adjudications.

Elsewhere in his dissent Grodzins notes that

the Department of Agriculture must . . . persuade farmers to be its clients before most ASC programs can become effective. Historically, community and county committees were inaugurated precisely so that they would aid in this persuasion job. And more than 25 years ago — when the programs were new, farms were smaller and almost twice as numerous, roads were bad, rural telephones a scarcity, and television nonexistent — committees may have been the only effective persuasive device. It is by no means certain that they still are . . . Most important, acceptance of ASC programs depends in very large measure on the financial incentive offered, almost $4 billion in direct subsidies in 1962. The committees are secondary to cash in persuading farmers to participate in ASC programs. This alone suggests that it should not be difficult to find substitutes for the committees in their role as persuaders.

The Agricultural Stabilization and Conservation Service is thus a two-headed administrative monster that would be exceedingly difficult to manage even under the best of non-political conditions. At the Washington and state levels the ASCS is a highly politically oriented operation, while in the counties elected committees, frequently dominated by farmers completely out of sympathy with the farm program, are given the crucial job of carrying out the subsidy and control programs farm by farm. In the Estes cotton allotment case it was hardly surprising to find county committees and the state committee approving a scheme that meant more cotton production for Texas. It is asking a lot of a county or state to turn down efforts to expand its own farm economy.

The Estes case revelations spurred Freeman to carry out badly needed administrative reforms and to expedite other changes in departmental operations that he had been planning to make before the Estes scandal descended on him. In addition to the ASCS reorganization, Freeman told the President in January 1963, the "management and marketing of CCC grain stocks will be converted to computer process — and provide up-to-the-minute reports on Government stocks. All grain operations will be centralized . . . Other Department-wide moves are under way, particularly to strengthen management control in the Office of the Secretary. An Inspector General on the Secretary's staff now coordinates and supervises inspection and audit services, placing stronger administrative control over agencies which once were nearly autonomous."

The administration of any governmental operation as

large and as diffuse as the Agriculture Department will always be difficult. A new Secretary chooses his own Undersecretary, Assistant Secretaries and a few personal aides, and appoints the directors of the major agencies and bureaus within the Department. Civil service rules, which were written for a Government of paper-shuffling clerks, prevent a Secretary from reaching deeply into the Department to revitalize moribund agencies and to put his own men in key positions in the lower echelons. In some key agencies, such as the Forest Service, even the director must be someone who came up through the agency's ranks.

The Agriculture Department has gone through a typically bureaucratic cycle during the last thirty years. Many of the men who by the late 1950's and early 1960's had risen to key civil service career jobs came into the Department in the early 1930's, when Henry Wallace infused its operations with a reformer's zeal. These were the men who were going to make over the face of rural America and turn it into a shining example of bucolic prosperity for the world to admire. Thirty years later most of these men have become encrusted bureaucrats. Their operations can be even slower than those of the celebrated paper-pushing drones in the State Department. Their attitudes can be more arrogant than those of a newly minted Ivy Leaguer. Under the pressures of politics, bureaucracy and time, the reformers of the 1930's have turned into the time-servers and clock-watchers of the 1960's.

On its own momentum, the monolith that is the Agriculture Department wallows. Under the whiplash of an aggressive Secretary like Freeman, the Department whimpers and occasionally laboriously lunges forward. A Secretary and his aides, however hard-working they may be, can do only so much. It takes at least a year, and sometimes two, for a new Secretary to become sufficiently knowledgeable about the operations of a huge Department like Agriculture to be fully in command of it. So much of his time must be devoted to legislation, lobbying and speech-making that at best he can be only a part-time administrator. After two years in office the Secretary has usually suffered humiliating defeats at the hands of Congress. These defeats serve further to dilute his influence within his own Department, where the free-wheeling administrators under him often have their own independent access to Congress and keep a constant weather eye on the Secretary's always tenuous relations with the denizens of Capitol Hill.

Secretaries of Agriculture from Wallace to Freeman have frequently complained of their difficulties in convincing agencies and bureaus within the Department to conform to Government policies established by the President himself. In the middle of the 1950's the Hoover Commission on Governmental Reorganization carefully studied the operations of the Department and concluded that it was "a loose confederation of bureaus and agencies."

The Forest Service, which employs a third or more of the people who work for the Agriculture Department, and the Extension Service, which is deeply conservative, are the most independent of the agencies. On several occasions during the 1930's the Forest Service openly defied Franklin D. Roosevelt's conservation efforts. The Extension Service has been hostile to much of the farm subsidy and control legislation. Both the Forest Service and the Extension Service have so many friends on Capitol Hill for whom the agencies have done so many favors that they can ignore with impunity the policies of a Secretary or a President.

Unfortunately, there are no easy solutions to the political and administrative problems of the Agriculture Department.

A strong Secretary backed up by strong aides in all of the major jobs in the Department is an absolute necessity. Even with the greatest possible strength at the top, however, operating a highly political Department while lobbying legislation through Congress and appealing for support for farm programs with speeches throughout the country is a Herculean task for any man. Furthermore, there are interests both within the Department and on Capitol Hill that benefit from loosely administered operations.

The problems of running the Agriculture Department in the public interest rather than for the special interests of groups with the loudest voices on Capitol Hill have become more acute as the costs of the farm programs have skyrocketed and the effects of the programs have been felt by more and more farmers. An Agriculture Department vitally affecting the livelihood of every farmer ought to be run with a minimum of politics and a maximum of efficiency. If this cannot be done, Government should begin to remove itself as quickly as possible from its presently extensive involvement in the day-to-day activities of American farmers.

The breakdown of the Agriculture Department that the Estes case revealed was all the more serious because it reflected the same kind of collapse in the values of both corporations and individuals. The story of Billie Sol Estes and the fertilizer tanks, to which we shall now turn, is a disturbing commentary not only on farmers and the farm program but also on American business and corporate and personal ethics.

9

"This Tank Deal"

ONE EVENING late in February 1962 two worried officers of the Pacific Finance Company of Los Angeles put in a conference telephone call to Dallas. They got their two Texas lawyers, Frank Cain and M. R. Irion, on the phone to try to find out whether the incredible information the company had just received could be true. Someone had anonymously sent the company two articles clipped from the Pecos *Independent and Enterprise.* The articles noted that fifteen thousand anhydrous ammonia tanks existed "on paper" in Reeves County in West Texas but that the tanks "are not to be seen in Pecos — or Reeves County for that matter." Records of thousands of additional tank transactions had been found in other West Texas county courthouses, but the tanks could not be found in the flat Texas country, which hardly has enough vegetation to hide a jackrabbit — or a thousand-gallon tank as large as an automobile.

"There are many unanswered questions concerning the ammonia tank transactions and how these financial operations could affect the economy of Reeves County," the second of the two articles concluded. "More important, however, is the effect this sort of financial transaction might have in the future on the individuals concerned."

There certainly were many unanswered questions, as far

as Maxwell King, president of Pacific Finance, and G. L. (Gil) McDermott, the company's credit manager, were concerned. Pacific held more than three million dollars' worth of mortgages on anhydrous ammonia tanks in West Texas. If the information published in the Pecos newspaper about the tank transactions was true, Pacific Finance had paid three million dollars for worthless paper. Lawyers Cain and Irion told the anxious officials that they did not know whether the articles were correct but would find out. After Cain was informed by the two Pacific officers that the tanks could be identified only through their serial numbers, he advised them to send to West Texas every man the company could spare to check up on the farmers whose names were on the mortgages held by Pacific.

The company hastily established an emergency outpost in Amarillo, Texas, where eighteen of its investigators converged and after receiving instructions drove off to interview farmers. It took the investigators less than a day to conclude there were no tanks to be found.

In the meantime, Cain and Irion had obtained copies of the newspaper articles, which mentioned no names. The lawyers soon learned, however, that the big fertilizer tank man in West Texas was Billie Sol Estes. Just five days after getting the alert from Los Angeles they arranged to meet Estes and his lawyers in Lubbock, Texas.

On the way to Lubbock, Cain dropped by the Superior Manufacturing Company plant in Amarillo. Pacific Finance had purchased the mortgages from Superior, which manufactured fertilizer tanks for dealers and farmers throughout West Texas. After looking around the plant, which employed only 110 men, and talking with some of the men in charge, Cain concluded that its capacity on a three-shift, twenty-four-hour-a-day, seven-day-a-week operation could not be more than 800 tanks a month. Yet if the chattel mortgage records in the courthouses of West Texas were correct, Superior would have had to turn out 3376 tanks in January. Such production was absolutely impossible, Cain concluded.

Armed with this disturbing information, Cain went on to Lubbock, where he and Irion met Estes in the law offices of Hobart and Bert Nelson.

"I would like for Mr. Estes to tell us the story about how he operated in connection with these tanks," Cain began, according to his testimony before a Texas court of inquiry.

Cain also recalled in his testimony that Estes did not respond to this tentative suggestion to tell all. So Cain went on to say: "Now, Mr. Estes, you would have had to have manufactured 3376 tanks in the month of January, alone, because you have over four and a half million dollars' worth of contracts of record for the month of January alone. That's utterly impossible."

There was an uncomfortable moment of silence and then Estes quietly said, "Well, there just aren't any tanks."

Cain and Irion were stunned. Then Cain quickly said, "Well, you realize, there not being any tanks, that you are subject to criminal penalties on this thing, as well as civil?"

Estes said he knew that, and then added, "If you fellows will work with me, we can work these things out. If you can get these finance companies to work with me on this thing we can work it out."

Cain and Irion had not yet recovered from the shock of Estes' admission that there were no tanks when Billie Sol tried to calm them down by suggesting how things could be worked out. Estes pointed out that he was the largest anhydrous ammonia dealer in the world and that he also was very big in the Government grain storage business. He neglected to go on to point out that Commercial Solvents Corporation had all of his grain receipts tied up.

"We can have a net income there after expenses of between four and five million dollars," Estes suggested.

"That's providing," Cain added, "we can keep the storage full."

"Yes," Estes answered, "but don't you worry about that. I can keep them full, if we just don't let this house of cards fall down."

"How are these companies going to trust you?" the puzzled Cain asked. "How can they trust you in a thing like this after you have just stolen I don't know how many millions of dollars? I know you've gotten four, approximately four and a half million, from us, or somewhere in that neighborhood. How much have you gotten before?"

Estes did not reply. He merely pulled a piece of paper from his pocket and handed it to Cain. On the paper were listed the names of twelve finance companies. Included were such big and highly respectable firms as C.I.T., Walter E. Heller, Commercial Credit and Pioneer Credit as well as Pacific. To the right of the name of each company were two columns of figures. One showed the monthly payments Estes was making to the company; the other was the amount of money Estes still owed each company. His debts to the twelve companies totaled $21,845,730.72, and his monthly payments amounted to $527,751.09. To Walter E. Heller, Estes owed $6,243,588.86, and his C.I.T. bill was $5,240,-318.27. He was into Pacific Finance for $3,264,859.16.

"He then told exactly how the plan worked," Cain recalled when he testified before a Texas court of inquiry in April 1962 about his strange interlude with Billie Sol Estes.

Despite the rapid growth of his farm and business enterprises during the 1950's, Billie Sol never seemed to have enough cash on hand. The lines of credit extended to Estes by the two banks in Pecos were never large enough to meet his ever-increasing needs. Although some of the smaller Estes enterprises, such as his concrete ditch-lining and trucking businesses, were profitable, they did not bring in the big money Estes needed to expand his operations for the sale of fertilizer, the storage of Government grain and the production of cotton. His cotton acreage, on which in 1961 he produced a crop worth nearly half a million dollars, brought him excellent profits, but all the money from his Government grain storage business went to Commercial Solvents and could be used only to finance his fertilizer purchases. As long as Estes persisted in selling fertilizer at below cost his unique arrangement with Solvents could not even pay for the fertilizer.

It was late in 1959 when Estes got into the fertilizer tank business in a big way. In his own fertilizer operations he needed many anhydrous ammonia tanks. The usual tank holds a thousand gallons of the liquid fertilizer. It is mounted on a chassis with rubber-tired wheels so that it can be pulled into the cotton and sorghum grain fields. There the fertilizer is injected into the ground by applicator devices drawn behind a tractor or is mixed with water as it is spread between the rows of irrigated crops.

In April 1962 in a court of inquiry held in Amarillo, J. D. Greeson, who farms near Hereford, Texas, told how he came to buy $300,000 worth of fertilizer tanks that he never saw.

"About twenty-two months ago," Greeson began, "I was

approached by Mr. Estes to buy tanks and lease them to him."

"How had you known him?" Texas Attorney General Will Wilson, who was examining Greeson, asked.

"I didn't," the witness replied. "I met him at a cafe in Hereford. It was over a cup of coffee . . . and he approached the matter to me that they were expanding and needed their capital loose to buy fertilizer, that is, workable, to pay for fertilizer when he had to pay for it, and that is why they wanted to lease equipment rather than owe for it; also he represented to me that he owned three million dollars' worth of tanks free and clear, and that his money was tied up and couldn't be used in the form of inventory, and so forth."

"What kind of proposition did he make to you?" Wilson asked.

"At that time he didn't make me any direct proposition," Greeson replied, "but wanted to know if I would be interested in an arrangement like that and I was approached about six weeks later by Mr. Orr [the president of Superior Manufacturing] and Mr. Estes."

"Where was that?"

"That was at the Hereford Airport and also it was discussed at Plainview at the Hale County Airport, where I had happened to meet him there. I fly and had landed there."

"What was the substance of that conversation?"

"They explained then," Greeson said, "that I was to buy tanks and in turn they would make the 20 per cent down payment for me and then in turn I would receive 10 per cent of the actual cost of the tanks."

It looked like a good arrangement to Greeson, who put his name to $300,000 worth of mortgages. For signing his

name, and thus lending his credit to Estes, Greeson got 10
per cent, which amounted to $30,000. It was not a bad re-
turn on a man's signature. Greeson did not even have to
worry about making the monthly payments on the tanks.
They were immediately leased by Estes at a monthly rate
equal to the mortgage payments. Estes took care of all the
paperwork, seeing to it that Greeson's payments were made
on time each month. Greeson never saw the tanks, which
Estes had told him would be used in his rapidly expanding
fertilizer business.

L. B. Johnson, who farmed five miles southwest of Pecos,
also got involved in what was becoming known in West
Texas as "the tank deal."

"I got a telephone call to drop by his office," Johnson told
Attorney General Wilson when he testified at a court of
inquiry in Pecos.

"What was this tank deal?" Wilson asked.

"He told me he was in so many businesses," Johnson said,
"that he had used up all of his credit rating. I thought I understood that. And that he was the biggest dealer in the
world. And that he had thirty-five places of distribution in
three states. And that he needed more equipment. And he
wanted me to lend him my credit rating to buy it for him."

"And what was the business deal that he proposed to you?"

"He proposed to lease the tanks," Johnson replied. "And
in five years, the lease would pay for the tanks and in return
he would give me 10 per cent."

Johnson said that he was "skeptical of the whole thing,
and every time I would stall him he would bring me something to satisfy me on that point." Johnson asked Estes what
would happen if he should fail to make his payments on
the lease. Estes assured him that Superior would take back

the tanks and hold him "harmless" on his purchase agreement.

Still, Johnson was uncertain. He would sit down and talk with Estes across his big desk in his modern, one-story office building on the outskirts of Pecos and then go home to think and talk about this strange but seemingly profitable arrangement.

"I went home and discussed it with my wife a little bit," Johnson said. "And then I called him back and told him that I didn't want to go, that I didn't want any part of it — just count me out.

"Well, he sounded like he was crying," Johnson continued. "I was able to stay with him over the telephone, but I couldn't do it in his office."

Johnson finally agreed to help Estes out and signed some papers committing himself to buy tanks. Later he changed his mind again, went down to Estes' office, and was given what he thought were all the papers. As he later recalled the incident, he "took those home and tore them in two and threw them in the wastebasket in my office." That night he and his wife went out to play bridge with some friends, happy to be rid of the Estes proposition at last.

Some months later Johnson got a mysterious telephone call from Oscar Griffin, editor of the Pecos *Independent*.

"He wanted to talk to me," Johnson testified. "I told him I would be glad to talk to him. I was curious to know what he wanted to talk to me about. He came down to my house, and we had a guest in the house. I tried to get him to set down, and he told me he wanted to talk with me personally. So I took him in my office, and he asked me if I would talk to him about these tanks. I told him I didn't know anything to talk to him about. So he informed me that my name was over here in the courthouse with a chattel mortgage. Well,

I told him right then that if there was one over there, it was unbeknownst to me. Of course, I got concerned."

Within ten minutes Johnson had A. B. Foster Jr., general manager of the Billie Sol Estes Enterprises, on the phone and demanded to know how his name got on a tank mortgage. Foster reassured Johnson that it was all a mistake and that "he would have that thing released" promptly. Foster kept his word. He sent the Estes pilot, Joe Henderson, in one of Billie Sol's two planes to pick up the release from the company that was supposed to be manufacturing the tanks.

Johnson was considerably more fortunate than many other farmers in West Texas whose names Estes put on mortgages "unbeknownst" to them. In some cases the farmers had agreed to "buy" a few tanks but later discovered they were purchasing many more than they had agreed to buy. Other farmers were like Johnson. They had considered helping out Estes but decided against it. Unlike Johnson, however, these farmers found their names on mortgages after it was too late for them to do anything except protest.

Businessmen as well as farmers were cut in on "the tank deal" by Estes. Two of the businessmen were "Coot" and "Bo" Worsham, who had been in the fertilizer business until Billie Sol ran them out of it with his price-cutting. The Worsham brothers also operated a profitable airplane service for dusting crops with pesticides. Estes told Coot and Bo the same stories he had been telling farmers. Each brother ended up with his name on half a million dollars' worth of tank mortgages.

Once when Coot Worsham asked Estes what he should do if someone from a finance company came around looking for the tanks, Estes told him to send the men to him and he would direct them to the tanks.

"Did he ever tell you anything like, 'Don't worry about those little bird dogs that come around,' that he 'took care of it with the big boys'?" Assistant Texas Attorney General Jack Price asked Coot.

"He did," Coot replied. "He made that remark to me. He said, 'Don't worry about the little boys, the higher-ups know about it; everything is all right.' "

Price then turned his questioning to another aspect of the Estes tank operation. "Were you ever mailed an inflated financial statement on yourself by Billie Sol Estes?" he asked.

"Yes, sir."

"About how much was this thing exaggerated — the financial statement?"

"Well, that would be hard to figure out," Coot said. "If the tanks and all of that stuff would have continued to have been paid for, it wouldn't have been too far off, but it just about doubled my financial statement the way it was."

Carol Wicker, a pretty, brunette, twenty-two-year-old former secretary and receptionist for the Estes Enterprises, told the court of inquiry in Pecos how credit reports on the farmers involved in the tank deals were prepared on a typewriter assembly line in the Estes offices.

"And were all of these credit reports written on the same typewriters?" the slightly nervous Mrs. Wicker was asked by Assistant Attorney General Price, a tall man who gave the impression of always being in complete command of his facts.

"No, sir, they weren't," Mrs. Wicker replied softly.

"Were they written on five different typewriters?"

"Yes, sir."

"On five different stationeries?"

"Yes, sir."

"With five different sets of secretary's initials?"

"Yes, sir."

Mrs. Wicker used the letterheads of five Estes companies — the Farmers Company, Equipment Service, Water Well Service, Pecos Transit Mix and the Fort Stockton Implement Company. Each letter purported to list the amount of credit extended to a farmer in the previous five or six years, the credit given to him in the current year, and his present credit standing with the company. The letters were signed by the managers of the companies.

"Did any of the managers ever complain that some of the farmers that they were giving credit reports on never even had done business with them?" Price asked Mrs. Wicker.

"One of the managers of a company one morning when he was signing shrugged and said, 'It's nice to know I do business with this man,' " Mrs. Wicker replied.

The credit reports were as essential to the tank operations as were the farmers themselves. Both the chattel mortgages signed by the farmers and the credit reports were sent by Estes to the Superior Manufacturing Company in Amarillo, which supposedly was making the tanks being purchased by the farmers who in turn were leasing them to Estes. Superior was controlled by three Estes associates, Coleman D. McSpadden, Harold E. Orr and Ruel Alexander.

Superior needed the credit reports to carry out the next step in this gigantic scheme. The firm sold the mortgages at a discount to one of the dozen finance companies that were on the list Estes pulled from his pocket to show to the astonished Frank Cain. The reports satisfied the companies that the farmers to whom Superior was supposed to be selling the tanks were good credit risks and were likely to meet their monthly payments on the tanks. The companies did not know that the reports had been prepared in the Estes offices. So the finance companies purchased the mortgages from Superior at discounts of up to 20 per cent.

When the companies were buying the mortgages they also did not know that every one of the tanks was being leased by Billie Sol Estes. The leases were not submitted to the companies. Estes' name appeared nowhere on the papers seen by them. All they knew was that fertilizer was in great demand in West Texas and that there certainly was a correspondingly expanding need for fertilizer tanks in this arid country. Given these conditions, there did not seem to be a particularly unwarranted rise in the demand for money to finance the construction of fertilizer tanks. Estes also carefully spread the mortgages among the dozen finance companies to avoid arousing the suspicions of any one of them.

Although some of the finance companies made sporadic efforts to check to see whether the tanks were where they were supposed to be, none of the companies seems to have been genuinely concerned that it was just possible there were no tanks.

Geron S. Wheeler of Hereford, Texas, who ran a fertilizer company in association with Estes, told the court of inquiry in Amarillo about Billie Sol's outspoken contempt for the finance companies. Wheeler said Estes told him, "Don't worry about the peons who come out and check you. I do business with the top brass."

"These people are stupid," Wheeler said Estes told him another time.

"I know a man who borrowed a lot of money one time from a Kansas City bank on cattle," Estes said, according to Wheeler's recollection, "and they came down and checked the cattle, and he took those city boys out to a water hole where they drove what cattle they had, and counted them.

Then they took the fellows to another water hole, and drove up the same cattle to this water hole, until they came up with the correct tally on cattle of what his mortgage consisted of. We can do the same thing with the tanks. We will starve them to death looking for equipment."

William H. King, a field representative for the C.I.T. Finance Company who later joined up with Estes as a vice-president of Superior Manufacturing, was one man who was run all over the country in search of tanks. Early in 1961 C.I.T. financed a dozen 12,000-gallon storage tanks for McSpadden. In recalling the incident in testimony before the Lubbock court of inquiry, King said C.I.T. sent him out to check on the tanks because McSpadden was an officer of Superior and "a finance company does not like to . . . finance merchandise for an individual who is creating the installment paper.

"The twelve tanks," King continued, "were supposed to be located three miles north of Summerfield, Texas, which is just west of Friona. I drove over there without saying anything to anybody and went to the Summerfield area and there wasn't tank one."

King remembered that he had once financed an airplane for the owner of a grain elevator who lived near Summerfield. King checked with him, but he said he knew of no tanks in the area except some that he himself owned.

"He said," King added, "none had been through there because I couldn't miss seeing something that large. When he told me that, I drove all over the country looking for the tanks and still unable to find them."

From the little town of Friona, he telephoned the C.I.T. credit manager in Dallas, who, as King put it, became "rattled" when he heard that no tanks could be found.

Attempting to soothe him, King said, "Sometimes these tanks are located where soil conditions or moisture conditions are right for the use of ammonia. Before you do anything, let me check into it a little further and make sure they haven't just been relocated."

King got back into his car and drove to Amarillo, where he tried to locate Harold Orr, the president of Superior.

"I asked the receptionist to talk to Mr. Orr, but I was told Mr. Orr was in conference and I couldn't see him," King testified. "So I asked her for a scratch pad and wrote him a note saying, 'Harold, I can't find those 12 tanks that belong to McSpadden, where the H are they?' I stapled the message together . . . so the girl couldn't read it. I asked her if she would give that to Mr. Orr when he came out of his inner sanctum."

Orr was out of the inner sanctum by 6:15 that evening and on the telephone to King, who lived in Amarillo. King said Orr apologized for not being able to see him that afternoon, "asked me what was wrong, and laughed because I couldn't find the tanks."

Only Jack Quirk, who worked for Superior, knew where the tanks were, Orr explained, but he would be happy to have Quirk show them to King the next day.

"I met with Mr. Quirk at 7 A.M. the next morning at the plant," King said, "and we drove 745 miles that day through about nine, well, it was actually nine counties. He took me to every one of the twelve tanks. I specifically designated exactly where they were located and how to get there, the farm roads and et cetera, sent a complete report to C.I.T. Corporation and they were satisfied with the collateral check."

One fertilizer tank looks just about like another, and, as

Estes knew, the only positive way to identify a tank was by its serial number. It was recorded on each mortgage purchased by the finance companies. If the tanks were not where they were supposed to be, according to the mortgage records, well, most of them were mounted on wheels and, as everyone who knew anything about the fertilizer business realized, the tanks had to be moved frequently from place to place.

Estes may never have had 33,500 fertilizer tanks for which he had mortgages written totaling $34 million, but he did have 33,500 metal serial number plates for fertilizer tanks. The plates were kept in paper sacks and in burlap bags in carefully guarded back rooms of Estes' buildings in Pecos, Amarillo, Hereford and elsewhere in West Texas. Sometimes a sack of plates was put aboard an Estes plane to be flown to a town where they were quickly and badly needed to forestall a puzzled investigator like King.

"Were you ever instructed to change serial numbers on tanks?" Joe B. Bridges, an employee of an Estes company at Hereford, Texas, was asked at a court of inquiry by Attorney General Wilson.

"Yes, sir," Bridges answered.

"And where were the tanks you were to change the numbers on?"

"Just anywhere . . . There on the property at Hereford I just went right out there where they were setting in the yard and chiseled the old plates off and put the new ones on."

"Was that daytime or at night?"

"Part of it in the daytime and part of it at night. They didn't specify no time."

"They were welded to the tanks?"

"Yes, sir."

"And you chiseled the old plates off and put the new ones on by weld?"

"Yes, sir."

"And did you paint over them?"

"Yes, sir."

"And what did you do with the old plates?"

"As far as I know they are still in the office. That is where I left them."

On at least one occasion, testimony before the courts of inquiry showed, two Estes employees armed with a sack of serial numbers kept one jump ahead of two C.I.T. investigators. The Estes men used a two-way radio in their truck to keep in touch with Billie Sol, who knew the itinerary of the investigators.

For nearly three years Estes himself managed to stay one jump ahead of not only the finance companies but also the law. At times it must have seemed to him that he had invented a perpetual motion machine for raising cash.

The tank deals were an expensive way to raise money. For every three dollars Estes eventually got out of a mortgage he had to extract at least four dollars from a finance company. Estes not only was paying the cooperative farmers 10 per cent for their signatures; he also had to cut in his friends and associates at Superior Manufacturing. It was still an easy way to get funds. Whenever more cash was needed there always seemed to be more farmers to be found who would cheerfully lend their credit to Estes for 10 per cent of the take.

The money the finance companies paid Superior was funneled to Estes through a dummy bank account. When Superior got a check from a finance company it placed the check in its own account in Amarillo. A Superior check was then written for a corresponding amount payable to the Texas Steel Company of Pecos. There was no such company. It was merely a Billie Sol Estes account in the First National Bank of Pecos.

On paper, though, everything seemed in order as the money went round and round into Billie Sol's pockets. The mortgages were carefully registered in county courthouses, as required by law. The credit reports on the farmers looked good. The finance companies knew that, under the stimulus of Government price supports, the production of cotton and grain sorghums was booming in West Texas. The companies also knew that Superior had been a reputable firm in the tank manufacturing business. Most important of all, the finance companies received their payments on time every month. The companies had been able to buy the mortgages at such fat discounts they could even afford to lose a few monthly payments without endangering their wide profit margins. The fertilizer tank paper soon became known in the finance business as an attractive bargain. For a time there was lively bidding among companies in an effort to get into this exclusive financial club. Billie Sol never distributed his largesse beyond the original circle of twelve companies. He was meticulous about meeting the payments on the mortgages. Early in 1962 the payments totaled more than half a million dollars a month. These high payments were a major reason for Estes' constant need to raise more money. They had to be made promptly to keep the finance companies from prying into his affairs.

Estes also used the expertise of at least two men who knew their way around the finance business. One was C.I.T. field man King, who was employed for several months as a $500-a-month consultant to Superior while he was still working for C.I.T. James A. Turiff, who worked out of Dallas for C.I.T., also joined Superior after the tank scheme got under way. Turiff received a Ford Thunderbird automobile from Estes as well as other gifts. Charles D. Lewsader, a former Estes pilot, told a court of inquiry that he delivered mysterious envelopes to Turiff. Orr said that he once gave to Turiff an envelope from Estes containing "twenty one-hundred-dollar bills."

One of the first persons to suspect that there was something strange about the large number of fertilizer tank transactions being recorded in the Reeves County Court House was a young Pecos physician named John D. Dunn. Dr. Dunn also happened to be one of the owners of the Pecos *Independent*. In February 1961 Dunn's widowed mother, who operated a small retail credit office in Pecos, told her son about farmers who had been registering an unusual number of chattel mortgages with the county. She knew that most if not all of these farmers had had many business dealings with Estes.

Dunn looked into the matter and concluded that the Federal banking laws probably were being violated. He had known Dan Smoot, a former Federal Bureau of Investigation agent and a well-known right-wing political figure who now lived in Dallas. Dunn took what information he had to Smoot, who put him in touch with FBI agents in El Paso. The FBI conducted a perfunctory investigation and turned over its information to an Assistant United States Attorney in El Paso. By then it was summer and both the FBI agents and the El Paso District Attorney's office were busy with an airplane hijacking case involving Cuba. In the circumstances, there appeared to be neither grounds nor time for investigating the Pecos mortgages further.

From the FBI Dunn turned to newly elected Republican Senator John Tower of Texas, but the doctor met with no success here either. Tower said he simply did not have the staff to carry out such an investigation and suggested that Dunn get in touch with Texas state authorities, which he did.

Dunn also decided this might be a case for his newspaper to expose. It was not surprising that he should look to the *Independent* at this particular time, which was the fall of 1961. In August Estes had started his own newspaper, the Pecos *Daily News*, to try to run the seventy-four-year-old *Independent* out of business. Estes, who boasted that he was a liberal Democrat, had had political differences with the arch-conservative *Independent*. Dunn himself was a member of the John Birch Society. Estes blamed his own defeat as a write-in candidate in the school board election the previous spring on the *Independent*'s opposition to him.

Neither the fledgling five-day-a-week *Daily News* or the well-established twice-weekly *Independent* was the kind of small-town newspaper that would attract attention out of its home county. There was hardly room for two newspapers in Pecos, and the *Independent* had an economic as well as a political interest in discrediting Estes and his upstart newspaper.

Alan Propp, an accountant who was general manager and one of the other owners of the *Independent*, began a systematic check of fertilizer tank mortgages. He hired some women to copy mortgage records in courthouses throughout West Texas. The investigation revealed that one farmer had ostensibly purchased $3 million worth of tanks, another more than $5.7 million worth.

Propp turned the material over to Oscar Griffin, the *In-*

dependent's twenty-nine-year-old editor. Griffin wrote a series of four articles that never mentioned the name of Billie Sol Estes. In tantalizing prose that later won a Pulitzer prize for him Griffin told about well-to-do but hardly rich farmers with mortgages amounting to millions of dollars filed in their names. To anyone familiar with the tank transactions that Pecos had been whispering about for some months, it was easy to put the articles together, read between the lines, and come up with the name of Billie Sol Estes.

The first two of these articles were what caused the Pacific Finance officers to call Frank Cain and M. R. Irion that night in February 1962. By the time Cain and Irion were in Lubbock learning from Estes himself that there were no tanks, the FBI, which had also received copies of the articles in the mail, was coming to the same conclusion. In the meantime, Cain made two trips to Estes' comfortable offices and ostentatious home in Pecos. During the first trip Estes told Cain more of the details of the tank transactions and again suggested that if all the finance companies that held mortgages on the nonexistent tanks would work together with him a profitable and perhaps even an honorable way out could be found for everyone. The second time Cain went to Pecos was for his celebrated Sunday after-breakfast conversation with Estes and Maynard Wheeler, president of Commercial Solvents.

Cain had no trouble rounding up anxious finance company representatives to meet with Estes and his lawyers in the board room of the Mercantile National Bank in Dallas. By then it was too late. The meeting came to no satisfactory conclusion, and two days later, on March 29, 1962, two

FBI agents walked into Estes' office in Pecos and quietly arrested him.

Estes spent that night, a Thursday, and the following weekend in the Pecos jail, where he vainly tried to raise the $500,000 bail a Federal judge in El Paso had set at the Justice Department's request. Estes used his telephone credit card to place long-distance calls to Dallas and all over West Texas and even to Washington, seeking money. One of those he called was his old Agriculture Department friend Red Jacobs. He also tried to reach his two best political friends, Senator Yarborough and Congressman Rutherford. Estes must have found it hard to believe that a few months earlier Yarborough and other liberal Democrats in Texas were thinking about running him for governor in the Democratic primary. Billie Sol's bail was finally reduced to $100,000, and the money was raised by his brother, Bobby Frank, and his father.

Within a week of his arrest a Federal grand jury sitting in El Paso indicted Estes on three counts of mail fraud, three counts of illegally transporting securities in interstate commerce and one count of conspiracy. One of the mail fraud counts listed fifty-seven separate acts of fraud. Indicted with him were his three associates who helped to run Superior — McSpadden, Orr and Alexander. All the indictments stemmed from the fertilizer tank deals. Later Estes was also indicted by a state grand jury in Pecos for theft, fraud and conspiracy in violation of Texas laws in connection with his fertilizer tank operations. A third series of charges was made against Estes when Attorney General Wilson filed a suit naming Billie Sol and Commercial Solvents as participants in a conspiracy to violate the Texas antitrust laws by seeking to control the anhydrous ammonia fertilizer market in West Texas.

A week after the first Federal indictments were returned against Estes, Attorney General Wilson began his courts of inquiry, which turned the Estes case into the first big scandal of the Kennedy Administration. For weeks new facets of the Estes story popped up all over Washington. One day it was the Agriculture Department, the next day the Labor Department, then up to Capitol Hill, to the House, to the Senate and back to the Agriculture Department. Finally, late in May, a House Government Operations subcommittee began public hearings on Estes' Government grain storage operations. In June, shortly before the Senate Investigations subcommittee opened the public phase of its study of Estes' cotton allotments, Billie Sol was indicted again by the Federal grand jury in El Paso. The new indictment combined the counts in the original charges of April with a host of additional ones, making a total of sixteen counts of mail fraud, twelve counts of illegally transporting securities in interstate commerce and one count of conspiracy — twenty-nine counts in all. McSpadden, Orr and Alexander were also indicted again with Estes on the same fraud, illegal transportation and conspiracy charges.

Billie Sol's three associates quickly pleaded guilty, and in September Federal Judge R. E. Thomason of El Paso sentenced McSpadden and Orr to ten years in prison and gave Alexander a six-year term. Thomason said that the three men were guilty of "one of the most premeditated, fantastic and ruthless frauds ever to come before any court in the Southwest."

For forty-five minutes the judge lectured the three men as they stood silently before him. "It was the old story of ill-gotten gains that will be found out," Thomason noted. He then went on to say that the law violations were "highly indicative of the deviated morality that now afflicts our system."

The day after the three Estes associates were sentenced, a San Antonio businessman named Morris D. Jaffe bought Estes' assets for $5.8 million, a figure which was only a tiny fraction of the $150 million that Estes once boasted he was worth. Harry Moore, an El Paso banker who had been the court-appointed trustee in bankruptcy for the Estes properties, said that Jaffe's price represented a fair appraisal of Estes' assets. (Under the Texas homestead law his palatial home was exempt from the bankruptcy proceedings.)

The $5.8 million sale price meant that Estes' creditors, to whom he owed at least $20 million, would get an average of slightly better than twenty-five cents on every dollar of debt. These creditors included the finance companies, who presumably could also collect from the farmers whose names were on the tank mortgages.

Estes was found guilty of fraud, theft and conspiracy by a jury in a state court in Tyler, Texas, in November 1962 and sentenced to eight years in prison in January 1963. Between the end of his trial and his sentencing Billie Sol hit the sawdust trail, speaking at Church of Christ revival meetings in Ohio and Indiana. After State Judge Otis T. Dunagan, a quiet, friendly man, passed sentence on him, Billie Sol walked up to the bench, shook hands with the Judge and wished him the best of luck.

Two months later Estes went on trial in United States District Court in El Paso, and on March 28, 1963, just one day short of a year after his arrest by FBI agents, he was found guilty on four Federal counts of mail fraud and one of conspiracy. He faced maximum Federal sentences of twenty-five years in prison.

It took the jury of ten men and two women forty-nine hours and forty-five minutes to reach their verdict after listening to testimony for eighteen days in the courtroom of Judge Thomason. During the trial the Federal prosecutors charged that Estes raised $24 million through phony mortgages on fertilizer tanks held by one hundred individuals and a dozen finance companies. Estes did not testify on his own behalf in either the Federal or the state trial, but his lawyers argued at both trials that Estes could not be guilty of fraud or conspiracy because the farmers with whom he dealt and the finance companies knew the mortgages were on nonexistent fertilizer tanks.

When the verdict was announced in the El Paso courtroom, Estes showed no emotion. He gazed steadily at the jurors as their decision was read and occasionally even smiled weakly.

After the court adjourned and his lawyers said they would appeal, Estes refused to comment on the verdict, maintaining the silence with which he has met all questions since his arrest. As he walked out of the courtroom his wife clutched his arm and said, "He looks just as good to me today as he did yesterday."

Two and a half weeks after the jury brought in its verdict Mr. and Mrs. Estes were back in court to hear the stern judge sentence Estes to fifteen years in prison for mail fraud and conspiracy.

"The record shows," Thomason told Estes, "that you were the author and perpetrator of one of the most gigantic swindles in the history of our country.

"Your actions in this case," the judge added, "have passed a cloud upon segments of our business world and upon the many victims of the scheme you successfully carried out for your monetary gain. Your defense was built mostly on the idea that you could pay off if left alone . . . There is nothing in the evidence to show you could have paid off. It is a sad commentary that would make you perpetrate a scheme, which amount of money exceeds anything in history . . . It is a disgrace to yourself and to your fine family."

Estes left the courtroom to resume his itinerant preaching on the Southern evangelical trail. One day he even showed up in Alabama at the place where a Baltimore postman had been shot to death as he was walking through the South to protest segregation. The demonstrators who were continuing the postman's march would have nothing to do with Estes when he tried to join their protest and they rudely told him to move on.

10

Farmer in the Treasury

FOR THIRTY years farmers have frightened politicians and
bureaucrats alike. Billions upon billions of taxpayers' dollars have been ladled out to farmers by a cowed Congress
and a supine bureaucracy. The handouts have been justified
in the name of the small family farmer. They have been
called the farmer's only answer to Big Business and Big
Labor. They have been defended as the guarantor of
rural prosperity. They have been described as the bulwark
against a sea of unmanageable farm surpluses.

There is only one thing wrong with them. They have not
worked. They have become a national scandal because political considerations rather than economic realities have dominated the farm subsidy program since it began in 1933 as a
hopeful New Deal effort.

Congress has deliberately designed farm legislation so that
its production control provisions would be ineffective. Congress has written farm laws primarily to benefit the big,
prosperous farmers who have the most political influence.
The legislation has also been tailored to meet the demands
of the highly influential small-town dealers in farm commodities and the equally influential big-city processors and
users of the commodities. Presidents and Secretaries of Agri-

culture have joined in the great game of farm politics in a shameless quest for rural votes.

Farmers have become as adept at outwitting production control legislation as they have been in bamboozling politicians. By utilizing new machinery, miracle fertilizers and pesticides, hybrid seeds and modern production techniques, farmers have plowed under Government programs.

Not even all the taxpayers' money and all the farmers' and politicians' ingenuity can put the good rural life of the American dream together again. Despite the annual injection of up to $5 billion in Federal subsidies into the farm economy, rural counties and small towns are rapidly drying up throughout the nation.

The rate of farm-to-city migration was greater during the 1950's than in any previous decade, but the movement off the farms was still not fast enough. Farmers who have stayed with the land have not shared equitably in the prosperity of the 1950's and 1960's. They are lagging behind businessmen and workers largely because the farm subsidy programs have frozen agriculture into inefficient patterns and have kept on the farm people who probably would do much better in the city.

So, as of December 31, 1962, the Government was storing surplus commodities valued at more than $8 billion. Although this figure was $1 billion less than the record high of $9 billion two years earlier, it was nearly $400 million higher than the December 1961 totals.

The biggest items were more than $2.5 billion worth of wheat, $1.8 billion worth of corn, nearly $800 million in grain sorghums, and cotton valued at over $1.5 billion. The quantities were still high even though the wheat and grain surpluses had been reduced since 1960 by 900 million bushels: 1.3 billion bushels of wheat, 1.6 million bushels of corn, over 800 million bushels of sorghums, 9 million bales of cotton, 350 million pounds of butter, 660 million pounds of powdered milk.

The farm programs became so complex and so difficult to understand that it took a Billie Sol Estes case to alert the nation to the dangers entangled in the vast web of agricultural subsidies. The Estes grain storage manipulations dramatized the way grain production had got out of hand and showed how both farmers and businessmen have taken advantage of the generous Government guarantees. Billie Sol's efforts to obtain more cotton allotments demonstrated the lengths to which farmers and businessmen will go to get Government planting permits. His phantom fertilizer tank deals were a stark commentary on what has happened to the puritanical ideals that are supposed to permeate rural living. The desperate efforts made by Estes to save his crumbling empire by appealing to his friends in high political places in Washington spotlighted the dangers of having economic powers of a life-and-death nature in the hands of politicians whose first concern is getting reelected.

The Estes case shocked the nation and shook the Kennedy Administration, but it led to no fundamental reforms in the farm subsidy program. The case was the legacy of thirty years of costly farm subsidy failures, but the subsidies have become so ingrained in the American farm economy and so sacrosanct to politicians that few influential members of a still rurally oriented Congress would risk their political future by demanding genuine reforms.

Farmers need some Government protection, particularly in a subsidy- and protection-oriented economy such as the United States has today. It hardly seems wise or necessary, however, for the Federal Government to hand out $5 billion a year in order to prop up 8 per cent of the country's population.

Unless the unconscionably high farm subsidies are soon brought down to realistic levels and unless surplus production is firmly controlled, the remains of the farm bloc on Capitol Hill may find itself with a taxpayers' and consumers' revolt on its hands that will make the farm uprisings of the early 1930's look like a hog-calling contest. Gradually but surely, the city and suburban Senators and Representatives are ascending to positions of power in a Congress that up to now has been dominated by rural and small-town legislators. In another ten years, when the results of the 1970 census are reflected in Congress, farmers and their representatives probably will be less secure on Capitol Hill than they are now. Long-suffering taxpayers and consumers will agree that it's about time. The longer the rural representatives take to adjust farm subsidies to realistic levels the harder the farmer's fall will be when the consumer and the taxpayer at last get their sweet revenge.

Whenever one of the farm subsidies is carefully examined it turns out to be an expensive handout that is usually costing taxpayers hundreds of millions of dollars without giving help to farmers who need it and without adequately reducing surplus production.

For thirty years cotton has been caught in a tug-of-war between political and economic forces. On the one side have been the Senators and Representatives from the Southeast, who are among the most powerful men in Washington. These are the Southerners who through seniority dominate Congress and who depend on farmers for much of their political support. They have written cotton legislation primarily to benefit the farmers of the Southeast.

This approach ignores the economic realities of cotton production. Cotton has been a dying crop in the Southeast since the 1920's. Boll weevil infestations took their toll then in a soil that had been exhausted years before by intensive cotton production. Furthermore, cotton farms in the Southeast were generally too small to make efficient use of modern machinery and production techniques.

Cotton has been moving West since the early 1930's because yields are much greater there than in the Southeast. Cotton is a more productive crop in the West because there it is grown on irrigated land where moisture can be carefully controlled. In the Western states of Arizona, California, New Mexico and Nevada — as well as in West Texas where Estes operated his farms — more than a thousand pounds of cotton can be grown on an irrigated acre. In the old cotton-producing states of the Southeast yields are little more than a third of those in the West. Even the rich black soil of the Mississippi River Delta regions in Mississippi, Louisiana and Arkansas yields average only a little over five hundred pounds of cotton to the acre — about half the Western yield.

If there had been no cotton price support legislation during the last thirty years practically all the nation's cotton production would probably have moved to the highly efficient irrigated acres of the West. The generous cotton subsidies provided by Congress have held back these economic forces. As a result the West and Southwest account for only about 55 per cent of cotton production.

In the absence of subsidies, many more cotton farmers in the Southeast undoubtedly would have left the farm for the city. Those who remained would have turned more quickly to the mass production of chickens and the raising of cattle, operations that are belatedly changing the face of agriculture in the Southeast and bringing a better life to more Southern farmers than cotton ever did.

To keep the incomes of Southeastern cotton farmers at a satisfactory if hardly munificent level, Southern Congressmen had to set cotton price support levels at a rate that has created a bonanza for the highly efficient Western producers. The price guarantee has been so high that for the last ten years it has been necessary to restrict cotton acreages. Without such restrictions the cotton surpluses would be unmanageable. Even with the restrictions production generally has outstripped the needs of both foreign and domestic markets.

Also complicating the cotton picture is the increasing competition of man-made fibers and the importance of foreign markets to American cotton. During the 1962-1963 crop year, 8.1 million bales of cotton were used by domestic textile mills, 3.5 million bales were shipped abroad, and another 11 million bales were being stored by the Government and by private warehousemen.

To sell American cotton abroad the United States must heavily subsidize every pound destined for a foreign textile mill. In the 1962-1963 crop year the Government guaranteed a cotton price to farmers of nearly 32.5 cents a pound. This was one third more than the world cotton price of about 24 cents a pound. The Government pays farmers 32.5 cents a pound for cotton and then gives exporters an 8.5-cent-a-pound subsidy so that they can sell American cotton at the world market price of 24 cents a pound.

This is not the end of the cotton carnival. Foreign textile mills can buy American cotton at three fourths the price that must be paid by manufacturers in the United States. Cheaper labor and more efficient textile machinery, particularly in Japan and Hong Kong, have meant that such finished foreign textiles as women's blouses and men's shirts made from American cotton can be purchased in the United States, even after the cotton has made the round trip on a slow boat, cheaper than can cotton textiles manufactured here.

Since 1955, when the cotton subsidy payments on foreign shipments began, American imports of finished cotton goods have more than tripled. The slowness with which American textile manufacturers have adopted new production techniques is partly to blame for the increased imports, but the principal cause is the crazy-quilt pattern of United States cotton subsidies.

During the presidential campaign of 1960 Mr. Kennedy promised to help the domestic cotton mills so that they would be able to compete on a more equitable basis with foreign manufacturers. In his first two years in office the President took several steps, including the negotiation of an international agreement regulating cotton imports, to ease the difficulties of the American textile industry, but the 8.5-cent-a-pound difference between domestic and foreign prices for American cotton remained.

Early in 1963 efforts to get Congress to extend the 8.5-cent subsidy to cotton sold in domestic markets got snagged in cotton politics. The efficient Western producers have long been willing to exchange a lower price guarantee for an increase in the number of acres they are allowed to plant. The Southeastern cotton farmers, on the other hand, must have the high price supports to survive. Not all the acreage to which the Southeast is now entitled is planted to cotton, because it is a dying crop in the area, despite the efforts of Southern Congressmen to make cotton king of their region once again. Smugly observing the tug-of-war from the sidelines are the Republican members of Congress, whose

Northern and Western districts include few if any cotton farmers. Why, ask the Republicans, should there be any increase in cotton production when the United States already has a perennial cotton surplus?

The lessons of the cotton fiasco are clear. The Southern Senators and Representatives who run Congress have turned cotton subsidies into a welfare program for Southern farmers. To keep their farmers — and voters — on worn-out acres the Congressmen passed legislation requiring establishment of cotton price supports at unrealistically high levels. For political reasons President Kennedy and Secretary of Agriculture Freeman acquiesced in this congressional conspiracy against the economics of cotton production. Shortly after taking office in 1961 Freeman himself increased cotton price guarantees to placate Southern Congressmen.

As powerful as they are, the Southerners and their allies in the Agriculture Department have not been able to hold back the westward movement of cotton; economic forces cannot be stopped even by the Southern oligarchy on Capitol Hill.

In seeking to protect their cotton farmers, the Southern Congressmen have not only failed to save the South's traditional farm economy; they have seriously hurt the Southern cotton textile industry.

In the midst of the debate over a new cotton program early in 1963 Olin T. Mouzon, a professor of economics at the University of North Carolina, pleaded in a letter to the Washington *Post* for

. . . appropriate action . . . to separate the cotton commodity high price support problem from the low income problem of the small Southeastern producers.

The present price support program [he added] has principally benefited large producers and while it has kept up the income of small producers, it has kept them producing unneeded cotton, and has interfered with competitive adjustments and the efficient allocation of resources . . . A recommended simple solution to the dual problem of high price supports and low income would involve a twofold plan. First, eliminate all cotton production controls and price supports (except as noted below) and allow the cost of cotton production and price to be pointed downward, and thus no export subsidy would be required. Second, support the price of cotton at the 1962 level of 32.47 cents a pound on up to ten bales grown on present acreage allocations of fifteen acres or less. This could be done by paying these growers the difference between the support price and the market price. This support program for small producers should be reduced to zero to the competitive price over a period of five to seven years.

In the meantime, since the second part of this program is obviously a welfare program, the areas affected in the Southeast should be given the benefit of other retraining and industrialization programs designed for areas of unemployment. The obvious intent of this phase of the program is to get high-cost cotton producers out of the industry and into more efficient production. In no event should we have a continuation of the present policy of local agricultural officials begging small producers not to give up their acreage allotments. The net profit of the recommended program might be that the Southeast would erect monuments to efficiency, just as Enterprise, Alabama, built a monument to the boll weevil when that area was emancipated from the shackles of King Cotton.

The wheat scandal is even worse than the cotton fiasco. Like cotton guarantees, wheat price supports have been set far above world wheat market prices and have encouraged wheat production greatly in excess of domestic needs. Year after year the wheat surplus has been twice the annual wheat consumption in the United States. Only by heavily subsidizing export sales has the Government been able to move large amounts of surplus wheat into foreign markets.

Western and Midwestern political forces on Capitol Hill are largely responsible for the wheat situation. Members of Congress from the Midwest and the West voted for high cotton prices in exchange for Southern support for high price guarantees for wheat.

In three decades wheat yields almost doubled. Better seeds, better fertilizer and other improvements in farm techniques combined with generally good weather to produce the high yields and record crops. It is unlikely, however, that yields would have increased as much as they did if farmers did not see intensified production as the way to circumvent Government controls.

To gain support for the high price guarantees, Senators and Representatives from the big Western wheat states agreed to exempt small plots of wheat of up to fifteen acres from the controls but not from the price guarantees. In the last ten years this provision has resulted in the proliferation of fifteen-acre wheat plots throughout the Midwest and the East, where little wheat had previously been grown. It was simply too good a gift for a farmer to pass up, but every fifteen-acre plot added its little bit to help build up the big wheat surplus.

Wheat farmers were able to push up their price support levels during the period of worldwide food shortages immediately after World War II and during the Korean War. Although the wheat price guarantee fell from a high of $2.24 a bushel in 1954 to $1.78 in 1960, it was back to $2 in 1962.

The $2-a-bushel Government-guaranteed price is more than twice what it costs many farmers to produce wheat. Studies made by Macalester College economists in North Dakota, Wyoming and Washington show that the cost of wheat production ranged from 89 cents to $1.30 a bushel.

Wheat farmers have been able to keep their price guarantees high because there are so many of them. The Agriculture Department has noted that 1.8 million of the nation's 3.7 million farmers — or almost half of them — get all or part of their income from wheat. In each of the last ten years farmers have received at least $2 billion for their wheat crop, but nearly half the wheat receipts have been from Government subsidies.

If it were not for the Food-for-Peace shipments to the underdeveloped countries of Asia, Africa and Latin America, the nation's wheat surplus would be even more embarrassing and costly than it has been in recent years. The United States has become a major exporter of wheat, to the distress of such well-established wheat-exporting countries as Canada and Australia. Most of the American wheat exports are for local currencies that cannot be converted to dollars.

Even commercial wheat exports that return dollars to the United States must be heavily subsidized because of the high wheat price guarantees. From 1949 to 1960 the Government had to pay from 44 to 79 cents a bushel to American wheat exporters so that they could sell in the world market. During the 1950's American price guarantees kept domestic wheat prices from 25 to 40 per cent above world market prices. American taxpayers and consumers thus had to pay first to maintain high prices for United States wheat farmers and then to subsidize the export of the high-cost wheat.

To try to reduce surplus wheat production, the Kennedy Administration persuaded Congress to approve two new wheat programs. Congress went along wih the Kennedy legislation because the wheat subsidies and surpluses were getting enough out of hand to invite trouble and retaliation for the farm bloc on Capitol Hill.

The first Kennedy wheat program was put into effect in 1962 and 1963. Under it farmers were paid to take additional wheat land out of production. This temporary program reduced both wheat acreage and the wheat surplus, but production remained far above the nation's needs.

In 1962 Congress approved by a narrow margin legislation to remove the floor from wheat acreage and to allow the Secretary of Agriculture to establish wheat production controls based on annual estimates of the nation's needs. Individual farmers would be allocated marketing quotas each year. By seeking to control production on a bushel basis rather than by acreage limitations, the Kennedy Administration hoped to bring wheat harvests into line with needs. The program also provided that the Secretary of Agriculture should support wheat grown in excess of immediate food needs at a price of only two thirds of the guaranteed price.

This "tough controls" approach to the wheat scandal was emphatically rejected by wheat farmers in a referendum in May 1963. The control program got less than 48 per cent of the vote, with 547,151 farmers supporting the plan and 597,-776 opposing it. Under farm legislation in effect since 1938, two thirds of the farmers who would be affected by a proposed production control program must approve the plan before it can go into effect.

It was the first time a referendum had become the subject of an intensely fought political campaign. The drive for a "yes" vote was led by Secretary of Agriculture Freeman and the National Farmers Union. The American Farm Bureau Federation was the principal opponent of the control program. Organizations of livestock producers were also opposed to it.

The choice given wheat farmers was essentially a question of controls and high prices vs. unrestricted production and no price guarantees, but farmers were not voting to sever the umbilical cord that has tied them to the Government for thirty years. In leading the campaign against the control program the Farm Bureau and its Republican allies on Capitol Hill promised farmers Congress would enact less onerous legislation once the Administration's wheat program was defeated. Farmers accepted these promises and voted accordingly. The rejection of the control program was not a vote to get the Government out of agriculture.

If the referendum had approved the program, farmers would have been guaranteed $2 a bushel by the Government for 80 per cent of the wheat they produced in 1964. The other 20 per cent would have been supported at $1.30 — 5 cents less than the world wheat price and about the same as the Government guarantees for corn, sorghums and other feed grains.

In exchange for the high price guarantee, which had been in effect in 1962 and 1963, farmers would have had to cut their wheat production 10 per cent. By introducing a two-price plan the Government would have been controlling production of the nation's 1.8 million wheat farmers for the first time on a bushel rather than an acre basis. The per cent of a farmer's crop eligible for the high, $2 support price would have been set in terms of bushels, not acres. It was this provision that turned the vote into the first real contest in the twenty-five-year history of farm price support and production control referendums. Bushel controls could not have been circumvented the way acreage restrictions have been.

In the referendum big farmers and little farmers, producers of only a few acres of wheat and farmers whose wheatfields stretch as far as the eye can see across the High Plains rejected the program. The total vote was twice that of any of the thirteen previous wheat referendums, the first of which was held in 1941. In the face of rising costs and increasing capital outlays — a typical Western Kansas wheat farm represented an investment of nearly $200,000 — farmers revolted against controls. The big, efficient farmer produced wheat for 85 to 95 cents a bushel and was willing to take a price guarantee considerably under $2 in exchange for the right to use his expensive tractors, cultivators, planters and harvesting machinery to produce more wheat. Like businessmen, farmers hate to see costly equipment standing idle. They think that the Government should be able to find markets for surplus crops.

Under the program that automatically went into effect with the defeat of the strict controls proposal, there would be only a $1.25 price guarantee for farmers who agreed to cut back their production by at least 10 per cent. Few farmers would participate in such a program, however, because a $1.25 price guarantee for restricting production is not attractive enough. Most farmers would prefer to plant all they want and take their chances on price. This was why the Administration had estimated during the referendum campaign what wheat would drop below the $1.25 support level to $1 a bushel if the control program were defeated. Most wheat farmers were, however, counting on Congress to put a floor somewhere between $1.25 and $2 under their income.

Four agricultural economists from state universities in the Midwest estimated in a report prepared for the Administration before the referendum that in 1964 the income of wheat farmers would decline by $700 million — a decrease of almost one third from the 1962 figure of $2.3 billion — if the control program were defeated. This figure was based on estimates that a lower price level and the absence of controls would stimulate increased production despite the 1.3-billion-bushel wheat surplus at the time of the referendum, a surplus large enough to feed Americans for two years.

All of the Kennedy Administration's grim warnings about the adverse effects of a "no" vote in the referendum were sharply challenged by the Farm Bureau during the campaign. Even if Congress failed to come to the wheat farmers' rescue, Farm Bureau economists maintained, the program that went into effect for 1964 as a result of the wheat vote would not necessarily spell disaster for farmers. With a high wheat price guarantee no longer spurring surplus production, according to the Farm Bureau's interpretation of the vote, many farmers would turn from wheat to soybeans, grain sorghums or other crops that would be more profitable.

Changes in crop patterns undoubtedly would occur, but it was doubtful whether the shifts by some farmers would be large enough to offset increased wheat production by others. In the 1920's, the 1930's, and again in the 1950's, when Ezra Taft Benson sought to move agriculture back to a free market, the response of farmers was to plant more to prevent their income from falling. The Farm Bureau wanted Congress to approve a wheat price guarantee of about $1.35 a bushel as part of a program that would include the systematic retirement of land from production.

The emphatic rejection of strict production controls by wheat farmers made it more difficult for the Administration to put into effect any farm program other than one following the uneasy and largely ineffective compromises of the last thirty years. In the 1950's Ezra Taft Benson found he could not move the Government out of agriculture, and in the 1960's Orville Freeman discovered he was unable to get farmers to accept the controls needed to restrict subsidized production.

The production of corn and the three other feed grains (sorghums, barley and oats) was finally brought under control in 1961 and 1962, but only at a direct cost of at least $1.7 billion to American taxpayers.

Secretary Freeman has claimed that taxpayers ultimately will save $1 billion under the new program. The Secretary's calculation takes into account the $1.7 billion in payments that were made in 1961 and 1962 to get farmers to cut back their corn production. The savings determined by the Agriculture Department constitute the difference between what the no-controls program of the previous decade would have cost and what the moderate-controls program instituted in 1961 costs.

Corn production has as broad a base as does wheat. Although corn is concentrated in the Midwest, it is also grown in the West, in much of the East and in the South, for expanding cattle operations. Unlike cotton and wheat, most corn and other feed grains are consumed on the farms where they are grown.

This means that corn production is much harder to control. Farmers are less willing to accept controls on corn than on wheat because corn is a raw material on the cattle assembly line and not an agricultural end product. Sporadic efforts were made during the 1950's to control corn production, but they met with little success.

Like wheat, the corn surplus had increased to scandalous proportions by the time the Kennedy Administration came into office in January 1961. Even so, it was necessary to offer farmers a fat reward for reducing their corn production. Every farmer who cut back his corn acreage was given a substantial Government payment, and only farmers who reduced production were eligible for corn price guarantees.

In 1961, the first year of the program, the Government paid out $765 million to get a reduction of nearly 800 million bushels in the corn crop. It thus cost taxpayers nearly a dollar for every bushel of corn that farmers did not produce in 1961. Farmers were guaranteed $1.20 for every bushel of corn they produced. During the second year of the program the ratio of Government payments to the non-production of corn remained about the same, but more corn land was idled than in 1961, so the total payments to corn producers came to $854 million. Taking into account some small payments to barley producers as well as administrative expenses, the first two years of the corn program thus cost taxpayers more than $1.7 billion.

The costly corn program of the late 1950's is generally blamed on Benson and scornfully pointed to as an example of the bankruptcy of the no-controls, low-price-guarantee approach to agriculture's ills. In Benson's defense it should be noted that the corn price guarantees of a little more than a dollar a bushel that were part of the program of the late 1950's were high enough to encourage production. The Benson corn program was merely another in the long and unsuccessful line of uneasy farm policy compromises of relatively high price guarantees without controls or with ineffective controls.

If we accept Secretary Freeman's "iffy" estimates of the difference between the high costs of his corn program and the still higher costs he claims would have resulted from continuing the Benson program, American taxpayers are now somewhat better off. Those economists and other observers of the wonderland of farm subsidies who have not cheered the new corn program as loudly as Freeman may be pardoned for their skepticism. The same seeds of potential disaster which have sprouted from previous programs are sown in the new program.

President Kennedy and Secretary Freeman tried but failed in 1962 to get Congress to approve mandatory corn controls that would have forced all corn producers to abide by acreage restrictions once two thirds of them had approved the program. In the absence of such legislation corn farmers can decide for themselves whether to enter the program and take advantage of its payments for acreage reductions and its attractive price guarantees or whether to stay out and produce as much as they wish.

At best the Kennedy Administration negotiated an uneasy truce in the battle against excess corn production. It was able to get no better solution because members of Congress from the Midwest and their farmer constituents do not want controls on farm production and because Southern Senators and Representatives feared that controls would freeze feed grain production for their prospering and expanding cattle industry.

Milk production is out of hand, too, and no solution is immediately in sight. In 1961 and 1962 milk surpluses increased as production continued to expand in the face of declining consumption. The increase in dairy production was spurred by high price supports and by Federal marketing regulations that set milk prices in 83 metropolitan areas where half of the nation's milk is consumed.

Farmers are learning how to squeeze more milk out of every cow. From 1952 to 1962 milk production went up by 9 per cent, while the number of dairy cows declined 19 per cent. The increase in productivity averaged 34 per cent per cow.

The Kennedy Administration is partly to blame for the increase in milk production in 1961 and 1962. Secretary Freeman raised milk price guarantees early in 1961, and this action contributed to an increase in production that sent the cost of Federal subsidies soaring by $600 million. In March 1962 Freeman lowered price guarantees, but the dairy program still cost taxpayers $500 million in 1962, while the income of dairy farmers declined by $100 million from 1960 to 1962.

More than 400 million pounds of surplus butter piled up in cold storage warehouses, and 600 million pounds of nonfat dry milk was stacked up in other warehouses. Not even vigorous efforts to distribute surplus butter and powdered milk to Americans on relief rolls and to hungry people abroad made a significant dent in the dairy stockpiles. In one of the ironic twists of farm subsidies high Government guarantees have priced butter out of the reach of a whole generation of middle-class Americans who now use — and apparently prefer — margarine.

Dairy farmers have an ideal political base. They are in every state, and the production of milk constitutes an important part of every state's farm income. So a solid majority of Senators and Representatives can always be put together without too much trouble by the dairy interests — if they can agree on what Congress should do for them.

Farmers who supply the nation's big cities with milk have interests quite different from farmers in the Midwest who sell most of their milk to plants that process it. Under the complicated milk price structure a considerably higher price is guaranteed farmers for milk to be bottled immediately than for milk to be turned into butter, cheese, ice cream mix and powdered forms. The argument among dairy farmers concerns whose production should be reduced, and by how much.

The Kennedy Administration tried to get Congress to approve legislation requiring all dairy farmers to cut back their production before they could get high price guarantees. The farmers have resisted these efforts to use controls to bring milk production in line with consumption, despite frequent warnings from Secretary Freeman that farmers who refuse to limit their production cannot expect open-end help from the Government indefinitely. So the taxpayers' milk bath continues.

One more example of the strange and expensive workings of the farm subsidy system should be cited: the tobacco program. For more than twenty years it has been praised as an almost perfect case of the way high Government price guarantees can work if they are accompanied with adequate production controls.

The Government's once highly touted tobacco program began to come apart in 1962 like a badly made roll-your-own cigarette because farmers were forcing too much production out of each acre. Rows of tobacco plants were placed closer together and increasing numbers of farmers were using a new chemical, maleic hydrazide (MH–30) to inhibit the growth of unwanted sprouts on the tobacco plants.

Before the chemical came into use farmers pinched off the sprouts by hand. It was a backbreaking job that took thirty-two hours to cover a single acre. Now the chemical does the work while the farmer sits comfortably in his rocking chair, but according to tobacco company experts the chemical produces an inferior product.

A spokesman for a major tobacco company told an Agriculture Department hearing on MH–30 in 1962 that "we . . . would not knowingly or willingly consider marketing a new cigarette which had a consumer acceptance level as low as that indicated for cigarettes made from a tobacco treated with maleic hydrazide."

Under the farm subsidy program a farmer who raised inferior tobacco got as high a price guarantee as one who produced a superior product. The principal interest of the nation's 500,000 tobacco farmers was to increase their income by planting as much tobacco as possible on their small plots.

Early in 1963 a tobacco surplus began to pile up in the midst of the industry's increasing dissatisfaction with the quality of a chemically treated crop. Farmers strongly resisted a suggestion made by the Tobacco Advisory Committee of the Agriculture Department that crops treated with MH–30 be given a Government price guarantee of only 50 per cent of the support level for tobacco not receiving this treatment, but such a discount was finally put into effect by the Department.

Tobacco farmers are a tiny minority in the United States, but they are concentrated in North Carolina, the home state of Chairman Cooley of the House Agriculture Committee, and in the other Southeastern states represented by powerful Democratic members of Congress.

As recently as 1940, two thirds of what economists call farm "inputs" were land and labor. Today land and labor constitute little more than one third of the "mix" in the agricultural economy, while such nonfarm inputs as machinery, fuel, fertilizer, pesticides, feed supplements and many other goods and services account for nearly two thirds of the farm economy's modern mix. Agriculture Department economist Harold F. Breimyer has pointed out in an article published in the August 1962 issue of the *Journal of Farm Economics* and reprinted by the Agriculture Department:

Since so much of the increase in use of purchased inputs in farming has taken place since 1940, those 20 years (from 1940 to 1960) can justifiably be called an age of transformation. After countless centuries of history, production from farms is no longer so closely predestined by the mineral content of soils, the vagaries of rainfall, and the assiduousness of the labor force tied to the land. Now it is subject also to the governing influence of the resources fed into it. This is the fundamental significance of widely heralded "galloping technology"; it is not that it necessarily expands farm output, but that it makes output expansible.

Land values in agriculture are probably destined for gradual subordination relatively even though they may hold up well in dollars per acre. Manifestations of this alignment are being obscured by various resistances and delaying actions. For instance, open-end price support to farm commodities has had such an effect. When support rates are at an incentive level, open-end support encourages liberal use of non-farm inputs in farming; but unless acreage allotments are very tight it also keeps land in productive use. Thus the Federal Government has subsidized both fertilizer manufacturers and landholders. Future changes in support policies, such as a shift to quantity marketing quotas, could change significantly both the amount and relative proportion of succor to each.

Breimyer found considerable hope in the new agricultural mix for the solution of the problem of overproduction.

The new kind of farming "ought to have a more responsive supply function. Non-farm inputs are a spigot that can be turned on and off fairly readily; they provide an output-regulating device that was not so available in the days of simpler organization of agriculture. Of itself, this would seem to offer a welcome prospect for more stability in primary agriculture, and perhaps even for an ending of any need for farm control programs.

In another sense, though, the new primary agriculture merely shifts the point of control. It posits it more on the forces and techniques by which the inflow of capital resources is managed.

It remains to be seen how, and how wisely, man uses his new power. The older agriculture, resistant to man's control, was protection against his errors. Its limited productivity, while not surfeiting consumers and often a harassment to farmers, yet served to prevent serious progressive declines of prices and values in farming. It was not so easy to overproduce then as it is now.

There are of course positive aspects to the farm subsidy programs. Although they have generally helped farmers who needed assistance the least, have encouraged unwanted production, and have kept too many people in farming, the programs have been an important factor in improving farm living conditions. Despite the hand-wringing and wails of so many farm politicians, life on the farms that have received most of the subsidies and produce most of the crops — and the surpluses — is not the dreary dawn-to-dusk existence of hard physical labor that it is so often still thought to be.

Still, the per farm and per capita farm income figures issued each year by the Agriculture Department present a depressing picture of the farm economy. In 1962, for example, net income per farm was figured at $3498, an increase of 4 per cent over 1961 and the highest on record. When 1962 farm income was reduced to a per capita figure it averaged $1430 per farm person, or a $57 increase over 1961. Of the total, $926 came from farming and $504 from nonfarm sources, including jobs off the farm and investments. The $1430 per capita farm income figure was only about 60 per cent of the per capita nonfarm income figure of $2440.

Per farm income in Arizona, where cotton is a major crop, totaled $24,223 in 1962, while the figure for West Virginia, where the mountainous landscape hinders any farming efforts, was only $898. Arizona and West Virginia represented the range from the best to the worst farming states.

A better way to look at farm income, particularly when it is being discussed in relationship to farm subsidies, is in terms of major kinds of agricultural operations. Such figures show that in 1961, the latest year for which data are available on this basis, income by types of farm ranged from $12,195 for wheat and grain sorghum operations on the Southern plains to $2909 for tobacco and dairy operations in the Kentucky Bluegrass region.

Other income figures by types of farm included $11,940 for wheat farms in the Pacific Northwest and $10,619 for wheat farms in the Southern plains. The income of Midwest corn belt farmers ran from $8878 for cash grain operations and $8126 for hog and cattle feeding farms to $6174 for combined hog and dairy operations. The income of dairy farmers ranged from $6938 in eastern Wisconsin to $4590 in New England.

The figures show that even with the large Federal farm subsidy payments of the last decade, farm income has not been increased to wholly satisfactory levels. Therefore, it is sometimes argued, Federal subsidies should be raised to even higher levels. A look at the record of the last decade reveals, however, that as the cost of farm programs went up farm income went down. In the 1951 fiscal year, for example, all Agriculture Department activities cost less than $650 million, while net farm income that year totaled more than $15 billion. By 1957 Federal spending for all agricultural programs had increased to $5 billion, while farm income hit its postwar low of $11 billion. The Federally sweetened pie that the farmers were dividing was not big enough to provide adequate incomes for large numbers of farmers, but it was large enough to keep millions of farmers on the land and to prevent them from seeking jobs in town or city.

In 1961, net farm income increased $800 million, to $12.5 billion, compared with $11.7 billion in 1960. This increase reflected little more than higher Government payments to farmers. In 1962 net farm income rose a mere $100 million to $12.6 billion. In its first two years in office the Kennedy Administration could claim credit for adding a total of $1.7 billion to net farm income, but during these two years the Administration's new feed grain programs alone resulted in the direct payment to farmers of the same amount. Thus, farm income was increased only at a high cost to taxpayers. Even higher and ever expanding farm subsidies hardly seem to be the answer to the farm problem.

11

What Must Be Done

THERE ARE two farm problems. One is overproduction. This has bedeviled the nation, the farmers, their organizations and the farm politicians for a century. Efforts to solve this problem have cost taxpayers billions over the last thirty years. It is usually identified as the only farm problem because its roots are primarily agricultural, because the many attempts to solve it have been so costly, and because it has been the focus of legislative attention since the depression days of the early 1930's.

The other major farm problem is part of a larger, nationwide problem. It is the problem of poverty in the midst of plenty. Louis J. Ducoff, an Agriculture Department economist, estimated in 1962 that "half or more of the farms . . . are too small to provide a minimum adequate living from agriculture."

"It is well to recognize," Ducoff told the Agriculture Department's Fortieth Annual Outlook Conference in November 1962, "the more acute and special nature of the problem confronting the low-income farm families and their heavy concentration in the South . . . While progress has been achieved in the improvement of levels of living of farm families generally and further progress may be anticipated, there are still wide discrepancies not only in income between farm and nonfarm families but also in educational preparation, health facilities and other measures of general well-being. The farm population has a disproportionate number of its people among the poorly remunerated, the poorly educated and among the underprivileged. The agricultural wage workers by and large have a more precarious and less adequate level of living than many low-income farm-operator families."

Among the low-income farmers are more than 404,000 semiretired persons who depend largely on social security payments and other pension checks for their livelihood and another 888,000 persons who either work in towns and cities much of the time or depend heavily upon outside income earned by members of their families.

This leaves less than 350,000 farmers who have no other cash income than what they net from their gross annual sales of $2500 or less. These are the people who sit on the porches of their unpainted houses watching the world pass them by. It was always difficult for them to make a living on their small farms, but it is impossible for them to compete with the mechanized and chemically fertilized agriculture of today. Forty acres and a mule are as obsolete as a wooden plow. Some in this group are tenants, but most own their land. Farm tenancy, which was one of the worst social problems in the early 1930's, particularly in the South, has declined dramatically. Today only 16 per cent of all farmers are tenants, compared with over 40 per cent twenty-five years ago.

The 350,000 farmers at the bottom of the agricultural heap are a social rather than a farm problem. Many of them are old or ill. Others are shiftless ne'er-do-wells. There is little room for many of them in farming or in industry.

Some of them can and ought to do what 888,000 other low-income farmers have already done — get nonfarm jobs to supplement their meager incomes from agriculture.

"The large numbers of farmers and farm families who have shifted to other major occupations while remaining nominally in farming are in a position to shift quickly and completely out of the farm classification," John H. Southern, an Agriculture Department economist, told the 1962 Outlook Conference. "Our rural development studies show that thousands of part-time farmers or small farmers can cease their current farm activity without decreasing money incomes. In many instances, money incomes might even be increased by ceasing to farm. The chief income feature of part-time farming or of rural living among thousands of families is the rental value of the home, some home-produced foods, and the security feature of owning a resource — small though it may be — that continues to increase in value at a rate comparable to returns that might be obtained if funds were invested elsewhere."

Southern went on to point out that drastic reductions in the number of farms would be necessary to consolidate small farms into units large enough to compete in today's agriculture.

"In three commercial farm areas of the South," he noted, "adjustments in farm size to return adequate labor-management incomes of $4500 would result in a reduction in farm numbers and labor requirements of some 50 per cent . . . In a low-farm-income county of eastern Oklahoma a system of farming suitable to the area and returning a labor-management income of $2500 would reduce the existing 1200 farms in the county to about 215 farms. In a similar but larger area in Missouri, adequate adjustments to obtain a net return of $2000 would reduce the number of farms from about 10,500 to about 3200 or to about 2800, depending upon the type of farming involved."

Since the early 1930's sporadic efforts have been made by the Agriculture Department and by Congress to help low-income farmers, through rehabilitation, resettlement, soil conservation, self-help and education programs, but these efforts have never had the political support that farm price guarantees have had year after year. The poor people of America, whether they be in city slums or in unpainted houses on worn-out land, are unorganized and unable to get Congress to enact legislation to meet their needs.

Some progress has been made in recent years. The $389 million depressed areas redevelopment program approved by Congress in 1961 set aside $100 million in loan funds to encourage the location of industrial plants in rural areas. The 1961 housing legislation included a $430 million loan fund for the construction, repair and remodeling of farm homes and buildings. Small, experimental loan programs to help farmers turn their land to recreational uses were established by Congress in 1962.

The Agriculture Department has also had a small Rural Areas Development program in operation since the mid-1950's. Although one of its ambitious goals is to eliminate the causes of rural poverty, the program has never had more than a few million dollars at its disposal in any year and has consisted largely of rhetoric and of demonstration projects under both the Eisenhower and the Kennedy Administrations.

Farm price guarantees and other agricultural subsidy programs have failed to solve the problem of rural poverty because poor farmers produce so little. If a farmer sells less than $2500 worth of commodities in a year even a Government program guaranteeing a 100 per cent greater return on his labor would hardly move him into the affluent class.

The most often heard suggestion for solving the over-production problem is to "get the Government out of agriculture." The United States Chamber of Commerce, the National Association of Manufacturers and most other business groups take the free farm economy approach. The American Farm Bureau Federation's long-range goal is a farm economy free from controls and Government guarantees, but under the Farm Bureau program complete Government withdrawal from the agricultural economy would take several years.

Although food costs declined from 27 per cent of consumers' disposable income in 1947 to 19 per cent in 1961, most workers and housewives still consider food too expensive. There is unquestionably a good deal of support among consumers for the abandonment of farm subsidies. This feeling has been reflected in recent years in the votes on farm subsidies in Congress. Fewer urban Congressmen have been willing to support the farm programs, even in exchange for votes for city legislation.

Both businessmen and workers separate the guarantees granted to them by the Government from the subsidies provided for farmers. There are certainly significant differences among the degrees of Federal assistance given to the various parts of the economy, but dollar for dollar the farm subsidies represent the largest direct Government expenditures for members of one group. If subsidies are bad for farmers, does not it logically follow that tariff protection is bad for industry and minimum wage and hour legislation is bad for workers? The level of farm subsidies can be attacked by other groups that are either directly or indirectly helped by the Government, but the principle of a subsidized agricultural economy is no different from the rationale for the substantial assistance given by the Government to so many other groups.

What would happen if farm subsidies and controls were abandoned? What would happen to the small-town merchants, to the big machinery, fertilizer and pesticide manufacturers, and to all of the other businessmen and workers who supply farmers with goods or process commodities produced by farmers?

During the farm depression of the 1920's and the general depression that began with the stock market crash of 1929, farmers responded to lower prices by planting more crops each year. The additional production drove down prices still further. If price guarantees and acreage controls were removed today, farm prices would decline and production would increase. The number of commercial farmers is too large for production to be regulated without Government controls. It is also easier for farmers to increase their production today because they depend more on science and technology and less on land and labor.

Big corporations can control both their output and their prices. Unions can negotiate wage rates for their members. Except through cooperative organizations, which have proved to be of only limited value to agriculture, farmers have been unable to control either their prices or their output without the help of the Government.

In the fall of 1960 the Joint Economic Committee of Congress prepared under the direction of its chairman, Democratic Senator Paul H. Douglas of Illinois, a study of possible economic policies for agriculture during the 1960's.

Among the alternatives discussed in the committee's report was the abandonment of farm subsidy programs.

John W. Lehman, acting executive director of the committee, noted that a panel of economists examined the question of an agricultural economy with no guarantees and no controls and found that "farm prices and income would fall sharply if current farm price support, production control, and conservation reserve programs were dropped and not replaced by an alternative program or combination of programs."

Without such Government programs, the report estimated, by 1965 wheat prices would decline 50 per cent from their 1959 levels, cotton prices 34 per cent, corn 28 per cent, rice 27 per cent, cattle 24 per cent, hogs 23 per cent, eggs 16 per cent, and milk 12 per cent. The report went on to say:

According to these projections, net farm income could be expected to drop from $11.3 billion in 1959 to $7.2 billion in 1965 of which $3.1 billion is inputed income from rental of the farm dwellings, and from home-produced food and fuel. Allowing for trends in farm consolidation, net income per commercial farm with sales of $2,500 or more in 1965 would be 30 per cent lower than in 1959.

Discussing farm income and adjustment problems in the same report, Walter W. Wilcox, senior specialist in agriculture for the Legislative Reference Service of the Library of Congress, noted:

Usual supply and demand forces do not achieve equilibrium in agriculture at satisfactory price and income levels under conditions of rapid technological advance. The extremely inelastic demand for farm products causes sharp price declines when supplies increase faster than population growth. Previously committed resources — tractors, improvements in land, specialized machinery and most farm operators — cannot shift out of agriculture in response to price declines. Thus the addition of new output increasing practices becomes the most profitable alternative to the individual farmer in spite of low prices.

As an industry agriculture differs from most others. Relatively little labor is hired and purchased supplies are a smaller part of total costs than in manufacturing. Economic incentives encourage the full use of all land, labor, equipment and unit cost-reducing technologies as long as the family continues to farm. In the present state of agriculture's development farm output may be increased with fewer farm operator families and workers as mechanization of crop and livestock production continues.

Agriculture has greater difficulties than manufacturing industries in assimilating rapid technological change. Farmers are price takers under current market organization in contrast to industrial firms which typically establish sales prices and produce to supply their markets at stable prices. Manufacturers typically make differentiated, trademarked products, often using patented processes. They utilize purchased materials and hired labor. New technological processes are adopted to lower costs. But, utilizing purchased materials and hired labor for the most part, they limit production to amounts that can be sold at prices in line with costs.

Workers displaced by labor-saving equipment suffer income losses but are cared for by unemployment insurance and welfare services until they find new employment. Industrial workers usually have less difficulty than farm workers in finding new employment, since they usually live in urban areas accessible to new employment opportunities. Also, their experience better fits them for other industrial employment than the experience of farm workers. It is these differences in economic organization of the industries which make it possible for most manufacturers to operate profitably at less than full capacity while assimilating rapid technological change and prevent agriculture from following similar practices.

Wilcox then tried to determine what would happen to farm income if price guarantees and production controls were dropped. His conclusions were much the same as those set out by Lehman. Wilcox wrote:

In the past seven years an average of $2.2 billion, or seven per cent of total farm marketings, were removed from commercial channels by surplus disposal and storage programs. If these programs were dropped without replacement by others, farm income would drop several billion dollars. Projections of farm production, prices and income for 1965 indicate a drop in net income of 36 per cent from 1959 and 45 per cent from 1958 if production controls and price supports are discontinued. Prices of the price-supported crops of cotton and wheat would drop 30 to 50 per cent. Prices of the uncontrolled feed grains and livestock also would drop 10 to 30 per cent below recent levels. The index of prices received by farmers would decline 21 per cent from 1959.

These projections provide (1) that existing surplus stocks be isolated and disposed of outside usual markets, and (2) that Public Law 480 exports from 1965 production be continued at about recent levels . . .

Land and capital investment values generally would shrink. Industries and financial institutions serving farmers in the towns and cities would feel the financial pinch in the rural areas. A prolonged period of severely depressed farm incomes adversely affecting all who deal with farmers appears probable if agriculture's full production potential is utilized in the 1960's.

Although the abandonment of farm price guarantees and production controls is sometimes discussed in terms of suddenly ending all the programs, any legislation that seeks to get the Government out of agriculture would have to establish a gradual process. No other approach to a free farm economy would be politically acceptable. Price supports and other guarantees would have to be reduced slowly but deliberately, over a period of at least five years. Assistance would need to be provided for hundreds of thousands of farmers who would have to move to industrial jobs.

A carefully developed outline of such a plan was presented in the summer of 1962 by the Committee for Economic Development, an organization of liberal businessmen. Called *An Adaptive Program for Agriculture,* the report was vehemently attacked by Secretary Freeman, by members of the farm bloc on Capitol Hill, by the National Farmers Union and by the National Farmers Organization. The report even led to hearings by the House Agriculture Committee; they were devoted largely to efforts to discredit the CED suggestions.

Most of the attacks on the report stemmed from the CED proposal that the number of workers in agriculture — both farm operators and hired hands — be reduced one third or by about two million during the next five years. The number of agricultural workers now totals more than 5.5 million. Actually, the rate of migration proposed by the CED was little different from the rate in the late 1950's and not as large as it was in the early 1950's. Furthermore, the CED did not advocate a program to force people off the farms, as some of its critics contended. The CED report noted:

Although the exodus from agriculture in the past decade or longer has been large by almost any standards, it has not been large enough . . . The need for movement has been disguised by temporary upsurges of demand for agricultural products, during World War II and the Korean War, and by the price-supporting programs of the government . . . The excessively high level of urban unemployment in the four years 1958-61 tended to keep the movement of labor out of agriculture less than it should have been . . .

The support of prices has deterred the movement of resources out of agriculture. It has given farmers erroneous expectations of the earnings their labor might yield in agriculture in the future. The high support prices, plus the technological change increasing the amount of land a farmer could efficiently work, have raised land prices and misled the farmer about the income he was actually earning. These same factors, plus the financial capacity created by the higher land values, have encouraged the investment of capital in agriculture.

Under the program proposed by the CED, farmers and farm workers would be retrained by the Government for jobs in towns and cities and would be eligible for loans to pay for the cost of moving to their new jobs. The CED report said that the Manpower Development and Training Act approved by Congress in 1962 should be amended to provide for the retraining of more farmers. The report added:

The retraining of farm workers leaving farming should be considered one of the principal objectives of the new Act. Those responsible for the administration of the Act should have it clearly in mind that farming is the leading case of misuse of resources in the American economy, that overcommitment of people to farming for their livelihood is the special form of the use of excess resources in agriculture, and that the Manpower and Training Act should consequently be applied with all vigor to solution of the farm problem.

In addition to encouraging the movement of people out of farming, the CED would eliminate farm price guarantees over a period of five years and would revive the soil bank to encourage with Government payments the retirement of cropland. The CED estimated that if its proposals were adopted total Government expenditures for agriculture could be cut in half. The CED concluded:

There are two ways to reduce government agricultural outlays without great losses to farmers. One is to tighten controls of production and marketing enough to reduce farm output to the point where all output will sell at the higher prices. This will make consumers pay more for farm products, and let the government pay less.

The other way is to attract and assist enough farmers out of farming so that farm income per farmer will be sustained without rising farm prices despite a decline in government spending on agriculture.

The first method reduces government costs by shifting them to consumers, forcing some resources out of productive use in agriculture without at the same time channeling them toward better alternative use. The second method results in a true net reduction of costs to the country as a whole. Government costs go down. Farmers' per family incomes are sustained. Many people now in farming shift to work more profitable to them and to the Nation. Consumers — including farmers — are not made to pay higher food and fiber prices.

Elsewhere in its report the CED rejected the "stringent, leakproof controls of production" on the grounds that this could not be done "without policing measures that would be intolerable in America." The report also noted that a tough production-control program merely "would change the evidence of waste from mounting stocks of surplus products to idle land, labor and capital, withheld from farm use and not channeled to other uses."

If a program like the one proposed by the CED is to work, the American economy must be operating at a high level. Only then will there be adequate employment opportunities for the men and women who must shift out of agriculture into industry if the farm problem is ever to be solved. During the 1950's farm migration was at its highest in the boom years of 1950, 1952, and 1956 and negligible in the recession year of 1954.

It is difficult to quarrel with the CED recommendation for a high rate of migration from agriculture to industry. The rural politicians, the leaders of farm pressure groups, the bureaucrats in the Agriculture Department and others

who have a vested interest in a large farm population would
— and did — find fault with the CED migration proposals.
They also were opposed by those Americans who sincerely
believe the countryside offers advantages and instills values
that can seldom be found in cities.

The real issue raised by the CED program and by the
many similar proposals that have been made in recent years
is the assumption that Congress could be persuaded to withdraw all subsidies from agriculture. If farmers were the
only group in the American economy receiving substantial
aid from the Government, the withdrawal of subsidies
would not be so difficult. As long as the Government pro-
tects other groups and other parts of the economy from the
vagaries of a completely free market, why should farmers
be the only ones to lose all Government protection?

Energetic leadership by the President and by the increasing number of city-oriented Senators and Representatives
could turn the farm program into a less costly and more
effective effort. It is most unlikely, however, that a majority could be found in Congress to end all farm subsidy
programs, even gradually over a period of five to ten years.

Once those who leave the farm obtain jobs, most of them
will be protected by wage and hour laws, unemployment
compensation and social security. Today in the United
States and in the other industrialized countries of the world
no one is completely on his own. There are always Government programs and assistance hovering over the modern industrial worker. So, whatever the magnitude of the faults of
the farm programs, the farmer still expects and is entitled to
have some Government protection.

Thus, there are sound economic reasons as well as practical political ones for refusing to cut off farmers without a

cent of Government assistance. No other country with an advanced economic system has turned its farmers loose.

In December 1962 T. A. Hieronymus, professor of agricultural marketing at the University of Illinois, discussed the farm policies of other countries at the annual convention of the American Farm Bureau Federation in Atlanta.

"The countries of the world," he said, "whose agricultural policies and programs are most like those of the United States are the highly industrialized, high-income countries of Western Europe and the United Kingdom. Important similarities are: (1) relatively small proportions of their populations are engaged in farming; (2) by the world's standards their agriculture is highly productive; (3) they enjoy high dietary levels; (4) they have great concern for the welfare of their farm populations and can afford to indulge this concern; and (5) a substantial proportion of their farm units are of less than optimum size in terms of area or volume of production. There is one very major difference: The United States is an agricultural surplus-producing country whereas the others are major importers of agricultural raw materials. The import position of Western European countries makes the implementation of a high price-income policy relatively easy. By restricting imports domestic prices can be easily maintained."

Hieronymus cited the farm programs of West Germany and Britain as being particularly relevant to the discussion of agricultural policies in the United States.

West German agriculture includes many small, unproductive farms as well as some large and extremely efficient units. The Germans must import much of their food and livestock feed. The small German farm population is a potent political force that has succeeded in maintaining farm income with two principal programs.

One is a system of production subsidies which, as Hieronymus noted, includes "rebates on fertilizers, purchase of seed, particularly potatoes, improvement of orchards, improvement of milk quality, purchase of machinery for co-operative use, and for land consolidation and settlement . . .

"The primary device for the maintenance of farm income," Hieronymus went on to point out, "is import restrictions. Germany maintains very high import restrictions on many agricultural products, particularly feed. As the import restrictions on feed grains are high the interior price of barley is high. As the price of barley is high the price of feed potatoes is high. As the price of feed potatoes is high livestock prices are high, etc. . . .

"This system has not solved the German farm problem. Many of the production units are so small and inefficiently organized that no feasible level of prices can result in parity income. The large, efficient units do very well but they are not really a part of the German farm problem. It is a system whereby the poor stay poor because they are not productive, and the rich live off the fat of the land."

The Germans are having some of the same difficulties in trying to attack their farm problems as the United States has had. In Germany as in the United States subsidies ostensibly designed to help small farmers have given the most aid and comfort to the well-to-do farmers who need assistance the least.

Like West Germany, Britain depends heavily on imports for her food. Britain is the world's largest importer of farm commodities and gets more than half of her food abroad, principally from Canada, Australia, New Zealand and other Commonwealth countries.

In his analysis of British farm policies Hieronymus noted that as a trading nation Britain must keep domestic manufacturing costs as low as possible to maintain competitive prices for its exports. This means, among other things, moderate food costs. Other considerations in the development of British farm policies have included maintenance of adequate incomes for farmers, development of a domestic agricultural economy to meet essential needs in case of war, and support of the agricultural economies of the Commonwealth countries.

"Within the framework of these policy considerations," Hieronymus pointed out, "the United Kingdom has developed an agricultural program that consists primarily of direct treasury payments. The first of these is a system of guaranteed prices. After conferences with agricultural organizations forward [future] prices for a long list of agricultural prices are established. The primary considerations involved in establishing these prices are the effects on farm income, effects on production of the various products, and the cost to the treasury. Market prices prevail and the difference between market prices and guaranteed prices is made by direct payments.

"Import restrictions are kept at relatively low levels so that the interior price level is very close to the world price level. The second system of direct payments is in production allowances. These subsidies have the effect of reducing input costs. In addition to what I identify as commodity subsidies there are indirect aids to agriculture in the form of credit, special tax treatment, education and extension, and land reclamation.

"The cost of programs can be identified readily because it is a matter of treasury payments. In recent years this cost has been held fairly constant . . . This system has much that is commendable. It results in relatively inexpensive food and is, therefore, desirable from a consumer point of view. It leaves a great deal of flexibility in the kinds of product so that inputs are used fairly efficiently. The cost is readily identifiable and so can be kept in reasonable bounds. It tends to maintain the status quo of agriculture and guarantee a minimum food supply level for whatever social values these things may have."

Hieronymus noted that "there are certain drawbacks to the system. If the subsidies did not exist and there were the same small import restrictions the cost of food would be very little, if any, higher. Imports would be greater and the size of the agricultural plant would be smaller. Resources would be freed for other uses. This more nearly optimum allocation of resources would increase the total economic output of the United Kingdom."

Hieronymus concluded, as have many other economists, that the British system of direct payments offers the best solution to the farm subsidy problem. This system has inherent advantages in a country that relies on imports for most of its agricultural commodities and thus is able to control domestic production by adjusting the level of its imports. Even though the United States imports little of its food, it still could use the direct-payment system to provide minimum subsidies for its farmers.

What the United States needs is a realistic farm program that recognizes the two surpluses of American agriculture. One is surplus people. The other is surplus production.

A realistic farm program should consist of four parts:

(1) The Government should help farmers get out of agriculture by retraining them for industrial and other non-farm jobs and by providing allowances for the resettlement of farmers in cities.

(2) The Government should permanently retire land from production by paying farmers who agree to put all their land into a soil bank.

(3) The Government should support farm income by making direct payments representing the difference between market prices and minimum prices established to assure an adequate income to farmers, with a ceiling on the amount of subsidy one farmer could get.

(4) The Government should attack the problems of rural poverty through vigorous efforts either to bring industry to rural areas or to move people where there are jobs.

This is a program that is politically realistic. It faces human and political facts by providing for ways to ease the transition from farming to jobs in industry.

Imaginative rural politicians would find a lot of votes in legislation to implement these proposals. What is envisioned here is a complete turnabout in the nation's rural economy. Rural politicians know that they cannot stem the tide of migration from farm to industry, but they have never been united behind a program to bring industry and other alternatives to farming — such as recreation facilities — to the countryside.

This program is designed to attract rural votes without offering uneconomic handouts to farmers. Unless a farm program can be combined with rural redevelopment efforts to get the support of rurally oriented leaders of Congress, particularly in the House, the program is doomed to failure before it can even be intelligently discussed.

The four-point program offered here would lead to substantial reductions in the cost of farm subsidies. The costs of retraining and resettling farmers would be nonrecurrent and would quickly decline to a modest amount once the mass movement from farm to city was completed. The Federal loans to attract industries to rural areas would be repaid over a period of years. Direct payments to the remaining farmers each year instead of Federal loans and purchases of commodities would quickly get the Government out of the expensive storage business. Even if the total proposed effort cost as much as the current $5-billion-a-year farm subsidies for the first three or four years, it would be a more constructive way to spend money than the present program.

A growing, prosperous economy is essential to any program shifting human and material resources from surplus areas to where they are needed. The depressed areas program has had only limited success in attracting industry to small towns and rural areas largely because the nation's entire economy has been sluggish. Such an industrial reorientation program can work only in an expanding economy where businessmen are constantly looking for new plant sites and more opportunities.

The depressed areas program has been a modest effort, given the needs of rural areas. The rural development programs in the Agriculture Department have been hopelessly underfinanced. This is largely because the cost of the present wasteful program of farm subsidies creates such pressures on the Federal budget that there is no money left for new programs like rural development.

Under the first part of the proposed program the Government would help hundreds of thousands of farmers move off the land. Many others could continue living on their farms while working in plants and shops in nearby towns. Under the Manpower Development and Training Act farmers are eligible for subsistence allowances while being trained for new jobs only if they have been earning less than $1200 a year from agriculture, but retraining benefits should be given to anyone who wants to get out of agriculture.

There are now no Government allowances to help farmers move to jobs in cities. Such allowances have been successfully used in several European countries, notably Britain and Sweden. President Kennedy asked Congress to provide relocation allowances in the Manpower Training Act, but opposition to the proposal from rural Congressmen killed it. If resettlement funds were coupled with expanded efforts to get industries to locate plants in rural areas, Congress probably would accept the idea of providing help to farmers moving to towns and cities. Only a relatively small number of farmers might have to move if increased efforts were made to bring industry to small towns and the countryside.

Retraining programs and resettlement allowances would help to create conditions and incentives that in the past have been left to the uncertainties of general economic conditions. Surely there can be nothing morally or economically wrong with such an approach to agriculture's basic problems of overproduction and underemployment.

As a corollary to the retraining programs for farmers, new vocational education programs should be established for their sons and daughters. In most rural high schools vocational education and other training programs are still operated as if all the boys were to become farmers and all the girls were going to be farmers' wives. Yet there will be no place in the farm economy for eight out of ten farm youths now in high school. The youths not planning to go on to college should be given the opportunity to learn trades needed in industry rather than learning farming skills they will never have an opportunity to use.

The second part of a realistic farm program would provide not only for the retirement of productive land on parts of farms; it also would allow farmers to place all their land in a Government soil bank. Previous proposals for the retirement of entire farms have been bitterly opposed by small-town businessmen. They fear that such proposals would administer a fatal blow to the already sick and dying economies of many small towns. Throughout the country small towns are in trouble because there is no longer any economic reason for their existence. They were established to serve a horse-and-buggy economy. Today farmers drive in their automobiles to fine stores in the cities. The farm program should not be used to prop up the economies of small towns. They are not going to be saved by Government subsidies designed to keep inefficient or unneeded farms in operation. A rural industrialization program might save some of these towns, but a subsidy program that keeps farm prices and production at artificially high levels will not do it.

Under the program proposed here most farmers probably would have to continue to withdraw some of their land from production to be eligible for price subsidies. If, however, enough farmers could be persuaded to leave farming, some of the land on the remaining farms would not have to be retired every year, except for normal soil conservation practices.

The retirement of entire farms is much to be preferred to the partial land retirement program that constituted most of the soil bank system tried by the Eisenhower Administration during the late 1950's. If whole farms could be put in the soil bank this would be a further stimulus to encourage farmers to leave farming. The whole-farm approach also would spur the retirement of farmers themselves. The farmer could continue to live in his farm home, and the money he would get from the Government for keeping his land out of production could be used to help finance his own retirement. The man who went to live in town or city after putting his farm in the soil bank could use his Government payments to help make the transition to city life.

A soil bank that encouraged the retirement of entire farms would also get land out of production that should never have been used for crops. This is particularly true on the Great Plains, where thin soil that should not have been taken out of grass has been planted to wheat because of high price guarantees. The lower subsidies coupled with the land retirement program would encourage the movement of this kind of land out of crops.

Land placed in the soil bank should be planted with grass or trees. With good grass cover and groves of trees, such land could be used for recreation purposes.

A soil bank program under which the Government would pay farmers to take land out of production and give them annual payments for keeping the land fallow could be an effective device for helping to move both land and human resources out of agriculture. A soil bank program is costly, but if the program emphasizes the retirement of entire farms it can be an extremely useful method for cutting back production.

The most controversial part of the program suggested here is the proposal for the support of farm prices through direct Government payments to farmers to make up the difference between market prices and prices that farmers should get for their commodities to assure them an adequate income. Such an income support program would have to be accompanied, at least in the beginning and probably for many years, by strict controls regulating production by bushels and pounds rather than merely by easily circumvented acreage limitations. There are, after all, no signs that the exploding agricultural technology of the last thirty years has run its course. The payments also would be limited so that large farming enterprises that need no Government aid would get none.

It would be preferable if all price guarantees and production controls could be eliminated, but even with the exodus from the farms envisioned by this program some income protection and production controls would unquestionably be needed. Controls would be needed because without them production would almost certainly expand beyond the nation's requirements as new farming techniques were developed. Controls would also be needed because no matter how low price guarantees are set they tend to encourage maximum plantings.

Direct payments to farmers would be a better way to subsidize the agricultural economy than the loan, purchase and storage programs relied upon during the last thirty years. The direct payments would get the Government out of the costly storage business. The Government might still have to maintain stockpiles for emergencies, but the technological changes in agriculture during the last three decades have clearly demonstrated the ability of farmers to step up their production quickly in an emergency. There no longer seems to be any need for huge stockpiles of farm commodities. The advocates of such stockpiles generally are the people who want to continue the costly farm programs in their present form. The stockpiles are looked upon as another way to hide the cost of the farm programs.

Another virtue of direct payments is that they would provide an easily understood accounting of the cost of farm subsidies. The payments would be made each year directly by the Government to the farmer. The cost would be known at once. There would be no need to wait several years for the Government to sell subsidized commodities, as is now the case, before costs of the farm programs could be fully determined.

This is one of the principal reasons for opposition to direct payments among farmers, their organizations and their political supporters. Farmers and their friends know that large subsidies would be far more difficult to justify if they were quite easy to identify.

Yet the British experience with direct payments is generally regarded by economists as evidence that they are the most satisfactory way to subsidize farm income. In the United States direct payments have been used to support wool prices and were approved by Congress in 1962 to help keep up part of the prices of wheat and corn and other feed grains.

American farmers are said to be opposed to direct payments. This, however, seems to be part of the mythology of American agriculture. If the taxpayers are going to subsidize farmers, why should they not do it as efficiently and as cheaply as possible? Thirty years of experience with farm programs have shown that farmers are far from bashful about taking money from the Government in whatever form it is offered to them.

The direct payment plan presented here is an adaptation of the Brannan Plan offered to Congress by President Truman in 1949. The plan was badly beaten then, but farm

programs have got so out of hand since that a direct payments approach cannot simply be written off because of
the 1949 experience. With vigorous leadership from the President and his Secretary of Agriculture, a direct payments
program could be moved through Congress, where even
some rurally oriented members are becoming concerned
over the costs of existing programs.

The fourth and last part of the proposed farm program
would seek to help the 350,000 farm families who live in
poverty. Theirs is not strictly a farm problem, but some of
the money that the other three parts of this program would
save should be used to help destitute rural areas and the
people in them to a better life.

Few of these people probably could make a living as
farmers. Their farms are too small, their land is too poor,
and their capital resources are too meager to earn an adequate income from agriculture.

These people could be helped with retraining programs
and resettlement loans. The location of industries in low-
income rural areas would help these people by bringing
jobs to them. Federal housing and other rehabilitation loans
should also be extended to them.

The men, women and children who live in poverty in
rural areas throughout the country have received little help
from the farm programs of the last thirty years. Their
problems have been ignored, but they have not gone away.
It is time that the Government did more than just pay lip
service to these problems.

A Billie Sol Estes would not like the four-point farm program proposed here. The program would take the Govern-

ment out of grain storage operations. This would mean that there would no longer be a lucrative storage business for people like Estes. The program would rigidly limit production as well as the amount of Federal subsidies one farmer could receive. This would mean that there no longer would be any incentives for men like Estes to amass Government planting permits to produce unneeded crops. The program also would clear the country air of the sharp practices that farmers have built up over the years to circumvent loosely administered control programs. These were the practices that Estes was able to build on with his phony fertilizer tank scheme.

This new farm program would not be a cure-all. There is no cure-all for the farm problem. The politics of getting farm legislation through Congress rules out simple solutions. To get such a program through Congress the President and his Secretary of Agriculture would have to speak some unpopular truths about the need for encouraging people to move out of agriculture into industry. These may be unpleasant things to say, but they must be said and faced up to if the costs of agricultural subsidies are ever to be substantially reduced.

The President also is going to have to tell the men who remain in farming that they must carefully control their production. In exchange they would receive some price guarantees through direct Government payments rather than through costly loan and storage programs.

It will not be easy to get Congress to accept farm legislation that recognizes the necessity for further mass migrations from agriculture, but the present unsatisfactory and unworkable farm programs cannot be continued forever.

The Billie Sol Estes case raised questions about farm subsidies that cannot be ignored for long without toppling the entire system of agricultural guarantees. From this sobering fact rises whatever hope there is for a rational approach to the farm problem.

APPENDIX
Some Basic Farm Statistics

TABLE 1.   FARM POPULATION 1941–1961

The farm population has declined in total numbers and in relation to the rest of the population.

Year	Total population (thousands)	Farm population	
		Number (thousands)	Percentage of total
1941	133,098	30,118	22.6
1942	134,498	28,914	21.5
1943	136,297	26,186	19.2
1944	138,027	24,815	18.0
1945	139,583	24,420	17.5
1946	141,039	25,403	18.0
1947	143,480	25,829	18.0
1948	146,051	24,383	16.7
1949	148,595	24,194	16.3
1950	151,132	23,048	15.3
1951	153,691	21,890	14.2
1952	156,421	21,748	13.9
1953	159,012	19,874	12.5
1954	161,761	19,019	11.8
1955	164,607	19,078	11.6
1956	167,509	18,712	11.2
1957	170,496	17,656	10.4
1958	173,367	17,128	9.9
1959	176,551	16,592	9.4
1960	180,007	15,635	8.7
1961	183,025	14,803	8.1

SOURCE: *United States Department of Agriculture.*

TABLE 2. FARM CLASSIFICATION BY PRODUCT VALUE
1939–1959

The decline in the number of farms has been the sharpest among the smallest and least productive farms.

Value of farm products sold	Number of farms (thousands)				
	1939	*1944*	*1949*	*1954*	*1959*
$10,000 or more	312	438	484	583	795
$5,000 to $9,999	585	723	721	707	654
$2,500 to $4,999	1,015	976	882	812	618
Less than $2,500	4,185	3,722	3,292	2,681	1,641
TOTAL	6,097	5,859	5,379	4,783	3,708

SOURCE: *United States Department of Agriculture.*

TABLE 3. FARM CLASS, NUMBER AND INCOME 1959
Two-thirds of commercial farmers have incomes of $5000 or less.

Economic class of farm	Number of farms		Per cent of sales of farm products	Average net income of farm operator families			
	Total (thousands)	Per cent of total		Net cash farm income	Off-farm income	Total Cash income	Total income including non-money income from farm food and housing
Commercial							
Farms with sales of							
$10,000 and over	795	21.5	71.9	$6,636	$1,978	$8,614	$9,960
$5,000 to $9,999	654	17.6	15.4	2,165	1,567	3,732	5,018
$2,500 to $4,999	618	16.7	7.4	1,288	2,077	3,365	4,572
$50 to $2,499	349	9.4	1.5	438	525	963	1,476
Other farms:							
Part-time	888	23.9	2.7	176	4,283	4,459	4,890
Part-retirement	404	10.9	1.1	116	1,846	1,962	2,363
ALL FARMS	3,708	100.0	100.0	$2,115	$2,247	$4,362	$5,275

SOURCE: *United States Department of Agriculture.*

TABLE 4. WHEAT ACREAGE AND YIELD 1951–1962

Better wheat varieties, the use of fertilizers, and Government price guarantees have increased crops despite Government programs limiting the number of acres that can be planted to wheat.

Year	Wheat acreage (thousands)	Yield per acre (bushels)	Production (million bushels)
1951	78,524	12.6	988
1952	78,645	16.6	1,306
1953	78,931	14.9	1,173
1954	62,539	15.7	983
1955	58,246	16.1	937
1956	60,655	16.6	1,005
1957	49,843	19.2	955
1958	56,017	26.0	1,457
1959	56,772	19.7	1,121
1960	54,919	24.7	1,357
1961	55,648	22.2	1,234
1962	49,127	22.3	1,096

SOURCE: *United States Department of Agriculture.*

TABLE 5. CORN ACREAGE AND YIELD 1951–1962

What better varieties, fertilizer and Government price supports have done to corn production.

Year beginning October	Corn acreage harvested for grain (millions)	Yield per acre (bushels)	Production (million bushels)
1951	71.2	36.9	2,629
1952	71.4	41.8	2,981
1953	70.7	40.7	2,882
1954	68.7	39.4	2,708
1955	68.5	42.0	2,873
1956	64.9	47.4	3,075
1957	63.1	48.3	3,045
1958	63.5	52.8	3,356
1959	72.1	53.1	3,825
1960	71.6	54.5	3,908
1961	58.7	61.8	3,624
1962	57.5	60.6	3,485

SOURCE: *United States Department of Agriculture.*

TABLE 6. SORGHUMS ACREAGE AND YIELD 1951–1962

The phenomenal push that better varieties, fertilizer and high Government-guaranteed prices gave to grain sorghums.

Year beginning October	Sorghum acreage harvested for grain (millions)	Yield per acre (bushels)	Production (million bushels)
1951	8.5	19.1	163
1952	5.3	17.0	91
1953	6.3	18.4	116
1954	11.7	20.1	236
1955	12.9	18.8	243
1956	9.2	22.2	205
1957	19.7	28.8	568
1958	16.5	35.2	581
1959	15.4	36.0	555
1960	15.6	39.8	620
1961	11.0	43.8	483
1962	11.3	43.0	487

SOURCE: *United States Department of Agriculture.*

TABLE 7. AGRICULTURAL SUBSIDY EXPENDITURES 1962

Where the $5 billion in "aids and special services" for agriculture was spent in the 1962 fiscal year.

Program	Expenditure (millions of dollars)
Commodity Credit Corporation and special export programs	
Sales for foreign currencies	1,455
Price support, supply and related programs	2,693
Losses on long-term sales contracts	29
Transfer to supplemental stockpile	193
National Wool Act	65
International Wheat Agreement	90
Special milk program	92
Agricultural Stabilization and Conservation Service	
Sugar Act	80
Other	10
Agricultural Marketing Service	
Removal of surplus agricultural commodities	215
Other	6
Other Department of Agriculture programs	71
Agricultural programs in other agencies	7
TOTAL	5,007

SOURCE: *United States Bureau of the Budget.*

TABLE 8.   AGRICULTURAL SURPLUS STOCKPILES 1962

As of December 31, 1962, the Agriculture Department owned more than $5.2 billion worth of surplus commodities.

Commodity	Quantity	Value
Grains		
Barley	28,208,176 *bu.*	$ 24,275,664
Beans, dry edible	893,290 *cwt.*	5,997,718
Bulgur	14,721,700 *lb.*	811,726
Corn	1,044,325,049 *bu.*	1,213,494,128
Grain sorghums	579,266,082 *bu.*	616,721,967
Oats	15,352,061 *bu.*	9,219,597
Rice	94,222 *cwt.*	844,056
Rye	984,004 *bu.*	1,001,744
Soybeans	36,710,649 *bu.*	87,433,158
Wheat	1,044,992,557 *bu.*	2,034,726,416
Wheat flour	6,000,000 *lb.*	344,768
Cotton		
Extra long staple	15,865 *bales*	4,350,337
Upland	4,688,689 *bales*	810,530,190
Dairy products		
Butter	350,791,487 *lb.*	207,118,200
Butter oil	48,339,956 *lb.*	38,957,025
Cheese	111,587,560 *lb.*	41,788,549
Ghee	737,188 *lb.*	598,857
Milk, dried	662,458,995 *lb.*	99,111,757
Oils and peanuts		
Cottonseed oil, refined	8,339,550 *lb.*	1,014,923
Peanuts		
Farmers' stock	14,118,584 *lb.*	1,438,503
Shelled	23,839,014 *lb.*	4,903,966
Vegetable oil	145,204,004 *lb.*	26,637,952
Turpentine	1,729,744 *gal.*	907,639
Honey	1,045,076 *lb.*	130,868
Commodities to be exchanged for strategic materials		38,221,767
TOTAL		$5,270,581,475

SOURCE: *United States Department of Agriculture.*

TABLE 9. OUTSTANDING PRICE SUPPORT LOANS 1962

The Agriculture Department had price support loans outstanding on December 31, 1962, amounting to more than $2.7 billion.

Commodity	Quantity		Value
Grains			
Barley	35,767,679	*bu.*	$ 29,229,410
Beans, dry edible	1,961,547	*cwt.*	13,954,662
Corn	559,925,887	*bu.*	616,199,485
Flaxseed	3,648,484	*bu.*	10,287,021
Grain sorghums	156,457,972	*bu.*	176,832,717
Oats	32,850,911	*bu.*	17,576,052
Rice	4,354,813	*cwt.*	21,661,704
Rye	4,705,243	*bu.*	4,321,847
Soybeans	58,269,509	*bu.*	130,134,369
Wheat	258,961,038	*bu.*	526,874,128
Cotton			
Extra long staple	8,921	*bales*	2,384,374
Upland	4,413,222	*bales*	705,927,966
Cottonseed	12	*tons*	558
Oils and Peanuts			
Peanuts	241,411,982	*lb.*	27,275,684
Tung oil	137,687	*lb.*	33,045
Rosin	166,410,409	*lb.*	17,152,711
Tobacco	657,078,845	*lb.*	461,218,738
Honey	2,854,875	*lb.*	351,878
TOTAL			$2,761,416,349

SOURCE: *United States Department of Agriculture.*

Notes on Sources

THIS BOOK was written in an effort to explain the hideously complex farm programs in simple terms. No attempt was made to suffocate — or impress — the reader with footnotes. Throughout the book sources have been cited in the body of the text. All figures are from official Government sources. What follows are some notes on sources for the reader who may wish to pursue further the fascinating story of Billie Sol Estes or the frustrating problems of farm surpluses.

1. "Just a Farm Boy"

Most of the material on Billie Sol Estes' life and on Pecos, Texas, was based on my own observations and interviews in West Texas. The best early accounts of Estes and his operations were written by Jimmy Banks in the Dallas *Morning News* in the spring of 1962 just before and after Estes' arrest. In its issue of May 25, 1962, *Time* carried a comprehensive account of Estes. Another good account, written by Cecil Holland, appeared in the Washington *Evening Star* of May 27, 1962. *U.S. News and World Report* for May 21, 1962, and *Newsweek* for May 28, 1962, also carried good accounts of the Estes case. More than any other reporter, Earl Mazo of the New York *Herald Tribune* focused national attention on the Estes case with a series of articles during May 1962.

2. More Hell — and Corn

J. D. Hicks's *The Populist Revolt* (Minneapolis, 1931) remains after more than thirty years the best single study of the origins of the agrarian reform movement in the United States. Shorter accounts of agrarian reform efforts can be found in Hicks's *The American Nation* (Cambridge, 1949) and in Arthur M. Schlesinger's *The Rise of Modern America* (New York, 1951).

3. Millions of Pigs, Billions of Dollars

The account of the little pigs' slaughter is based on United States Agriculture Department records made available to the author through the courtesy of Harold R. Lewis, the Department's Director of Information. The best account of Henry A. Wallace and the beginnings of the New Deal farm program is in *The Coming of the New Deal* by Arthur M. Schlesinger, Jr. (Boston, 1959). Russell Lord's *The Wallaces of Iowa* (Boston, 1947) is also useful. Wallace's own books include *New Frontiers* (New York, 1934) and *The Price of Freedom* (Washington, 1940). *Roosevelt's Farmer* by Dean Albertson (New York, 1961) is valuable not only for its account of Claude R. Wickard's years as Secretary of Agriculture but also for its description of Wickard's experiences as an administrator of the New Deal farm programs. The reader who wishes to investigate further the careers of Clinton P. Anderson and Charles E. Brannan will have to rely on contemporaneous newspaper and magazine articles; their careers have not yet been put between hard covers. Ezra Taft Benson has described his frustrations as Secretary of Agriculture in *Cross-fire* (New York, 1962). For an economist's account of farm programs and agricultural legislation, see *Can We Solve the Farm Problem?* by Murray R. Benedict (New York, 1955). *After a Hundred Years*, the Agriculture Department's 1962 Yearbook, is a complete if bland account of the Department's first century. The 1962 Yearbook also is a readily available source for basic agricultural statistics.

4. Powerful Peasants

Books of interest to the student of present-day farm politics include *The Farm Bureau and the New Deal* by Christiana M. Campbell (Urbana, Illinois, 1962), *The Agricultural Bloc* by Arthur Capper (New York, 1922), *The Farm Bureau Through Three Decades* by Orville M. Kile (Baltimore, 1948), *The Farm Bloc* by Wesley McCune (Garden City, New York, 1943), and *Who's Behind Our Farm Policy?* by Wesley McCune (New York, 1956).

5. *"A Real Ball"*

The account of the Estes grain storage operations is based on testimony before a series of six courts of inquiry conducted by Texas Attorney General Will Wilson in April and May of 1962 and hearings held by the Intergovernmental Relations Subcommittee of the House Government Operations Committee in May, June and July of 1962. Unfortunately, at the time of writing, the records of neither the courts of inquiry nor the House hearings were available in printed form. Typescript transcripts were made available to the author by Assitant Texas Attorney General Richard Wells and James D. Naughton, counsel to the House subcommittee. The author attended practically all of the House hearings, which were held in Washington. The transcripts of the House hearings are available in the office of the House Government Operations Committee. The courts of inquiry were held in Potter County Court, Amarillo, Texas, on April 10, 1962; in Hale County Court, Plainview, Texas, on April 11; in the Justice of the Peace Court of Precinct 1, Place 1, Dallas, Texas, on April 12; in Reeves County Court, Pecos, Texas, on April 14; in Justice of the Peace Court, Precinct 1, Place 2, Lubbock, Texas, on April 19; and in Justice of the Peace Court, Precinct 1, Place 1, Dallas, on April 20. The transcripts of the courts of inquiry are available in those courts and in the office of the Texas Attorney General in Austin, Texas.

6. *Subsidies, Everyone?*

It is difficult enough to define "subsidies," let alone find qualified sources where subsidies are discussed from a disinterested point of view. One of the best sources the author discovered is *Subsidy and Subsidy-like Programs of the U.S. Government: Materials Prepared for the Joint Economic Committee, Congress of the United States."* Written by Julius W. Allen of the Legislative Reference Service of the Library of Congress and published by the Joint Economic Committee in 1960, the study is an excellent summary of subsidy programs, few of which have changed much since the study was prepared. The study is available in an unnumbered Joint Committee print of the 86th Congress, 2nd session. A report on *Grain Storage Operations of the Commodity Credit Corporation* was published in 1960 by the Special Investigating Subcommittee of the Senate Agriculture and Forestry Committee. The subcommittee also published its hearings in four volumes in 1960. Representative L. H. Fountain, chairman of the Intergovernmental Relations Subcommittee of the House Government Operations Committee, summed up hearings that he began in 1958 into the operations of the Commodity Credit Corporation in a typescript statement issued by his office in November 1960. Many of the examples of waste and maladministration used by Senator John J. Williams in speaking out on the Senate floor on the inadequacies of the farm programs have been based on audits of Agriculture Department programs conducted by the General Accounting Office. The cases from Senator Williams' files which are cited were discussed by him on the Senate floor in 1958, 1959, 1960, 1961 and 1962 and may be found in the *Congressional Record* for those years.

7. *In the Land of Cotton*

The fullest account of Henry H. Marshall's mysterious death is contained in an article by Donald Hamilton, "Who Murdered Henry Marshall?" in the November 1962 issue of *Argosy*. The story of the incredibly complex Estes cotton allotment case was developed in an exhaustive series of hearings held by the Permanent Subcommittee on Investigations of the Senate Government Operations Committee. The hearings began in June 1962 and continued into September of that year. The printed record of *Hearings on Department of Agriculture Handling of Pooled Cotton Allotments of Billie Sol Estes* cover 2788 printed pages and have been published in eight volumes. The author attended most of the hearings. Throughout them, Donald F. O'Donnell, acting chief counsel of the subcommittee, was always ready to help puzzled reporters unravel the cotton allotment case.

8. Bureaucracy Unbounded

Much of the material on which this chapter is based can be found in the Senate Investigations subcommittee hearings cited above in the notes on Chapter 7. The Agriculture Department's unique farmer committee system is discussed in *Review of the Farmer Committee System*, the report of a committee set up to study the system. The report was issued in typescript form by the Agriculture Department in December 1962. The conclusions in this chapter are based in part on the author's own observations of the workings of the Agriculture Department.

9. "This Tank Deal"

The records of the Texas courts of inquiry, which were cited in the notes for Chapter 5, contain the best account of the Estes fertilizer tank transactions. An unsigned article, "Estes: Three-Sided Country Slicker," in the July 1962 issue of *Fortune* is an excellent summary of the tank transactions and Estes' dealings with other businessmen. Clyde H. Farnsworth of The New York *Times* wrote several articles in April and May of 1962 explaining the complicated tank transactions. Testimony taken in Estes' trials in State District Court in Tyler, Texas, in October and November of 1962 and in Federal District Court in El Paso, Texas, in April 1963 revealed some additional details of the Estes tank transactions. Oscar Griffin, editor of the Pecos *Independent and Enterprise*, first documented the phantom tank deals, and received a Pulitzer Prize for his investigation.

10. Farmer in the Treasury

The analysis of farm programs is based on hearings held by both the House and Senate Agriculture Committees. All figures cited are from official Agriculture Department sources. *Food and Agriculture: A Program for the 1960's*, a pamphlet published by the Agriculture Department in March 1962, is a good summary of the farm problem as seen by Secretary Freeman. For basic statistics see *The Balance Sheet of Agriculture, 1962*, Agricul-

ture Information Bulletin No. 270, a publication of the Agriculture Department's Economic Research Service. A bird's-eye view
of the agricultural economy, in the form of both charts and
statistics, can be found in *Agricultural Chartbook: Outlook 1963*,
which was issued in November 1962 by the Agriculture Department. A good analysis of the cost of producing wheat can be
found in *The U.S. Wheat Crisis*, a study by Harold I. Lunde
and James B. McComb of Macalester College in St. Paul, Minnesota. The study was published by the college in 1963.

11. What Must Be Done

An Adaptive Program for Agriculture, a statement of national
policy by the Research and Policy Committee of the Committee for Economic Development, is the best current summary of
the argument for the abolition of all farm subsidies. It was issued
in July 1962. Another Committee for Economic Development
publication, *Farming, Farmers and Markets for Farm Goods*,
contains papers prepared by economists Karl A. Fox, Vernon W.
Rattan and Lawrence W. Witt as background for the CED's national policy statement. It, too, was published in 1962. *Farms and
Farmers in an Urban Age* by Edward Higbee (New York, 1963)
is a study made for the Twentieth Century Fund which also
argues for the abolition of farm subsidies. *Economic Policies for
Agriculture in the 1960's: Implications of Four Selected Alternatives* is an excellent study published in 1960 by the Joint Economic Committee. Its authors are economists Walter W. Wilcox,
John A. Schnittker, Dale E. Hathaway, Harlow W. Halvorsen
and George E. Brandow. *Farm Prices: Myth and Reality*
by Willard Cochrane (Minneapolis, 1958) shows how farmers
have responded to falling prices with increased production.
Cochrane has been Secretary Freeman's principal economic adviser. A good discussion of the farm problem and its possible
solutions can be found in *Farm Trouble* by Lauren Soth (Prince-
ton, 1957). For a moving glimpse of what is happening to the
small, farm-oriented towns of America, see *The Talk in Van-
dalia* by Joseph P. Lyford, a study published in 1962 by the
Center for the Study of Democratic Institutions (Santa Barbara,
California).

Index